Fuses, Chains, and Backlashes

Fuses, Chains, and Backlashes

China, the United States, and the Dynamics of Conflict Contagion and Escalation

STEVE CHAN

OXFORD
UNIVERSITY PRESS

Oxford University Press is a department of the University of Oxford.
It furthers the University's objective of excellence in research, scholarship,
and education by publishing worldwide. Oxford is a registered trade mark of
Oxford University Press in the UK and in certain other countries.

Published in the United States of America by Oxford University Press
198 Madison Avenue, New York, NY 10016, United States of America.

CIP data is on file at the Library of Congress

ISBN 9780197812877
ISBN 9780197812860 (hbk.)

DOI: 10.1093/9780197812907.001.0001

Paperback printed by Marquis, Canada
Hardback printed by Bridgeport National Bindery, Inc., United States of America

The manufacturer's authorized representative in the EU for product safety is Oxford University Press España S.A., Parque Empresarial San Fernando de Henares, Avenida de Castilla, 2 – 28830 Madrid (www.oup.es/en)

Contents

Chapter 1
Introduction to the Dynamics of Conflict Contagion and Escalation

Overview

This study seeks to understand the dynamics of conflict contagion and escalation. It tries to draw lessons from international relations scholarship to illuminate the ongoing competition between China and the United States, especially the danger that it may become a serious confrontation such as over Taiwan's status. This inquiry is not *just* about Sino–American relations. It is more accurate to say that this is an effort to apply the cumulative knowledge developed by past studies on interstate conflict to understand the danger that these countries' evolving relationship presents to international peace and stability.

This book is as much about seeking a general understanding of the causes and processes of interstate conflicts as it is on Sino–American relations, perhaps even more the former than the latter. In any case, it is an effort to embed the study of this relationship in the general literature on interstate conflicts. Specific discussion of the Sino–American case will only come in the final chapter after previous ones have laid the necessary groundwork from the pertinent literature on interstate conflicts in general. Thus, this study departs from the usual tendency to "essentialize" China or the United States, emphasizing their respective uniqueness at the expense of their shared commonalities with other countries' conflict experiences.

Power-transition theory (Organski and Kugler 1980) and Thucydides' Trap (Allison 2017) have been in vogue recently. These formulations argue that the danger of war becomes elevated when a latecomer catches up to a leading, established state. My earlier research (Chan 2008; 2020a) has raised various objections to these formulations. I will not repeat these objections in this book, which actually agrees with them in two respects. First, like these formulations I focus in this book on the danger of armed conflict between great powers, specifically China and the United States. Second, I consider power shifts among the great powers to be a significant variable that, along with other variables, creates a dangerous brew that presents a conducive environment for war to break out, spread, and escalate. We all know that power shifts alone, not to mention power transitions, are not necessary for war to occur (power shifts between two

Fuses, Chains, and Backlashes. Steve Chan, Oxford University Press. © Oxford University Press (2025).
DOI: 10.1093/9780197812907.003.0001

countries do not necessarily mean a power transition, which entails a country overtaking its counterpart). There were wars in the absence of power shifts and power transitions that were peaceful.

How do this book's perspective and arguments differ from many other studies on war? Many of these studies, such as power-transition theory and Thucydides' Trap, present monocausal explanations of war. Instead of privileging any single master independent variable such as power shifts, I contend that it is more useful to apply a conjunctive logic—one that gives emphasis to the multiplicative effects of several variables, such as power shifts, armament races, alliance dynamics, and enduring rivalries—to study the causes of war. These variables combine to create a combustible environment conducive to war. The whole is more than the sum of its individual parts. Naturally, the more tightly the components of a system are coupled, the more likely that "one thing leads to another."

Moreover, I resist historical determinism and stress in this book the contingent nature of many political phenomena, including war. To use power-transition theory and Thucydides' Trap again as examples, I am not satisfied just to know that power shifts and war may be correlated or, for that matter, that armament races, alliance formation, and enduring rivalries are also correlated with war. I am interested in the mechanisms that can trigger these conditions to produce war. Specifically, I introduce the idea of a catalyst—or a *fuse* in my language—that ignites the combustible mixture produced by these variables' interactions. Contingency argues that in the absence of this catalyst, a powder keg does not explode, and the timing of this catalyst can be highly random and thus unpredictable. It takes a conducive environment and a trigger to initiate the process leading to war and its expansion.

Contingency also means that whether alliances can trap their member states in a larger conflict or, conversely, restrain them from reckless behavior depends on considerations such as these states' relative power and policy preferences. Similarly, whether power shifts or transitions can lead to war also depends on other variables, such as whether the pertinent states have cultural affinity and ideological compatibility, as shown by the peaceful Anglo-American transition. As a third example, a more balanced distribution of interstate power—such as when China closes the power gap separating it from the predominant United States—does not necessarily have to be destabilizing, at least not when considered in the context of the traditional realist tenet that a balance of power enhances the prospects of international peace and stability. Thus, it seems to me too facile to make blanket assertions claiming that these and other such variables will necessarily increase (or decrease) the danger of war. The answer is typically "it depends."

Most international relations studies do not present theory as this term is used in the physical sciences. I also do not see myself presenting a competing "theory" that challenges other formulations such as power-transition theory or Thucydides' Trap. These latter formulations and others like them posit that X causes Y—where X can be power shifts, alliance dynamics, enduring rivalries, or some other variable and Y is the occurrence, contagion, or escalation of war. Although these formulations posit that X causes Y, they are in my view deficient because they do not tell us the intermediate steps leading from X to Y. These steps are usually missing in their accounts and/or are not explicitly incorporated in empirical models. An example to fill in the missing links may be to argue that power shifts produce various cognitive or psychological dysfunctions such as anxiety, arrogance, overconfidence, or "gambling for recovery" on the part of leaders, cognitive or psychological impairments that in turn produce misjudgment and misinterpretation, raising the danger of war. In this example, power shifts do not in themselves make war more likely. Rather, their influence on war is mediated by various decision errors. My work in this book addresses some such missing or overlooked links that take us from X to Y. Knowing that X is correlated with Y does not tell us the intermediate steps that are responsible for this correlation.

In other words, I hope to illuminate several causal chains and pathways for wars to occur, spread, and escalate. I do not, however, claim that these chains and pathways are the only possible ones. On the contrary, the idea of equifinality suggests that different combinations of factors or pathways can produce similar outcomes. For example, states may go to war as a result of the push of their domestic politics, the pull of alliance dynamics, or cognitive or psychological dysfunctions (Welch 2015; 2018). These explanations need not be mutually exclusive. Life is too complicated for us to be dogmatic or to try to force explanations of complex phenomena into binary choices.

To be more specific, I address three common pathways which are highlighted by my references to the ideas of *fuses*, *chains*, and *backlashes* in the book's title. As just stated, these are not the only possible pathways to war but are in my view common ones that have happened in the past. Nor do I contend that these pathways lead inevitably to conflict enlargement because leaders have often been able to abort the contagion/escalation process before a large conflagration occurs. This is not a trivial point. History is only destined to repeat itself if people do not learn from the past. If they do, we should actually expect some of our propositions about war to be self-nullifying—which is another way of saying that we need to reconsider propositions such as that power shifts produce war. For example, if today's Chinese leaders learn from the mistakes made by Wilhelmine Germany (Wolf 2014), perhaps we have a good chance of avoiding Thucydides' Trap.

This book tries to give some historical and theoretical context to the question about why wars occur, spread, and escalate and why longstanding rivalries persist. Its basic theses are that large interstate wars have often (though not always) originated from local feuds that subsequently become enlarged due to intervention and counter-intervention by major states. These local feuds thus serve as the fuse for larger conflicts, and alliances often (though not always) serve as the transmission mechanism for this enlargement. The metaphor of chains as in chain-ganging points to this process. Sometimes, aggressor states behave recklessly. They do not know when to stop attacking other states, and this behavior expands interstate conflict and usually ends in their downfall. The idea of backlash describes their self-defeating policy. Backlash can also describe situations involving moral hazard, such as when the international community intervenes in a local conflict to arrange a ceasefire, supply humanitarian aid, and even provide political and military assistance to rebel groups or secessionist movements—thereby encouraging unintentionally copycats to start future wars or insurrections in the hope of receiving foreign support. By lowering the costs of conflict and raising its potential benefits, foreign intervention can also unintentionally cause some local feuds to persist and for the parties involved to initiate recurrent rounds of conflict. In other words, by preventing the belligerents from fighting it out till the bitter end, international peace efforts actually have the perverse effect of prolonging conflicts, and even making them more likely or more severe in the future.

The General Ideas behind My Perspective

Why do some local disputes ensnare third parties and turn into large conflagrations? World War I is a paradigmatic case to study this phenomenon, as it is for many other topics of interest to international relations scholars. It stemmed from a feud between Austria–Hungary and Serbia. The assassination of Archduke Ferdinand, Austria–Hungary's heir apparent, in Sarajevo precipitated a crisis that eventually involved all the world's major powers in a war engulfing Europe. Sarajevo provided the *fuse* that ignited this systemic war.

Not all local disputes, however, develop into systemic wars that threaten to reshuffle the interstate hierarchy while causing great havoc and enormous destruction to the world. In fact, most of these disputes involve minor states and are likely to go unnoticed by officials and scholars alike because they do not pose a serious threat to international peace and stability. They do not portend intervention and confrontation by major powers. As a result, they are underreported and even overlooked entirely in the annals of international relations. For example, Ecuador and Peru fought a war in 1941, known in Spanish as *Guerra del 41*. Although this conflict occurred during World War II, neither the Allied nor the Axis powers became involved. The remoteness and brevity of this war between two minor powers (fought over a small portion of the Amazonian basin and lasting from July 5 to July 31, 1941) was for all practical purposes a "non-event" for the wider world, even though it had caused over a thousand combat fatalities (mostly on the Ecuadorian side).

As just alluded to, the involvement of third parties in what was originally a bilateral dispute is a common pathway for a conflict to spread and escalate. This involvement stems typically from security ties, including but not limited to formal alliances. Thus, to return to the example of World War I, Germany became embroiled in this conflict because of its ties with Austria–Hungary and France likewise because it was allied with Russia, which was in turn allied with Serbia, Austria–Hungary's sworn enemy. Relations among Europe's major powers were tightly coupled, and the distribution of power was delicately balanced between the two opposing sides (the Triple Alliance and the Triple Entente). Thus, even a small disturbance to the system can cause large cascading effects. The spark set off by Sarajevo induced a *chain* reaction, eventuating in a wider and more devastating war.

Alliances therefore appear to be an important mechanism for producing conflict contagion and escalation. This factor helps to explain why some local disputes remain contained while others escalate to become larger and more intense multilateral struggles. Yet countries that have ended up fighting on the same side are not always formal allies in the sense of being signatories of a security treaty. World War II provides two prominent examples of this phenomenon. The Soviet Union only became belatedly a de facto ally of Britain and France after it was attacked by Nazi Germany. Similarly, Japan was already at war with China when it attacked Pearl Harbor in 1941. As with Adolf Hitler's invasion of the USSR, this action forged a Sino–American joint effort to fight back even though these two countries were not formal allies bound by a defense pact.

These two examples suggest another pathway for a conflict to diffuse and escalate. The reckless conduct of aggressor states is often responsible for rallying their victims to form a countervailing coalition to oppose them, thereby producing a wider and more intense conflict. By lashing out against multiple victims, these states create their self-encirclement and eventual defeat (Schroeder 1994a; 1994b; Wolf 2014). In addition to the two examples introduced in the last paragraph, Napoleon's France and the Habsburgs repeatedly attacked their neighbors and, in so doing, left no choice for them but to join hands and fight back. The aggressor states' behavior causes a backlash against them, an effect resulting in a wider and larger war that ends badly for them. Napoleon's and Hitler's own actions created a powerful countervailing coalition that eventually defeated them—something that British diplomacy had sought but failed to accomplish. More surprising perhaps, foreign intervention to arrange a ceasefire, provide humanitarian aid, and support insurgency against authoritarian governments can create a moral hazard by lowering an actor's threshold for starting or repeating a conflict and encouraging others to imitate its behavior—thus unwittingly causing a backlash effect by inviting more conflicts and even more severe ones because the weaker side in these disputes has an incentive to provoke escalation to attract foreign support.

The metaphors of *fuses*, *chains*, and *backlashes* point to ingredients that often abet conflict diffusion and escalation. Fuses by their very nature serve as a trigger or catalyst that puts in motion a sequence of events. In the context of this discussion, these events refer to steps leading to a wider and more intense war. Significantly, a spark can start a conflagration only if there is a conducive environment for a blaze to occur. Wars do not suddenly happen out of the blue. There must be preexisting conditions that increase their probability of occurrence. Recurrent crises, enduring rivalry, power shifts, armament races, tightening alliances, and diplomatic brinksmanship constitute elements of a combustible environment that abets warfare.

The analogy of a forest fire comes to mind. Several years of protracted drought, accumulation of dry debris, inaccessible terrain, and strong winds are ingredients providing an environment conducive to a large wildfire. A lightning strike, a downed power line, an unextinguished cigarette butt or campfire could all have ignited the blaze. The circumstances already existed to set off the tinderbox. On the eve of Sarajevo, conditions in Europe were ripe for a conflict to break out. William Thompson (2003) has used another metaphor to describe incidents that can serve as a fuse to produce a large conflict. Sarajevo is a "streetcar" that comes around and around. If it had not happened to precipitate World War I, some other incident *could* or *might* have done so. Some would go even further, claiming that some other incident *would* bring about the same outcome. Ned Lebow (2000/2001, 591) quotes British historian F. H. Hinsley, stating that "If the Sarajevo crisis had not precipitated a particular great war, some other crisis would have precipitated a great war at no distant date." To varying degrees, analysts see Europe in 1914 as a powder keg waiting to explode. Yet, it took a confluence of events and conditions in addition to a precipitant for war to happen.

Fuses do not inevitably produce fire. They may be disarmed by timely and effective human intervention or disabled by serendipitous circumstances. The local government of Lahaina in Hawaii has filed a lawsuit against the Hawaiian Electric Company, alleging its negligence for keeping the power lines energized despite warnings of strong wind and fire hazard. The point of this example is, of course, that timely and effective human intervention can defuse a combustion, literally or figuratively.

Formal alliance ties are not the only chains that can ensnare a country in a conflict. The ongoing Russo–Ukrainian War, the armed conflict between Hamas and Israel, and tension across the Taiwan Strait show that a third party such as the United States can become deeply involved even without being formally allied with one of the disputants. In fact, the United States does not even recognize Taiwan as an independent sovereign state, and yet there is a palpable danger that it can become more directly involved in a military confrontation with China over this island's status.

In addition to alliance ties, the idea of a chain reaction can refer to a tit-for-tat dynamic whereby action begets reaction, thus causing a conflict to spiral out of hand, such as in Lewis Richardson's (1960) classic model of an arms race when leaders do not stop to think about the consequences of their actions. The metaphor of a mirror image, referring to reciprocal perceptions of hostility, can involve a similar dynamic in the formation of elite and mass opinions such that antagonistic feelings and belligerent rhetoric in one country are responded to in kind by its counterpart. In this way, hardliners in both countries become partners in a tag team, sustaining and heightening a hostile atmosphere. Their reciprocal animosity tends to produce a self-fulfilling prophecy that vindicates their worst suspicions about the other side. The metaphor of a chain therefore refers generally to the idea of a runaway process with one thing leading to another.

I use *backlash* to refer to situations when a state's policies cause harm to itself. This term can therefore be used to describe self-defeating or self-injurious policies undertaken by a state. Susan Shirk (2023)uses the term *overreach* to describe these policies, such as when she argues that Beijing's assertive policies have caused adverse reactions abroad. In this work, I use *overreach* in another way, referring to when an actor makes the mistake of taking on more challenges, obligations, or commitments than it can reasonably manage. It can, for example, refer to the idea of "imperial overstretch." Paul Kennedy (1987, 515) has coined this term, warning that "the United States now runs the risk, so familiar to historians of the rise and fall of previous Great Powers, of what might be called 'imperial overstretch': that is to say, decision-makers in Washington must face the awkward and enduring fact that the sum total of the United States' global interests and obligations is nowadays far larger than the country's power to defend them all simultaneously." Naturally, overreach or imperial overstretch is a self-inflicted error, producing self-defeating or self-injurious policies. The distinction that I am trying to draw here, however, is that *backlash* is used to refer to a situation when a policy backfires on the actor initiating it, whereas *overreach* refers to a mismatch between this actor's objectives and the resources available to it to pursue them—that is, when the available resources are inadequate to achieve the objectives being sought.

Equifinality, Conjunction, and Contingency

Complex sociopolitical phenomena like war do not lend themselves to simple answers. Thus, monocausal explanations are suspect, especially when the evidence invoked to support them has not accounted for the influence of other plausible factors that could have been responsible for or contributed to the occurrence of the event or outcome being studied. It is usually more accurate and useful to think in terms of a combination of several factors that increases the likelihood of an event or outcome. In studies of the war phenomenon, this perspective suggests that rarely does any specific variable among those typically considered by international relations scholars present a sufficient condition for its occurrence. I favor explanations that point to the influence of a confluence of factors, or ones that adopt the conjunctive logic. Moreover, as already stated, there can be multiple pathways or combinations of factors that produce the same outcome.

Ned Lebow (2000/2001) argues that World War I happened due to a confluence of three independent streams involving Gestalt shifts in Berlin, Vienna, and St. Petersburg. German leaders came to believe that they could still win a war in 1914 but not soon afterward, when Russia would have completed its military modernization and rail construction, Austrian leaders were eager to confront Serbia to stem pan-Slavic nationalism threatening the disintegration of their multiethnic empire, and Russian leaders were determined to stand their ground after having been pressured to yield in prior crises in the Balkans. Each of these shifts alone in the mindset of the relevant leaders was not sufficient to bring about a large war, but in combination they were. "Timing was everything in 1914, and that timing was fortuitous" (Lebow 2000/2001, 600). The Gestalt shifts happened practically concurrently in the three European capitals. Lebow argues that if the Sarajevo incident was delayed for even only two years, the perceptions and calculations of European leaders would have undergone further transformation so that World War I could very well have been avoided.

The conjunction of factors is therefore critical according to this perspective. Each of these factors may be necessary, but none of them is sufficient for an event to occur. Lebow (2000/2001) offers an example of a house fire started by an unattended lit candle left on a window ledge according to the neighborhood's tradition for a commemorative occasion. The window was left ajar so that a strong breeze blew the nearby curtain to be ignited by the candle. What is the cause of the resulting house fire? The neighborhood tradition, the lit candle, its proximity to the curtain, the open window, the windy weather, or the absence of the house's residents? Each is a necessary condition, but none is itself sufficient to bring about the house fire, which results from their joint contribution. In other words, if one of these conditions was missing, this accident would not have occurred. Because they all played an indispensable role in bringing about the fire, we may speak of them as a causal chain. This accident required a conjunction of facilitative conditions. Moreover, each condition in this example has an independent source.

The above example of a house fire is obviously different from a situation of equifinality, when the same event or outcome can be due to different causes. Equifinality suggests, for example, a child's poor academic performance may be due to a dysfunctional family environment, disadvantages in socioeconomic circumstances, a lack of appropriate mentorship or a role model, and/or inadequate school facilities and unmotivated or poorly trained teachers. There are therefore multiple factors and intersections for a social worker to consider and act on to assist this student to improve. In contrast, it is easier to imagine steps that could have prevented the house fire. By removing just one of the conditions described above, we could have avoided it. International relations, however, are more complex; and they resemble more situations of equifinality, suggesting the existence of many pathways to war, thus making efforts to prevent it more difficult. The more independent pathways there are, the more interventions are necessary to alter an outcome; and the more coupled are the pathways, the more contagious a situation becomes.

There is an obverse side to this phenomenon. In situations involving complex social or physical systems, success depends on the proper functioning of all their parts. In the above example, it takes the removal of all handicaps and hindrances as well as the introduction of positive support and reinforcement to improve a student's academic performance. Similarly, the operation of a nuclear plant requires all its subsystems to work properly in conjunction. Significantly, a failure by any of the critical subsystems to perform satisfactorily can cause the system to shut down. The entire system is vulnerable to its weakest link.

The movie *A Bridge Too Far*, based on a book by Cornelius Ryan (1977) with the same title, recalls the Allies' Operation Market Garden during World War II to create a path to invade northern Germany. Their plan entailed simultaneous assaults by ground and airborne forces on multiple targets in German-occupied the Netherlands. Among its objectives was the imperative of overcoming six water obstacles in their path. The inability of the US airborne troops to seize the bridge over the Rhine at Arnhem caused the entire campaign to fail even though the Allies had successes in carrying out the other parts of the plan.

Thus, *A Bridge Too Far* signifies that malfunction or failure at any juncture of a complex network or operation of interlocking parts can produce a system breakdown.

Unlike the example of the house fire, the elements of a combustible environment conducive to war tend to be interrelated and can be traced to a common source of tension. Recurrent crises, arms races, alliance politics, economic sanctions, commercial rivalry, hard-ball diplomacy, and hawkish domestic opinion tend to abet, support, and reinforce each other—or, in the words of social scientists, to create and sustain a system of positive feedback. All of them originate from mutual antagonism among the relevant states due to their dissatisfaction over some unsettled issues.

John Vasquez (2009a, 133) states succinctly, "war and violence occur because of *grievances* and not just power" (italic in original). In this view, power transition, competitive armament, alliance entanglement and competition, and other conditions and actions promoting war-proneness could all have contributed to the occurrence of World War I; but they were themselves the consequences of the rivalry and hostility that were already present or developing among the then future belligerents. One may conceive of those elements that I have mentioned in describing the combustible environment of pre-1914 Europe as derivatives of grievances over contested issues. Naturally, the dynamics of their interactions can acquire a life of their own to increase the probability of war and hasten its onset.

In this context, the idea of path dependency enters the analytic picture. Relations between countries have a past and a future. How officials act reflects their memories of the past and their expectations of the future. A particular policy undertaken today will foreclose some options in the future while also opening other possibilities. One example of such serial dependency is the well-established tendency for each episode of militarized dispute between two countries to increase the probability of another such dispute in the future.

China's military intervention in the Korean War offers another example. This action caused relations between Beijing and Washington to be locked in hostility and mistrust for many years until President Richard Nixon visited China in 1972. Similarly, the estrangement between Moscow and Washington caused by the current war in Ukraine would take many years to reverse. More pertinent to the present discussion, the various elements describing a combustible environment conducive to war can become entrenched in relations among the countries concerned so that processes such as armament escalation and confrontational diplomacy can gain a self-sustaining momentum and become more difficult to arrest or reverse.

Even in the presence of a combustible environment, war is not inevitable. This environment is permissive, but it does not mean that war is thus inevitable.

It makes this occurrence more likely but not certain. We know the phenomenon of spontaneous combustion, and yet a dry pile of wood does not usually catch fire by itself—even though it is more likely to do so if it has been previously doused with gasoline. A catalyst, such as a lighted match, is usually necessary to ignite a blaze.

Thus, it helps to distinguish the idea of cause between a precipitant, on the one hand, and the underlying structural conditions, on the other hand. A precipitant or catalyst represents the immediate cause, as in the case of the assassination of the archduke and his wife in Sarajevo triggering the onset of World War I. Besides a lighted match, we can easily imagine other fuses setting off a blaze, such as a downed power line, a lightning strike, or a cigarette butt that has been discarded carelessly. Any of these fuses could have lit the fire. By their very nature, however, it is difficult for analysts to predict the specific catalyst or precipitant that starts a fire. Similarly, given the tensions and antagonisms gripping Europe in 1914, one can easily imagine different incidents—an unexpected or unauthorized border clash, a coup d'état, or a false alarm of enemy invasion—that could have launched a chain of events to bring about war. There can be many alternative plausible candidates of precipitants or catalysts. They are interchangeable or substitutable, with all of them being capable of triggering war, hence making it difficult to predict them because they are random and there can be so many of them.

Past as Prologue?

Naturally, today's world is not a replica of past situations such as Europe in 1914, and there is always the danger of misapplying historical analogies (Khong 1992). Yet, as Mark Twain reportedly said, "History does not repeat itself, but it rhymes" (https://quoteinvestigator.com/2014/01/12/history-rhymes/).

William Thompson (2003) stresses three components of Europe's political landscape on the eve of World War I. First, there were multiple ongoing rivalries. These rivalries stem from "serial" clashes; that is, there were repeated militarized disputes, with each encounter increasing the probability that there would be another subsequent round of contest. Second, major European states were lining up in opposing camps. This bifurcation pattern in states' alignment decisions and the tightening of the alignment clusters meant that the European system was becoming more vulnerable to unexpected and even uncontrollable breakdown. Third, there were ongoing power shifts which were transforming Europe's pecking order in a nonobvious and nonlinear manner. In a multilateral setting even a small increment of power gain by a second-tier major state like Russia can have profound and unexpected effects on the relative positions of other members of this cohort and the overall European balance of power. These three elements combined to create a highly unstable system prone to breakdown. Although each of these elements was itself important, their interaction effect was more important in pushing Europe over the brink.

It does not take much imagination to see that these developments are emerging and converging in contemporary East Asia. Taiwan has always been a point of friction in Sino-American relations, but the danger of escalation had been mostly contained since these countries' rapprochement in 1972—until the last several years when relations between Beijing and Washington deteriorated to such an extent that this relationship no longer serves as a ballast to stabilize not only cross-strait relations but regional ties more generally. We are also seeing incipient but unmistakable signs of states in the region taking positions in opposing alignments, perhaps even alliances. The Quadrilateral Security Dialogue group consisting of the United States, Japan, Australia, and India is one example. Joint exercises among these countries' (except India) navies with that of the Philippines provide another example. There has also been a Sino-Russian rapprochement, a partnership "without limits" according to Beijing and Moscow. The Shanghai Cooperation Organization and the BRICS (Brazil, Russia, India, China, and South Africa) group with new members such as the United Arab Emirates, Iran, Ethiopia, and Egypt also show signs of possibly developing into anti-Western coalitions in the future.

Although East Asian countries have not ramped up their defense expenditures in the past in response to a rising China, this situation may be changing. Of course, one of the most transformative developments in international relations in the past four decades or so has been the ongoing power shifts between China and the United States. China has made relative gains, while the United States has suffered relative decline—especially in its economic position, even though it remains the predominant military power.

Some of the processes just mentioned have been going on for some time, but others such as emerging patterns of interstate alignment and military expenditures are more recent. Of the more recent developments that augur for a more contentious future is Washington's declared intention to decouple economically from China and its overt steps to move closer to committing it to defend Taiwan—an issue at the core of Beijing's interests. The spillover of political frictions to trade tariffs, technology embargoes, and investment restrictions suggests that we are entering a more worrisome era. As in Europe, the euphoria accompanying the Cold War's end has also disappeared in East Asia. The days when China and the United States were practically strategic partners in their joint opposition to the USSR are now a distant memory. We may very well be entering a second Cold War.

World War I took on the connotation of a fight between a declining global hegemon (Britain) and a rising regional powerhouse (Germany). Such conflicts tend to be rare historically, but when they occur, they have seldom remained dyadic (W. Thompson 2003, 466). They tend to become multilateral affairs because they impinge on the important interests of other countries, and these wars tend to be deadlier and more destructive compared to those involving bilateral disputes between two minor powers (Rasler and Thompson 1994).

Unlike most other (spatial) rivalries, China and the United States do not have any territorial disputes. Theirs is more a positional rivalry for regional or global leadership status. This kind of competition is necessarily linked to ongoing changes in their bilateral balance of power, one of the structural variables in creating a more combustible international environment (W. Thompson 1995, 218). The most dangerous kind of rivalry is between a declining global hegemon and a rising regional powerhouse.

There is, however, an offsetting consideration regarding the historical tendency for such contests to become large multilateral wars, suggesting that "the greater the distance between the home bases of these actors [i.e., positional rivals], the less likely full-scale warfare has been" (W. Thompson 1995, 209). Proximity, in this case sheer physical distance, means a looser coupling (such as for the United States and Japan with respect to their lesser sensitivity to European developments in 1914 in comparison to countries located on that continent) and has in the past acted as a barrier to conflict diffusion—assuming, of course, all else being equal.

As the reader may have surmised, I see what is different and perhaps relatively novel in my effort to understand a more volatile East Asia is my emphasis on framing this inquiry in a broader historical and geographic context beyond this region or, in other words, to introduce knowledge from other times and places to inform our understanding of East Asia—as opposed to focusing on the more idiosyncratic aspects of the countries in this region. As should also be obvious by now, I emphasize multifactor explanations and historical contingencies. Thus, I eschew a focus on just one variable such as power shifts as the ostensible cause of war, and I am also skeptical about our ability to make specific predictions—even though international relations analysts have a reasonably good idea about factors that tend to generally abet or inhibit war.

Further Thoughts on the Dynamics of War

As William Thompson points out, interactions among elements of the conflict complex (enduring rivalries, bifurcation of states' alignments, and ongoing processes of power shifts) can produce nonlinear changes so that we can speak of an acceleration of momentum, a spiral of conflict, and a rush to war. A nuclear meltdown due to a runaway chain reaction spreading and escalating beyond the control of relevant personnel conjures up a similar image. The conditions described here constitute the central focus of this inquiry and most other similar kinds of research. Analysts can point to and warn about the emergence and consolidation of those elements that abet armed conflicts in general without, however, being able to predict the specific trigger that initiates a particular war.

My view corresponds largely, although not entirely, with Ned Lebow's. He argues that "underlying causes, no matter how numerous or deep-seated, do not make an event inevitable. Their consequences may depend on fortuitous coincidences in timing and on the presence of catalysts that are independent of any of the underlying causes" (Lebow 2000/2001, 591–92). He sees World War I as a highly contingent event. What made war possible was the interactions among causes. War was a product of "a non-linear confluence of three largely independent chains of causation [the Gestalt shifts in Berlin, Vienna, and St. Petersburg described earlier]" (Lebow 2000/2001, 592). It is hard to disagree with Lebow on these points. Indeed, I share his view on the importance of timing and the often unintended and unexpected results of interactions among multiple variables.

This said, precisely because coincidences tend to be fortuitous and there are many plausible catalysts, analysts should focus on the more easily recognizable patterns and regularities without denying the possibility of contingency. Although we can try to estimate the range of empirical uncertainties and the probability of accidents, it is difficult to specify catalysts represented by unexpected and rare incidents because they are by their very nature unknown. Accidental conjunctures are accidental and thus irregular and hard to predict (the best we can do, for example, is to say that a traffic accident is more likely if a motorist has consumed alcohol and drives at a high speed during a rainy night on a poorly lit, winding country road crossed frequently by wildlife). Moreover, few social scientists would maintain that complex sociopolitical phenomena like war are inevitable or foreordained. Most are likely to acknowledge that their conclusions are probabilistic, even though they may not be able to assign a numerical figure to this probability and even though they may only be able to say that an outcome is more probable under given circumstances. I am in these colleagues' company.

A few additional words are necessary about the role of a trigger or precipitant. The metaphor of Sarajevo as a streetcar is pregnant with several implications. A streetcar can, of course, come around and around. This imagery implies that Europe in 1914 was a powder keg primed to explode—if not this time, then next time, or the one after that when something presents itself to activate the fuse. Yet a streetcar can also be late, and it may even never arrive. Ned Lebow (2000/2001) argues that had the dual assassinations not occurred in 1914, or had they occurred two years later in 1916, Europe could have avoided World War I.

That is, the underlying structural conditions might have changed sufficiently that in the calculations of German, Austrian, and Russian officials about war, this option would have become much less attractive or feasible in the meantime. That Sarajevo happened at the time that it did was accidental but critical for war to occur at that moment. Analysts can say something about the combination of factors that makes a war likely, but they are unable to predict its exact timing.

Still another implication of this discussion is that occurrences such as World War I are contingent. History could have taken a different turn. What if the archduke had decided not to go to Sarajevo or not to visit its city hall? What if the lead car in his motorcade had not made a wrong turn to cause a traffic stop? What if the assassin, Gavrilo Princip, had missed his shot? Any of these small changes could have altered history. Lebow (2000/2001) contends that if Sarajevo did not happen, it was doubtful that World War I would have happened in 1914. Thus again, international relations analysts can have some important things to say about those conditions and actions that heighten the danger of war without, however, being certain about when and how it will happen.

Former US secretary of defense Donald Rumsfeld is known for his quip "there are known knowns; there are things we know we know. We also know there are known unknowns; that is to say we know there are some things we do not know. But there are also unknown unknowns—the ones we don't know we don't know" (https://en.wikipedia.org/wiki/There_are_unknown_unknowns).

As an example of a known unknown, we know that there is a danger of afternoon storms when we go mountain climbing in Colorado during the summer. There are also unknown unknowns when we are unaware of situations that are risky. There are, of course, also "unknown knowns" when people engage in risky behavior such as the hypothetical drunk driver described above. Sarajevo in Lebow's (2000/2001; 2003) discussion falls in the category of known unknowns, whereas for at least some of the archduke's entourage it could have been an instance of an unknown unknown. However, some of the archduke's other close associates had tried to talk him out of visiting Sarajevo due to concerns for his security. Therefore, for him it would have been a case of a known unknown. Because, by definition, unknowns are unknowns, it would be more fruitful to try expanding our knowledge about what we can learn and know. As explained later in Chapter 2, instead of focusing on catalysts or precipitants that are idiosyncratic and therefore unpredictable, I will focus on patterns of behavior that can serve as a fuse to cause conflict to spread and escalate.

Finally, even when a streetcar arrives, a person may decide not to get on board. President Lyndon Johnson's national security advisor McGeorge Bundy described the Viet Cong's attack on the US military outpost at Pleiku in February 1965 as a streetcar and urged the president to initiate a sustained bombing campaign against North Vietnam in retaliation (Hoopes 1969, 30). The context of

Bundy's advice, however, indicates that the communists' assault on Pleiku was a pretext for the United States to escalate the war. In this context, many other similar incidents could have served the same purpose. Because such incidents are frequent and recurrent phenomena, officials can always find an excuse to undertake and justify a policy course that they prefer or have already decided on.

Indeed, officials are known to have sometimes contrived or fabricated an incident to engage in this conduct, such as the Gulf of Tonkin incident alleging two episodes of North Vietnamese attack on US naval vessels in August 1964, enabling the Johnson administration to ask for a congressional resolution that gave it the authorization to expand and escalate the Vietnam War. Subsequent investigations concluded that the US Navy was providing covert support for South Vietnamese raids against North Vietnam and that at least the second alleged attack had never occurred (Hallin 1986; Moise 1996; Wells 1994). In this instance, a fuse could have been deliberately set. This possibility speaks to the role of human agency, structural conditions can push and shove, but human beings still exercise choices and make decisions. However, analysts do not usually have access to officials' decision processes, which are shrouded in secrecy and may still be the subject of heated debate after the relevant documents were made public many years after an event. Therefore, many studies, including this one, gravitate to the analysis of structural conditions. Even though these conditions may not necessarily be the most decisive determinant of an event's occurrence, they are more observable, and they present important information about the environment in which choices are deliberated and decisions are undertaken.

This last caveat or confession may remind some readers of the story about the drunk sailor looking for his keys under a streetlamp. A passerby asked him whether he was sure that he had lost his keys there. The sailor replied that he was not sure, but the light was brighter under the streetlamp. This story may not be fair to international relations analysts, suggesting that they are looking at the wrong place just like the sailor. It does, however, inject a sense of humility. Perhaps a better analogy is Plato's parable of a prisoner raised in a cave, who was never allowed to see things directly but only the shadows they cast on the cave's wall. Being outsiders usually without access to officials' decision processes, international relations analysts are also forced to make inferences about things that they cannot observe directly.

My Perspective's Policy Implications

East Asia is a large and complex region with many problems. Obviously, a single book cannot address all the relevant issues. This said, most people would agree with the proposition that Sino–American relations represent the key to this region's peace and stability and that relations between Beijing and Washington have deteriorated seriously in recent years. Consequently, one may say that the region is facing some danger of becoming "unhinged." What was the main reason for the deterioration of Sino-American relations? Both Beijing and Washington would probably agree that it was due to a power shift between them—although Beijing is likely to argue that this shift has caused the United States to undertake more aggressive steps to contain China's rise, and Washington is likely to contend that increased capabilities have caused China to act more aggressively.

How likely is a particular malfunction to cause a system failure or collapse? One consideration is the presence of a buffer that can prevent or mitigate contagion. In this light, the war in Ukraine is concerning because it and other parts of Europe such as Finland, Austria, and Sweden have traditionally served this purpose. They provide a neutral zone separating western Europe and the USSR/Russia, enhancing a sense of security for both sides and reducing points of potential friction between them. The eastward expansion of NATO (North Atlantic Treaty Organization) and the European Union has removed this barrier and increased Moscow's sense of insecurity. One can imagine how Washington would have reacted if Mexico were to come under the sway of Russian or Chinese influence.

Another consideration comes to mind as a possible restraint or constraint against a conflict spreading and escalating. It pertains to the amount of slack in the system and the existence of shock absorbers. When countries line up in tight alliances that oppose each other, there is less "give" or slack in the international system. Put differently, if relations and developments are tightly coupled, changes in one part of the system affect the rest of the system more easily, quickly, and seriously. Thus, a pattern of tightly organized and bifurcated alignment is concerning. A perturbation in one part of the system can be transmitted more easily and quickly to other parts of the system.

Similarly, when the system is delicately balanced, even a small disturbance can have wide and unanticipated ripple effects. The example of the German invasion of Belgium in August 1914 was pivotal because it impinged on Britain's and France's vital security. This reasoning also explains why Moscow cares so much about Ukraine's status—and China cares about Taiwan and Korea, and the United States cares about Cuba and Mexico for obviously similar geostrategic reasons. William Thompson (1995, 219) argues that wars between a global hegemon and a regional powerhouse in the past have usually stemmed from attempts by a regional leader to seize territory that would enhance its strategic position. He mentions as examples France's invasion of northern Italy in the late 15th century and the Netherlands in the late 17th century. These attacks were motivated more by positional considerations than territorial ambitions in France's rivalry with Spain and later with Britain. Of course, as Thompson acknowledges, both positional and spatial (i.e., territorial) motivations could be present. The ongoing war in Ukraine and tension over Taiwan are also prime exhibits in this line of reasoning.

The idea of slack is related to another idea that can soften or deflect the effects of destabilizing developments. Are there "shock absorbers" that can perform this function? As mentioned earlier, Sino–American trade and their economic interdependence more generally have served as a ballast to steady their relationship despite their many disagreements. In other words, the two countries managed to compartmentalize their disagreements and, despite these disagreements, continued to cooperate in other areas such as trade and nuclear nonproliferation for mutual gain. More recently, however, their disagreements have spilled over to other areas so that, as mentioned earlier, Biden could describe their relationship as "extreme competition" politically, economically, and militarily. US financial sanctions, technology embargoes, investment restrictions, and its policy of "economic decoupling" point to the dismantlement of an important shock absorber. Disruptions to and cancellations of academic exchanges are also disturbing because they provide important venues of communication and even avenues for building friendship and mutual trust. The opposite of a shock absorber is an accelerant that can add fuel to an already tense relationship. Armament race, commercial competition, bellicose rhetoric, and domestic politics encouraging a belligerent policy against the other country can exacerbate the further deterioration of this relationship. In the absence of shock absorbers and evident brakes available to stop or at least to slow down this process, the trend of deteriorating Sino–American relations is alarming.

These observations also apply to domestic discourse. Politicians sometimes engage in exaggerated rhetoric, and their words can backfire on them. Rhetorical trap was one of the reasons the United States had such difficulty extricating itself from the quagmire of the Vietnam War (Thomson 1973). In their effort to justify Washington's involvement, politicians "oversold" the stake that the United States had in that conflict. By saying loudly and repeatedly that Vietnam was vital to US strategic interests and represented a test of American will, US officials made it so; and when Washington finally left, its withdrawal was all that more damaging to its reputation.

The density and proximity of rivalry fields are also relevant (W. Thompson 2003). The number of concurrent rivalries matters, but the extent to which they are connected is also important. When there are multiple, intersecting rivalries and these rivalries are closely coupled, there is obviously a greater danger that a local dispute between two neighbors can more easily spread to other members of the international system. In 1914 Europe, Franco–German rivalry was closely linked to Russo–Austrian rivalry, which was also linked intimately to Austro–Serbian rivalry, to mention just a few. Moreover, Franco–German rivalry and Russo–Austrian rivalry obviously provided the strong glue binding the Franco–Russian dyad. They had a similar effect on German–Austrian solidarity. Naturally, when several rivalries are interlinked or "nested," it is more difficult to untangle them and contain a conflict's contagion. Obviously, recent developments in Europe, Asia, and the Middle East presage that conflicts such as those in Ukraine, across the Taiwan Strait, on the Korean peninsula, and involving Iran and its proxies may become intertwined. We have already seen NATO establishing closer ties with Australia, Japan, and South Korea and Iran, Russia, and China moving closer to one another.

Physical proximity is also a consideration. States that became belligerents in World War I were located within a short distance from one another, and some of them were contiguous to each other. Being close means a more acute sense that a country's security would be affected by its neighbors' actions. In contrast, a country (such as the United States) separated by great distance from Europe would be more insulated and less vulnerable to perceived threats emanating from that continent in comparison to European countries residing in a congested neighborhood. John Mearsheimer (2001) has also emphasized the importance of a water barrier in protecting a country's security from foreign assault, such as the Atlantic Ocean separating the United States from Europe. Geographic proximity indicates security sensitivity. There are obvious, good geostrategic reasons for Washington to care about Cuba's status and for Moscow and Beijing to care, respectively, about Ukraine and Taiwan/Korea.

When members of an international system are aligned in tight clusters of opposing alliances, the danger for a bilateral conflict to become multilateral is greater. Close ties, or tight coupling, among components of a system make it more likely for a local event to have system-wide ramifications. The idea of proximity does not, of course, have to be limited to physical distance; it can also refer to political affinity, economic interactions, security connections, and even emotional and historical ties. In all these senses, members of NATO are "tight" or "proximate" and have become more so since Russia's invasion of Ukraine. By comparison, the Russo–Chinese pair is more "loose" and "distant" even though these countries are contiguous neighbors. As in domestic politics, cross-cutting cleavages tend to soften partisan conflict and facilitate political compromises, whereas rigid and overlapping cleavages have the opposite effect of sharpening divisions and intensifying struggles of "us versus them" (Deutsch and Singer 1960). Finally, the idea of proximity can refer to the timing or, more specifically, the coincidence of several ongoing processes. The war in 1914 reflects the product of "separate but simultaneous and overlapping antagonisms" (W. Thompson 2003, 472).

This discussion also suggests that neutral countries provide important buffers not only to limit the potential for conflict to start in the first place and to subsequently spread and escalate but also to play a role as a bridge between the opposing parties. Helsinki, Vienna, Stockholm, and Geneva have served as hosts for important international organizations, sites for summit meetings, and useful conduits for confidential communication and impartial mediation. They serve an important role as objective observers and trusted intermediaries (such as the role that Sweden played as a liaison to reach out to North Korea and Austria, Finland, and Switzerland in hosting summit meetings between East and West during the Cold War). Finland's and Sweden's recent joining of NATO thus removes them from serving these important functions. In general, the more ties and exchanges between members of opposing coalitions or camps, the greater the prospects of stabilizing the international system. The more states share membership in many different international organizations, the more promising are these prospects. These organizations provide fora to exchange views, search for agreements, and conduct multilateral diplomacy. In fact, when a state decides to join such an organization, this decision itself conveys its interest and intent to cooperate with other members. When states withdraw from these organizations, as Japan and Germany did in leaving the League of Nations before World War II (the United States never joined this organization), this action is also informative, although it sends the opposite signal.

Agreements on the basic rules of international order can also serve as another protection against unwanted escalation of conflict. Charles Kegley and Gregory Raymond (1994) remark that when states agree on and abide by norms that restrict the use of force, stress the sanctity of treaties, respect one another's sovereignty, and refrain from encroaching on one another's traditional sphere of influence, these periods of restrictive international order experience more peace and stability. Conversely, during periods of permissive international order when these norms are abandoned and when states resort to force arbitrarily and unilaterally, disregard their treaty commitments, challenge the legitimacy of other countries' ruling elites, and fail to agree on the boundaries of their geostrategic competition, conflicts were more pervasive and intense.

In the years since the collapse of the USSR and the end of the Cold War, the world has paradoxically seen more frequent application of military force whether in the form of covert drone attacks on terrorist suspects or open military intervention, armed attack, and even brazen invasion. Iraq, Afghanistan, Panama, Libya, Serbia, Syria, Georgia, and Ukraine are just the more notable examples. Under the Trump administration, the United States has also withdrawn from a considerable number of important international treaties and international organizations, such as the Anti-Ballistic Missile Treaty, the Trans-Pacific Partnership, the Joint Comprehensive Plan of Action (intended to restrict Iran's nuclear program), UNESCO (United Nations Education, Science and Cultural Organization), the World Health Organization, the Paris Climate

Accord, and the United Nations Human Rights Council (the Biden administration returned the United States to the latter three institutions and accord, but in the early days of his second presidency, Trump withdrew the United States from them again for a second time). Unlike China, the United States never joined the United Nations Convention on the Law of the Sea.

Spheres of influence have recently gotten a bad name, but they have historically played a role in reducing conflict among major powers (Allison 2020; Etzioni 2015; Hast 2014). With the significant exception of Cuba, the USSR and the United States had generally refrained from interfering in their counterpart's zones of control. Thus, Washington did not act beyond verbal support when Moscow intervened militarily in Hungary in 1956 and Czechoslovakia in 1968. Nor did Moscow actively support insurgent movements in the Western Hemisphere, with Cuba representing an important exception. These two major powers, of course, competed in regions outside their traditional turf, such as in the Middle East and the Horn of Africa; but they did not confront each other directly, and as already mentioned, they also refrained from intruding into each other's backyard. Washington's policies to promote regime change (or color revolutions) and interventions in the name of protecting human rights ("responsibility to protect") since the Cold War's end have challenged old understandings of spheres of influence. NATO has increasingly encroached on Russia's near abroad referring to its immediate neighborhood.

Importantly, the United States has never recognized a Chinese sphere of influence as evidenced by its alliances and military bases encircling China. It has fought three large wars on China's doorstep in the recent past (Korea, Vietnam, and Afghanistan), and of course, tension over Taiwan's status is in Beijing's eyes an even greater affront to China's claim to great-power status. The breakdown of traditional recognition of spheres of influence is concerning. Notwithstanding that the Monroe Doctrine is clearly still intact and alive, we are missing today one important traditional guardrail that has helped in the past to reduce the danger of clashes between major powers.

Finally, there is a severe limit to how much we can do to cope with contingencies such as Sarajevo if we see them as unexpected random accidents introducing shocks to the international system. I will take a different tack in the next chapter where I look for general patterns of behavior that can produce systemic ramifications. The inclination of parties ensnared in protracted local disputes to internationalize their feud is a likely fuse to initiate larger multilateral warfare. The idea of a fuse is therefore used to refer to a general phenomenon rather than an unexpected accident brought about by a unique set of circumstances. This approach puts us in a better position to manage contingencies conceived as a class of recurrent phenomena rather than isolated and idiosyncratic incidents. Although insurance companies cannot predict which house will catch fire, they consider whether a home is equipped with a fire alarm in setting their policy premium. They also charge a higher premium for mountain homes near wooded areas and with poor access for firefighters.

My Larger Research Program

This book is part of a larger research program that I have been pursuing over the past dozen or so years. Publications produced by this research program have been motivated by a common concern about the danger of an armed confrontation between China and the United States, currently the world's two largest economies. I have pursued this topic in a manner that differs in some important respects from many, even most, studies on this topic.

Scholars who write about China tend to treat this country in isolation and therefore eschew comparing it with other countries. Moreover, they tend to emphasize the idiographic approach, calling attention to China's special, even unique, characteristics to explain Beijing's conduct. Finally, these scholars do not usually embed their research in theories of international relations and especially this field's scholarship reflecting quantitative research. In contrast, I have tried to integrate my work on China with these theories and the quantitative research tradition, taking on their insights and at the same time using China as an example to sometimes challenge conclusions drawn from analyses based on them. I have tried to place my study of China in a cross-country and trans-historical context.

There is another tendency characterizing studies on China. These studies tend to be China-centric. Their authors usually see China much more in the role of acting rather than reacting: China initiates and other countries are forced to respond. There is less attention given to how China may be reacting to what other countries are doing and how its environment is changing. Harry Harding (1976, 1) wrote some time ago that this tendency lends an air of omnipotence to Chinese leaders and presents China as if it is a ship on automatic pilot, "plowing its way single-mindedly through the oceans of international affairs, relatively uninfluenced by the waves and storms around it." Most such studies tend to be descriptive, presenting a sort of "slow journalism" that is not grounded in contemporary social science research.

This book builds on my previous publications and fills in several topical areas that have not been heretofore fully addressed. As explained earlier, it focuses on the question of why some local conflicts escalate and spread to become large conflagrations we call systemic war, while others are limited in intensity, duration, and scope and are frequently overlooked or underreported in the chronicles of history. Given my concern with the danger of a Sino–American conflict, this book tries to understand and identify those conditions and dynamics that can produce a systemic war and, conversely, those steps and circumstances that can help avert such a catastrophe.

To situate this inquiry in the context of my larger research program, I have advanced the following broad arguments in my prior studies.

1. Like other complex sociopolitical phenomena, wars are due to a constellation of factors. Therefore, monocausal explanations such as resorting to the ongoing power shift between China and the United States to warn about a possible collision between them tend to distort and mislead. They also tend to be sensationalist and alarmist. Ongoing and recurrent disputes, enduring rivalry, armament races, commercial competition, alliance politics, diplomatic brinksmanship, nationalist and xenophobic sentiments, and domestic partisan incentives that promote hostility directed against ostensible foreign threats are also frequently present to contribute to the dangerous brew that abets war (Chan 2008; 2013; 2017b; 2019; 2020a; 2020b; 2021a).
2. Systemic wars rarely stem from a direct challenge or assault by an ambitious rising state to displace the existing hegemon ostensibly over which one of them should rule the world and determine the international order. Much more frequently, multilateral and systemic wars happen because of a local conflict or one involving one of the great powers becoming enlarged due to the subsequent involvement of other great powers, including possibly the existing hegemon trying to protect an ally or to check the influence of another competing great power, or a combination of these motivations.
3. Power shift is not irrelevant to war occurrence, but it is just one element, albeit an important one, when combined with other elements contributing to a combustible mixture that is likely to encourage war (Chan 2012a; 2014). It is neither a necessary nor a sufficient condition for war to occur. In the one and only case in the modern era when the baton of world leadership changed hands—the Anglo-American case—power transition happened peacefully. There were, however, several instances of "near misses" when these countries came close to war. Much current discussion of this pair reflects hindsight bias and revisionist reconstruction of history. Moreover, history is replete with wars fought in the absence of a power transition (Chan 2017b; 2020a; 2020b).
4. This said, a power shift between China and the United States explains better the rising tension between these countries than other reasons such as China's communist ideology, its authoritarian government, or its abuse of human rights (Chan 2023a; 2023b). These latter attributions

were also valid during those years when relations between Beijing and Washington were amiable, such as when they were practically strategic partners in opposing the former USSR. In the years since they established formal diplomatic ties in 1979, China has opened its economy, become deeply embedded in the global economy, renounced its support for armed insurrection abroad, and increased its support for international organizations and multilateral diplomacy—all these changes should improve rather than worsen its relations with the United States (Chan 2023a; 2023b). Much of the current Western discourse on deteriorating Sino–American relations overlooks these historical changes.

5. Power shifts are not the same thing as power transitions. Thus, although China has made relative gain in its national power while the United States has suffered relative loss in recent decades, this phenomenon does not mean that China has already overtaken the United States or is poised to do so imminently. In fact, the United States continues to enjoy a large edge over China, especially in its structural power to determine the rules of the game and in its soft power to appeal to and convert people abroad. Thus, proponents of power-transition theory and Thucydides' Trap tend to offer an alarmist prognosis that is not warranted by the available evidence, and they may be producing a self-fulfilling prophecy to the extent that people are swayed by their warning of a coming collision between China and the United States. Moreover, although this collision may occur, this possible occurrence can be due to other causes and thus does not necessarily vindicate or confirm the reasons they give.
6. Although the danger of a Sino–American collision is real, it does not follow from the logic and evidence given by proponents of power-transition theory and Thucydides' Trap (Chan 2008; 2020a). International structure, such as that which results from power shifts, can push and shove; but agency continues to be important. People still make choices, even though these choices may be constrained or shaped by their environment. The domestic environment is usually more important in influencing foreign policy than the international environment. Officials' paramount incentive is usually to maintain their domestic power and authority. Their foreign policies are therefore often an extension or reflection of this incentive.
7. Shifts in the balance of international power are due to the uneven rates of states' economic growth. Thus, the main and original source of power shifts among states is their respective economic performance, specifically their differential rates of economic growth which are influenced by a variety of factors including government policies and socioeconomic institutions. An especially important determinant of economic

performance is a country's culture which, for example, distinguishes East Asia with a Confucian heritage from other regions of the world with less dynamic economies (Chan 2024a). To be sure, culture is not destiny, and its influence tends to be mediated by other variables such as government policies and political institutions. Culture is not a fixed entity. It evolves and is not exportable.

8. It is more within the power of officials to promote the economic growth of their own country than to impede that of their competitors or adversaries. The primary determinants of economic growth are located inside a country. Moreover, avoiding self-defeating policies that hinder one's own growth or that cause overreach or backfire is as important as pursuing effective policies to counteract those of one's opponents, if not more important. Success often goes to those countries that have the least burden of self-imposed disadvantages. Pericles cautioned his countrymen, stating "I am more afraid of our own mistakes than the strategy of our opponents" (quoted in Kagan 1969, 192).
9. Power shift is a relative concept pertaining to not only how well one is doing but also how others are doing. The relevant others include not just one's competitors or adversaries but also one's partners and allies. Systemic wars involve opposing coalitions of states. Many current narratives on the shifting power balance between China and the United States overlook the fact that the United States has many powerful allies, whereas China can count on only a very small number of countries to support it in any confrontation with the United States. Although China's economy has been growing faster than the US economy, other countries that are likely US allies or partners may be growing nearly as fast as and may grow even faster than China in the future. International relations are rarely strictly dyadic and are instead usually *N*-adic, referring in international relations parlance many pairs. Moreover, interstate competitions are marathons rather than sprints.
10. Prevailing Western discourse on China's rise tends to reflect political and ideational construction (Chan 2021b; 2023b; 2024c; He et al. 2021). A prominent feature of this discourse is China's ostensible revisionism, a concept that is usually poorly defined and rarely supported by systematic evidence. Attributions of ostensible Chinese revisionism tend to be exaggerated and usually fail to account for changes in Beijing's policies since the Maoist days or to compare its conduct with that of other countries such as the United States now or in the past when they were rising powers (Chan 2015; Chan, Hu, and He 2019; Chan et al. 2021a). For example, how different or similar is China's current conduct under Xi Jinping compared to that of the United States during Theodore Roosevelt's

administration? How does Xi's alleged assertiveness on national reunification with Taiwan compare with Abraham Lincoln's adamant rejection of the Confederacy's right to secede from the Union?

11. Territorial contests have been the most common source of dispute and conflict among states. Thus, neighboring countries are more likely to fight than others that are separated by large physical distance (which also implies emotional or psychological detachment or remoteness). China's sovereignty claims (such as in the South China Sea and East China Sea and over Taiwan) are the most likely reason for it to come into conflict with its neighbors (Chan 2016). The United States also has had its share of boundary disputes and contentious relations with neighbors in its home region, but it has settled them through negotiations with Britain and war with Spain and numerous armed interventions in Central America and the Caribbean. Although China and the United States do not share a border, US support for those countries that have competing sovereignty claims with China can embroil it in a conflict with China.
12. Involvement by third parties in disputes that were originally bilateral can stem from the pull of alliance politics or the push of domestic politics, or a combination of these two pathways to war (Chan 2019; 2023a). The weaker side of asymmetric disputes often plays a role in encouraging this involvement by instigating conflicts in the hope of inducing foreign intervention (Chan 2010a; 2011; 2012b). International reactions to human tragedies caused by local conflicts and intervention by great powers in these conflicts engender the risk of moral hazard and tend to have the effect of perpetuating conflicts and inviting their recurrence. Recent wars in the former Yugoslavia, Ukraine, and Syria and between Hamas and Israel exhibit some of these features.
13. Rationalist explanations of war (Fearon 1995) stress two factors that stand in the way of states reaching an agreement to avoid war. Such bargaining failures can be due to the parties' inability to commit themselves credibly to abide by a deal in the future should circumstances change and their suspicions about their counterparts' truthfulness in disclosing important information (or, to state this concern differently, suspicions that their counterparts will lie or bluff about their capabilities or intentions). Mutual trust is therefore important to alleviate, even if not to remove entirely, these barriers to reaching a deal to avoid war (Chan 2017a). Trust, however, is a rather fragile thing that takes a long time to build but can be easily breached or broken. Leaders in both China and the United States nowadays are deeply suspicious of their counterparts' intentions. Their relationship lacks mutual trust.

14. International relations are inherently ambiguous, thus highlighting the importance of trust (giving the other side the benefit of the doubt when interpreting ambiguous signals). In a security dilemma (Jervis 1978), neither party trusts its counterpart, and each therefore decides to defect, causing a suboptimal outcome for both. Misplaced trust and efforts to boost trust, however, can also be dysfunctional and even dangerous. Had it not been for the fact that the European great powers sought to reassure their respective allies that they could be trusted—such as Berlin's "blank check" to support Vienna—a large conflagration would have been less likely in 1914. Similarly, the weaker party in recent asymmetric conflicts may be less inclined to instigate an armed confrontation, if they can be sure of their patrons' backing. This said, being assured that their patron "has their back" can also have the reverse effect of encouraging it to provoke its stronger adversary. I will discuss conditions influencing these seemingly contradictory expectations in Chapter 3. Trust is not necessary for cooperation, which only requires reciprocity and convergent interests (Axelrod 1984).
15. Alliance ties can serve as a mechanism for a local conflict to spread and escalate into a larger conflagration as depicted by the metaphor of chain-ganging. These ties, however, can also have a dampening effect on conflict occurrence when allies restrain their confederates from bellicosity. Paradoxically, tight alliances are conducive to both of these opposing tendencies. Moreover, formal treaties or defense pacts are not necessary for conflict contagion to occur—strong, informal security ties and convergence of strategic interests can produce the same phenomenon. In addition, by attacking or threatening multiple targets an aggressor state's own actions can cause a conflict to expand, including these actions' effect on its targets to form a countervailing coalition to defend themselves or fight back.
16. If China and the United States come to an armed clash, Taiwan is the most likely cause. A combination of factors, including increased Chinese capabilities, shifting Taiwanese identity, and intensifying Sino-American competition, is increasing this danger for a local dispute to become a much larger multilateral conflict. As with other conflicts, resolution of this dispute requires the window for a negotiated settlement to be open simultaneously for all three parties. In addition to this difficulty in synchronizing three different political clocks, domestic partisan politics hinders resolution by raising the bar for ratifying any negotiated deal. The larger a chief executive's "selectorate" (those key constituents whose support the chief executive depends on to stay in power; Bueno de Mesquita and Smith 2012; Bueno de Mesquita et al. 2003) and the

> less secure a leader's domestic political position, the more constrained is this official's "win set" (that is, his or her range of an acceptable deal) and the less likely that it will overlap with those of his or her foreign counterparts (Putnam 1988). Ironically, it is easier to reach an accord with an authoritarian leader who is accountable to a smaller "selectorate," who is more powerful to override domestic opposition to a foreign deal, or who has less need for this deal to be ratified by domestic stakeholders.

As these propositions suggest, I seek to embed my study of Sino–American relations in the larger literature of international relations. Rather than "essentializing" China or the United States and treating these countries as sui generis, my approach is to place the study of their relationship in a broader context of historical patterns and generic propositions about how states behave generally, focusing especially on conduct and circumstances that can abet armed confrontation and conflict. Given this approach, my discussion in the next three chapters presents theories and evidence on how interstate disputes can occur, spread, and escalate. Consequently, its focus is not on China or the United States specifically. In fact, these countries appear in these chapters only as instances or cases of some general phenomenon being discussed. This discussion, however, is necessary as important background information to inform the analysis in the book's final chapter, where I address Sino–American relations more specifically.

The Rest of the Book

In the following pages, I will elaborate and expand on some of the arguments or propositions mentioned in the summary presented in the previous section. Specifically, I will address a series of puzzles presented by studies on interstate rivalries. Why does the weaker side of asymmetric conflicts often choose to initiate an armed confrontation? Why does it engage in this behavior repeatedly even after having suffered prior setbacks? Moreover, why do these disputes defy a resolution; or, in other words, what prevents the victor from imposing its terms of settlement on the vanquished? Why do these disputes linger? These questions are taken up in Chapter 2. As the reader will see, this chapter makes the case that a subset of chronic, lopsided disputes involving local or regional actors can provide the *fuse* for a larger conflict. The weaker side of these disputes often has a strong incentive to internationalize their conflict. They often deliberately instigate or escalate a conflict with their stronger counterpart to get outside powers involved in their bilateral quarrel. This phenomenon, however, is not inevitable and occurs only under some circumstances. Since World War II, the world has avoided the pathway described in this chapter for a local conflict to spread and escalate, but this danger still lurks and persists.

Just because a large earthquake has not happened in California for some time does not mean that it won't happen in the future. The consequences of a systemic war, as for a devastating earthquake, are so catastrophic that we need to be watchful of these contingencies and be prepared to cope with them effectively. Naturally, there is a critical difference between these two phenomena: one is caused by nature and the other by human action. By studying the past, we hope to avoid self-inflicted errors responsible for avoidable disasters.

An obvious variable determining whether a local feud will spread and escalate into a larger conflict pertains to decisions by third parties. Do great powers, including those located outside the immediate vicinity of a conflict, decide to intervene and, if so, under what conditions? Whether the intervention of one state leads to counter-intervention by others is also relevant. How do variations in the international structure shape these states' motivations to intervene and the manner and form of their intervention? As just implied, this intervention is not inevitable. Moreover, it can take the form of mediating or enforcing a truce rather than creating the conditions for the original conflict to spread and escalate.

When the latter phenomenon occurs, alliance ties are likely to have played a role. These ties are the most visible and obvious transmission mechanism for a conflict to expand. But they are not always necessary for this phenomenon to occur. Recall, for example, the US intervention in the Korean War which led to China's counter-intervention when US and South Korean forces (fighting under United Nations auspices) did not halt at the 38th parallel despite Beijing's warnings. Washington and Seoul did not have a defense treaty when the United States intervened, nor did such a legal instrument exist between Beijing and Pyongyang. Thus, it appears that formal alliances are not necessary for conflict contagion and escalation to occur. Informal security ties and officials' perceptions of their national interest in a particular case can substitute for formal legal commitments obligated by a defense treaty. Significantly, the United States does not have such a treaty commitment to defend two parties mired in perpetual tension—Israel and Taiwan. Naturally, the absence of a formal defense treaty does not mean that Washington is unwilling or unlikely to intervene in a contingency involving them. In Chapter 3, I will discuss circumstances in which a *chain* reaction is likely to transform an initial local bilateral conflict into a larger and more destabilizing, multilateral struggle. Under what circumstances are multiple third parties likely to jump into a fray or, perhaps against their better judgment, to become "dragged" into it and engulfed by the flames of war?

What can cause a countervailing coalition to form against a great power? More specifically, how can this country's own conduct cause such a backlash, producing a harmful effect resulting in its self-encirclement? Wars often become enlarged due to the reckless behavior and insatiable appetite of an aggressor state. Realists of different stripes expect states to rally against the strongest one among them (e.g., Mearsheimer 2001; Waltz 1979). We know, however, that this expectation does not always pan out historically. Countries that are threatened by a strong, aggressive state do not always balance against it, or at least that is often not their initial response. They have instead often reacted to their predicament in other ways such as to accommodate, hedge, hide, and even bandwagon (Schroeder 1994b; 1995). Balancing against an imminent threat is often not their first choice.

As remarked earlier, Napoleon's own conduct did more to encourage various coalitions against him than British diplomacy. The one that drove him into exile to Elba, for example, consisted of Britain, Russia, Austria, Prussia, Spain, Sardinia, Portugal, Sweden, and several smaller German states—all victims of his earlier aggrandizement. The forces that eventually defeated him at Waterloo came from Britain, Prussia, the Netherlands, and several smaller German states such as Hanover and Brunswick. This joint opposition coalesced only slowly and belatedly after he had repeatedly lashed out against his neighbors. Under what conditions are we likely to see the formation of a countervailing coalition? When does a large power arouse collective action to oppose it, and when and how is it able to subdue, diffuse, or deflect this threat? Chapter 4 takes up these questions. This chapter also discusses the moral hazard caused by foreign intervention, which tends to encourage conflict recidivism and persistence.

Finally, Chapter 5 concludes by recapitulating the major takeaways from the preceding discussion, and it discusses possible policy implications and lessons derived from it. Whereas Chapters 2, 3, and 4 engage international relations research in general, drawing insights from studies of historical cases and theories of war, enduring rivalries, and alliance politics, I direct my attention in Chapter 5 more specifically to Sino-American relations. I embed the discussion of this relationship in the context of empirical patterns, theoretical formulations, and policy dilemmas presented by the earlier chapters. I thus try to bridge the usual gulf between international relations research and more country-specific studies concerned about the danger that sparks created by an initial local conflict can spread and escalate into a much greater danger to world peace and stability.

Conclusion

To recapitulate, this book presents three pathways whereby interstate conflicts have spread and escalated in the past to become a large, destructive conflagration. Given the idea of *equifinality* introduced earlier, there is obviously more than one pathway for major wars to break out. Wars can be precipitated by an event or action, inadvertent or deliberate, as suggested by the idea of *fuses*. Large, intense conflicts can result from alliance ties or some other reason such as the tit-for-tat exchanges of mutual recrimination or the serial consequence of falling dominoes such as when prisoners are tied together by their ankles, as suggested by the idea of *chains*. Moreover, they can engulf countries beyond the initial belligerents due to the aggressor states' reckless actions that expand the zone of conflict—self-defeating policies captured by the idea of *backlash*.

We all know that some wars—such as the Russo-Japanese War and the Franco-Prussian War—were bilateral struggles without the presence of a third party. We also know that in some cases, such as the repeated armed conflicts between India and Pakistan and those between Israel and its Arab neighbors, a wider war has been averted thus far. Extra-regional powers had cooperated to contain this danger. Thus, the process of contagion and escalation is not inevitable.

History shows considerable serendipity so that events that did happen were not preordained and they could have turned out differently. It is difficult to anticipate accidents, which are by definition beyond people's control. This remark may be disappointing to those who want to make specific predictions about the future, but it does not deny that we can still come to a general understanding of the dynamics tending to favor certain outcomes. It also suggests serious reservations about whether it is possible to rule some variables "in" and other variables "out" by running a simple regression analysis, especially given the contingent nature of these variables' impact as it is dependent on some other yet unspecified variable(s).

As already stated, I do not consider most works, including this book, in international relations to constitute theory, although I continue to use this word when referring to popular formulations such as power-transition theory, balance-of-power theory, and attribution theory. Although obviously some explanations are more persuasive than others, they should not always force a binary choice of either acceptance or rejection. Thus, I do not see my work to be in competition with other studies as if they are in a horse race entailing only one "winner." *Equifinality* means that the same outcome can result from different paths.

To argue that an outcome is *contingent* means that this outcome can be altered. One reason for studying the dynamics of conflict contagion and escalation is the hope that we may be able to apply the knowledge thus gained to influence this process by removing or reducing those factors abetting the danger of war. There are usually several critical points in the development of a crisis when officials can take the exit ramp to avoid further contagion or escalation. Even though "streetcars" such as Sarajevo can present recurrent opportunities for a conflict to spread or intensify, officials still have the option of declining to get onto them.

The reference just now to several factors affecting the dynamics of conflict process points to my belief that social science inquiries, including the study of war, entail *conjunctive logic*. In other words, these inquiries should attend to the interactions of multiple factors rather than presenting monocausal explanations, which are in my view not likely to advance our understanding of complicated social science phenomena. Instead, it would be more rewarding to attend to the *confluence* of conditions conducive to an outcome's realization.

To anticipate the next chapter, my inquiry was inspired and motivated by a series of puzzles disclosed by quantitative research showing that local rivals often get into repeated rounds of armed conflicts even though their relationship is characterized by lopsided capabilities and even though the weaker side has often suffered setback and defeat in prior encounters. I explain this odd phenomenon in terms of the weaker state's incentive to internationalize its conflict by recruiting outside parties to assist its cause. This involvement by outside parties can transform local conflicts into larger, multilateral struggles—but it can also sometimes stop the fighting and restore peace. This view in turn suggests that we need to understand the incentives of these third parties. The universe of cases pertaining to the so-called enduring rivalries (Diehl 1998; Diehl and Goertz 2000; Goertz, Jones, and Diehl 2005) provides the reference group for this book. The relevance of this research to Sino–American relations should be obvious in that the dispute between China and Taiwan over the latter's status, a local feud, has the potential to ensnare Washington in a larger conflict with Beijing. This conflict between the world's two largest economies can also potentially engulf other states such as Japan and South Korea.

Chapter 2
Local Rivalries as Possible Fuses for Larger Conflicts

Overview

Several seeming puzzles present themselves when we review the large body of literature on interstate rivalry. These puzzles are interrelated, and they challenge students of international relations to take up a series of questions concerning the origins of interstate conflicts and the processes that lead to their expansion and escalation. As I will show in this chapter, they point to an important source for the possible enlargement of local conflicts to become more dangerous confrontations and sometimes even devastating wars among great powers, including those states that reside outside the immediate conflict zone.

Put in the context of the last chapter's discussion, this chapter is motivated by an attempt to search for a common precipitant (or catalyst) that can set off a large conflagration. The adjective *common* is important because it distinguishes my approach here from the conception of a precipitant (or catalyst) as a unique incident such as the assassination of Archduke Ferdinand in Sarajevo (Lebow 2000/2001; 2003). As I argued in the last chapter, the latter view will make it practically impossible to make any prediction about precipitants (or catalysts) because they are seen as accidents, which, by definition, are contingent and unexpected. This is not the approach I adopt in this chapter. I search for a class of events, or a general phenomenon, that can trigger a chain reaction leading to an intense multilateral conflict. I choose the term *fuse* to distinguish my approach from the way in which *precipitant* and *catalyst* have been used by some people to refer to a unique, unexpected incident. There is, of course, no reason why these two terms cannot be used to refer to some common pattern or regularity.

In the discussion below, I will combine two approaches in international relations scholarship that one does not usually see in the same study. There is a body of literature that one may call "conflict studies," relying usually on quantitative methodology and data with a large *N* (i.e., a large number of cases that is required for statistical analysis). I draw from and focus on the empirical patterns that this research approach has found. Many of these patterns are intriguing because they appear to be counterintuitive. They provide the starting point for

Fuses, Chains, and Backlashes. Steve Chan, Oxford University Press. © Oxford University Press (2025).
DOI: 10.1093/9780197812907.003.0002

my inquiry to search for possible answers. There is also a body of international relations research that one may call "security studies." These studies typically apply a qualitative approach to analysis, engaging in detailed examination of a few historical cases to understand their origin, evolution, and outcome. As the reader will see, I develop my propositions about how a local bilateral conflict may spread and escalate from insights provided by this second body of literature. These propositions raise important policy questions, including the problem of moral hazard.

The Genesis and Development of Local Feuds

Most interstate conflicts originate from local disputes involving close neighbors. In his compilation of rivalries, William Thompson (2001) reports that about two-thirds of these contentious dyads have involved quarrels between minor powers. These disputes are typically about contested territory or sovereignty, which he calls "spatial rivalries" to distinguish them from positional rivalries discussed in the last chapter. A long list of such disputes comes easily to mind: Israel versus Egypt/Syria, Somalia versus Ethiopia, Iraq versus Iran, Pakistan versus India, Greece versus Türkey, Ecuador versus Peru, North versus South Korea, and Morocco versus Algeria. Some conflicts do not have nearly as long a protracted history as these disputes, but they are still relevant to this inquiry. They include recent feuds involving the constituent parts of the former Yugoslavia, such as those pitting Serbia against Bosnia and Kosovo. Going back further in history, we have examples of other wars among minor powers, such as the one Paraguay fought against Argentina, Brazil, and Uruguay and the Second Balkan War waged by Bulgaria against Serbia, Macedonia, Greece, and Romania. I am interested in learning from these rivalries how to avoid small local conflicts from becoming global conflagrations. The ongoing war between Ukraine and Russia and rising tension across the Taiwan Strait suggest this inquiry's contemporary relevance. Of course, in these last two cases we have a conflict between a minor power and a major power; and in this respect, they offer parallels to the quarrel between Serbia and Austria–Hungary preceding World War I.

Local conflicts frequently heighten diplomatic tension and sometimes even lead to armed clashes. The following features stand out about these conflicts. First, and as already mentioned, these *local conflicts* typically involve neighbors over quarrels about land and sovereignty (Senese and Vasquez 2008; Vasquez 1993; 2009b; Vasquez and Henehan 2011). They sometimes precipitate intervention by extra-regional powers, causing these originally local conflicts to spread and escalate. Second, these episodes threatening peace and stability happen repeatedly; that is, these are recurrent conflicts involving the same pairs of disputants, and they make up the world's list of chronic hot spots. Therefore, they have been described as *enduring rivalries* (Diehl 1998; Diehl and Goertz 2000; Goertz, Jones, and Diehl 2005). Third, and perhaps to the surprise of some people, they usually involve contestants with lopsided capabilities (Colaresi, Rasler, and Thompson 2007; Klein, Goertz, and Diehl 2006). The stronger side in these disputes is usually much stronger than the weaker side by most conventional measures of national power, with a power disparity between them characterized by a ratio of at least three-to-one and often of much greater magnitude. Thus, we describe them as *asymmetric conflicts*. Fourth, and perhaps surprising again to some people, many of these disputes escalate to armed violence because of instigation by the weaker side (Chan 2010a; 2012b; Diehl and Goertz 2000; Grieco 2001; Paul 1994). Fourth, and as already mentioned, these local conflicts often engage extra-regional powers, which intervene sometimes to mediate peace and occasionally to bolster their local clients or junior partners. The latter course of action can and has led to a large conflagration involving great powers supporting opposing sides of the initial conflict. The dynamics leading to World War I, stemming originally from a dispute between Serbia and Austria–Hungary comes to mind. Finally, even though these asymmetric local conflicts happen repeatedly over a long time, many of them continue to defy a definitive resolution. They linger. They may be dormant for a while but tend to flare up time and again (Colaresi and Thompson 2002; Goertz, Jones, and Diehl 2005; Hensel 1999; Leng 1983; 2000).

I will try to explain below the reasons for these conflicts' recidivism, pointing especially to the motivations of the weaker side of these local disputes. One plausible reason for the protracted nature of these long-running feuds and their repeated flare-up is that the weaker side has an incentive to internationalize its conflict with a stronger opponent (another plausible reason pertains to its domestic politics). This view, however, only addresses one part of the story. We need to account for not only the local disputants' "demand" for outside intervention but also the outside powers' willingness to "supply" this intervention. Why do extra-regional powers, such as the United States and the former Soviet Union, sometimes interject themselves as mediators to arrange a ceasefire in, for example, the Yom Kippur War between Israel and its Arab neighbors? And yet, why do their efforts to restore peace fail to bring about a lasting settlement? And why, on some other occasions such as when China and the United States fought in the Korean War, were third parties self-motivated to get involved with scant evidence that the local disputants made any systematic effort to entrap these outsiders in their quarrel?

Those contentious issues motivating local conflicts often continue to fester and threaten to escalate to another round of violent confrontation. Why do these conflicts recur, and why do they defy attempts to resolve them? Of course, extra-regional powers do not always get involved directly and extensively in a local conflict. What can account for their decision to sometimes eschew active intervention? For instance, in contrast to the ongoing Russo–Ukrainian War, Western reaction to the war between Russia and Georgia in 2008 was muted. The latter conflict was terminated quickly in a matter of days after France took the lead to arrange a ceasefire (Kofman 2018).

Naturally, outside powers do not always take on the role of peacemakers. They can take sides in a local conflict, providing aid and support for one of its belligerents. NATO members are openly and actively assisting Ukraine in its current war against Russia. One may recall that the United States had similarly financed and supplied the mujahideen in Afghanistan to resist the Soviet invasion and occupation of that country. The former USSR and China undertook similar action to assist their ally in Hanoi during the Vietnam War. Furthermore, Moscow furnished assistance and support to Beijing and Pyongyang during the Korean War. All these episodes took on the appearance of a war by proxy, whereby outside powers sought to wear down their principal adversary, dissipating its energy, and draining its resources without fighting it directly.

US president Joe Biden ruled out the option of direct US intervention before Russia invaded Ukraine in February 2022, and his public statements to this effect, made before this invasion, diminished the effectiveness of Washington's deterrence threat against the then prospective Russian invasion. For many years since China and the United States established formal diplomatic relations, Washington adopted a deliberate strategy of ambiguity, declining to pre-commit itself to any specific course of action in the event of a military crisis regarding Taiwan's status. On at least four recent public occasions, however, Biden answered in the affirmative when asked by reporters whether the United States will intervene militarily in this contingency. Officials in his own administration walked back his statement on each occasion, claiming that the United States has not changed its policy on Taiwan. Nevertheless, Biden's statements were hardly a slip of the tongue. They indicate that Washington's policy to support Taiwan has become less ambiguous, although it is still unclear whether the United States will commit its own troops to fight the Chinese. Of course, President Harry Truman had famously reversed an earlier statement by his secretary of state, Dean Acheson, that had put the Korean peninsula outside the US defense perimeter; and he ordered US military intervention in the Korean War under United Nations auspices. In the leadup to the two world wars, we also saw major allies of the participants in the initial quarrel becoming increasingly engaged in direct military action. The immediate precipitant for Britain's and France's entry into World War II was Nazi Germany's invasion of Poland, a country that London and Paris had pledged to defend.

Thus, major powers have responded differently to local conflicts and disputes. What can explain variations in their response (Chan 2010a), the supply side of the question of their involvement (or non-involvement) in these local quarrels? The demand for outside intervention has also varied. Although some parties to a local conflict have actively sought foreign intervention—the actions of Bosnians and Kosovans in their fight against the Serbs to secede from Yugoslavia (Kuperman 2008) and those of Kuwaitis in their resistance to Iraqi invasion provide perhaps the most vivid recent examples—this feature is less evident or even absent in other cases. The settlement of the boundary disputes between Russia and China and between the United States and British Canada in an earlier era exemplifies the latter type.

This variation begs the question about those circumstances that motivate one or both sides of a local dispute to internationalize their conflict. As an example, Taiwan clearly seeks US involvement to protect its de facto independence, whereas China insists that this island's status is a matter of Chinese domestic affairs. Beijing is therefore firmly set against outside interference. It has also preferred to address its sovereignty disputes regarding the South China Sea in a bilateral fashion with the other claimant states. This stance is not difficult to understand because China is in a stronger bargaining position when it negotiates separately with each of the other claimant states in a bilateral setting. It is also natural that the smaller states would rather not be put in a one-on-one match with a much stronger counterpart, thus explaining their inclination to internationalize their disputes with the latter to even the odds in their lopsided bilateral contests. However, sometimes even the weaker party in a dispute can want to conduct its negotiation bilaterally with its stronger counterpart. For example, North Korea has demanded bilateral talks with the United States for reasons of gaining diplomatic recognition and driving a wedge in Washington's relations with Seoul. Parenthetically, that a strong country wishes to maintain its control over a weaker counterpart and to avoid the danger of entrapment has also been the primary motivation behind Washington's pursuit of bilateral security relationships in East Asia as attested by its hub-and-spokes alliance system in that region (Cha 2009/2010; 2016).

Metaphorically, certain local conflicts can provide the *fuse* to ignite a larger conflagration, and the transmission mechanism for this enlargement and escalation is alliance or security ties that serve as a *chain* that locks their respective members in an adversarial situation. I will address the first part of this observation (on fuses) in this chapter, postponing the discussion of the second part (on alliances or informal security relationships) until the next chapter. So that the escalatory potential of local conflicts can be placed in a broader theoretical and historical context, I turn next to reviewing the current dominant narrative on why and how great powers come to exchanging blows.

Theoretical and Historical Background

The danger of an armed confrontation between China and the United States has caught the attention of both the scholarlly and official communities. Graham Allison (2015; 2017) popularized this topic as Thucydides' Trap, referring to this ancient Greek historian's remark that the rise of Athens and the consequent fear felt by Sparta was the root cause of the Peloponnesian War.

Allison warns that history may repeat itself as China's rise can put it on a collision course with the United States. He claims that on 12 of 16 past occasions when a rising power caught up to an established power, this process ended in war between them. His warning of the danger of a Sino–American war has reached the highest levels of government. In a speech given in Seattle in 2015, China's president Xi Jinping remarked pointedly that there was "no such thing as the so-called Thucydides trap in the world," reminding his audience that "should major countries time and again make the same mistakes of strategic miscalculation, they might create such traps for themselves" (quoted in Shirk 2023, 10). Thus, Xi sounded rather skeptical of the proposition that power transitions presage war between the relevant countries.

Xi's remarks echoed Lebow and Valentino's (2009, 408) caution:

> Should war come between the United States and China in the future it will not be a result of a power transition. The greater risk is that conflict will result from the misperception that such a transition is imminent, and the miscalculation by decision-makers in the United States (or China) that China will soon be in a position to do what no state has done before—unilaterally dictate the rules of the international system. Power transition theory would be made self-fulfilling—generating its own corroboration where history has failed to oblige.

Allison was not the first one to warn about the danger of war precipitated by power shifts between the world's major states. Organski and Kugler (1980) have formulated their power-transition theory based on the same argument that as the power gap between the world's established, dominant power and a rising challenger narrows, their struggle over which country should rule the world and decide the international order will become more acute, ending usually in a destructive systemic war. In contrast to Allison, however, Organski and Kugler's theory was supposed to be limited to the two most powerful countries in the world, although in actual practice power-transition theory has been applied also to wars between states with lower rankings, such as the Russo–Japanese War and the Franco–Prussian War (Organski and Kugler 1980). Furthermore, when they characterized the two world wars as a challenge mounted by a rising Germany against a preeminent Britain, they had excluded the world's leading power, the United States, from their analysis.

Allison's selection of cases to support his thesis of Thucydides' Trap is even more eclectic. He includes quite a few major states in his analysis, although his criteria for designating these states and their wars and for incorporating them in his analysis are unclear. For example, his case files include the First Sino–Japanese War of 1894–95 but not the Second Sino–Japanese War of 1937–45, both the First and Second Opium Wars (pitting China against Britain in 1839–42 and China against Britain and France in 1856–60), nor the Nomohan War fought between Japan and the USSR in 1939.

These errors of commission and omission cast doubts on the validity of theses advanced by Thucydides' Trap and power-transition theory. Their analytic logic and evidence have been criticized and challenged (e.g., Chan 2019; 2020a; 2020b; 2021a; Lebow and Tompkins 2016; Lebow and Valentino 2009; Welch 2015). For example, does the rivalry between Athens and Sparta offer a suitable analogy for contemporary Sino–American relations? Athens, the rising state, was a maritime power and a democracy by the standards of its time, whereas Sparta, the supposed established state, was an agrarian oligarchy known for its militarist spirit and austere lifestyle. Its power derived from its infantry fighting in phalanx formation. It was also constantly fearful of a rebellion by its slaves. Do people really believe that these profiles fit appropriately today's China (with its counterpart as ancient Athens) and United States (with Sparta as its analog)?

Moreover, the one and only unambiguous case of world leadership being passed from one country to another, namely the Anglo–American transition, was in fact peaceful. The contention that the two world wars represented Germany's armed bids to replace Britain as the world's dominant power is questionable because by 1914, and certainly by 1938, the United States had already become the world's most powerful country, and Germany never came close to matching US power, not to mention overtaking it. Instead of challenging an established, dominant state directly, a rising state is more likely to pick on lesser states. As Swaine and Tellis (2000, 227) observe,

> the fact remains that direct attacks on a hegemon by rising challengers are rare and infrequent in modern times. The best example of such a war . . . remains the French attack on the Dutch United Provinces under Louis XIV. Most systemic wars in fact occur because (a) some rising states attack other rising states to consolidate their power but nonetheless manage to precipitate systemic war because the existing hegemon enters the fray on behalf of the weaker side to preempt a future challenge that may be mounted by the stronger rising power (the

> Italian wars); or, (b) some rising states attack key allies of the existing hegemon or important neutrals in a search for regional gains, which nonetheless precipitates systemic war because the existing hegemon enters the fray on behalf of the ally or the neutral to prevent a shift in the future balance of power (the Spanish wars, the Napoleonic wars, and the First and Second World Wars).

This observation corresponds much more closely with historical reality than the depiction offered by Thucydides' Trap and power-transition theory, suggesting that systemic wars originate from a direct confrontation between an incumbent hegemon and a rising competitor. Contrary to this depiction, large multilateral conflicts have been more frequently the result of an initial attack on some minor state that became subsequently enlarged because of the existing hegemon's intervention. Rarely does a rising power challenge an established hegemon directly. Systemic wars tend to instead occur due to a process of contagion and escalation originating from a local conflict. This historical pattern underscores and motivates the rationale behind my inquiry, suggesting that local conflicts often provide the impetus or fuse for larger, more intense wars.

The histories of the two world wars bear out this proposition. World War I broke out not because Germany had wanted to pick a fight with Britain. Rather, Berlin's diplomacy was unable to persuade London to stay on the sideline. This conflict was precipitated by the assassination of Austria–Hungary's heir apparent, Archduke Ferdinand, in Sarajevo, which developed into a conflict between that country and Serbia's patron Russia, which in turn engulfed these latter countries' allies, Germany and France, respectively. Moreover, this was not a war stemming from a German challenge to Britain's global leadership. Berlin was focused more on the evolving distribution of power in Europe, specifically the rise of Russia. German leaders started a preventive war against Russia, hoping to eliminate an emergent threat to their country's future security before its window of opportunity closed after Russia improved its military position (Albertini 1980; Berghahn 1973; Copeland 2000; Van Evera 1999).

In the European theater of World War II, it was again the defense of an ally that brought third parties into a war that did not initially involve them directly. Britain and France declared war on Germany because it had invaded Poland, a country that London and Paris had pledged to defend. The characterization of World War II as originating from a German desire to replace Britain as the global hegemon is mistaken. For one thing, Britain was by 1938 certainly no longer the world's dominant power. And for another, Germany had again sought to avoid fighting Britain. Adolf Hitler averred, "Everything I undertake is directed against the Russians; if the West is too stupid and blind to grasp this, then I shall be compelled to come to an agreement with the Russians, beat the West, and then after their defeat turn against the Soviet Union with all my forces" (quoted in

Copeland 2000, 135). On another occasion, he declared, "Originally, I wanted to work together with Britain. But Britain has rejected me again and again. It is true, there is nothing worse than a family quarrel, and racially the English are in a way our relatives. . . . It's a pity that we have to be locked in this death struggle, while our real enemies in the East can sit back and wait until Europe is exhausted. That is why I do not wish to destroy Britain and never shall" (quoted in Higgins 1966, 55). Therefore, power-transition theory's depiction of World War II as an Anglo–German struggle for world domination distorts historical reality. Moreover, even though these two countries found themselves at war, this conflict was much more about a contest over mastery in Europe rather than one for world domination.

In the Pacific theater of this war, Japan attacked Pearl Harbor in a desperate gamble, believing that the United States would defend its allies (Britain, France, and the Netherlands) and would oppose its attempt to seize these countries' colonies in Southeast Asia. The key point here is that Japan's leaders were not keen on picking a fight with the United States, which they knew to be eight or nine times stronger than their country (Russett 1969). They nevertheless decided to attack the United States because they were convinced that Washington would intervene against Japan if it were to seize the European colonies in Southeast Asia in its desperate attempt to overcome the shortfall of strategic materiel created by the Western (including US) embargo against it. In other words, Japan attacked because its leaders were convinced by the US deterrence threat to fight it should Tokyo get into a war with the European colonial powers.

We have here again a situation of conflict contagion originating from a clash of interests involving third parties, albeit in this case the diffusion and escalation of the conflict stemmed from an anticipatory judgment, namely, Japanese leaders' belief that war with the United States (which stood in Japan's way to acquire resources from Southeast Asia) was inevitable and that Japan should therefore capitalize on the element of surprise by initiating the first blow (Barnhart 1987; Wohlstetter 1962). Significantly, Western countries' sanctions against Japan—the source of its desperation to overcome shortages of critical materiel for waging war—originated from their demand that Japan give up the gains it had acquired in its invasion of China. Thus, we see here again a chain of events that can be traced to a local or regional conflict, which became enlarged subsequently. As in the case of Germany, it would be a stretch to argue that Japan's attack on Pearl Harbor was the initial shot in its armed bid for world domination. Japan did harbor expansionist designs, but its aspiration was limited to mastery of East Asia.

Moreover, although Japan did assault the United States directly, the dominant world power in 1941, the Pearl Harbor attack represented more a desperate gamble than a cocky, overconfident upstart eager for a fight with the world's premier power. Japanese leaders realized that inaction would have meant the fate of slow economic strangulation by the Americans. In about 18 months, their stockpile of oil would have been depleted, and the Americans would have won the war without having fired a shot. In the words of Japan's navy chief of staff Osami Nagano, "In various respects the Empire is losing materials; that is, we are getting weaker. By contrast, the enemy is getting stronger. By the passage of time we will get increasingly weaker and we won't be able to survive" (quoted in Ike 1967, 130–31). Japan's wartime prime minister Hideki Tojo expressed the same sentiment when he remarked, "I fear that we would become a third-class nation after two or three years if we just sat tight" (quoted in Ike 1967, 238). This sense of foreboding and even dread about an increasingly unfavorable future is a common feature in many cases, fueling the preventive motivation of the relevant leaders.

In sum, this discussion of the abbreviated history and dynamics of the two world wars questions the conventional narrative of a rising power challenging an established, dominant state to claim the mantle of global hegemon. It is much more accurate to describe these conflicts as a struggle for regional mastery. Neither Germany nor Japan had aspired to dominate the world. Moreover, they ended up fighting the United States and Britain not because they had actively sought such a confrontation but rather because they were unable to avoid it given their agenda. This observation naturally does not absolve their leaders' complicity in launching wars of aggression, but the important point being made here is that this aggression was directed initially against weaker victims and not intended to dislodge the world's dominant power, whether it is construed to be Britain or the United States. It is, of course, true that Britain and the United States became involved in the fighting, but the pathway leading to their involvement originated from local conflicts involving other lesser powers. Entanglement in these conflicts was the reason for their involvement.

The implications of these conclusions are straightforward. It is an exaggeration to characterize the current Sino–American tension as resulting from a Chinese bid to displace the United States as the global leader. China remains today a regional power whose primary attention and interest are focused on its immediate neighborhood and whose military reach does not extend very far from its borders. Although China has gained influence abroad, it can hardly match US structural power (Chan 2023a). Moreover, if there should be a clash between these two countries, it would be because Chinese diplomacy has failed to persuade the United States to stay on the sideline in a crisis involving Taiwan. Fighting the United States would be Beijing's last resort and not its first choice. As just mentioned, a conflict over Taiwan is the most likely fuse for a

Sino–American clash. Similarly, the war in Ukraine, again a local conflict, can be the fuse igniting a larger conflict. In both cases, foreign intervention to support the weaker side of these local disputes is the likely pathway for them to become a more intense multilateral fight.

Rationalist Explanations of War

James Fearon's (1995) seminal article argues that wars are inefficient. That is, wars are a risky and costly business for those who undertake them. If the belligerents could have anticipated the outcome of a war and reached a deal based on this anticipated outcome, they would have spared themselves the costs and risks of fighting. They bear not only the costs of waging war in blood, sweat, tears, dollars, and physical destruction but also the danger of losing their territory, country, political power, economic fortune, and even lives. If the prospective belligerents had foreseen the outcome of a conflict, they would have been better off by settling their dispute on that basis rather than having to pay the costs and risks of fighting a war for the same result. That they are unable to settle their dispute without war means that they have discrepant expectations about how this war will turn out. Obviously, at least one party must have believed that it could do better on the battlefield than the other party was willing to acknowledge, and this party's optimism therefore leads it to expect to come out of this conflict better off in getting whatever it wanted than its counterpart was willing to concede without war. Therefore, the parties' inability to agree on the outcome of a prospective war impedes their ability to reach a settlement without having to fight.

From this rationalist perspective, when a war happens it indicates that there has been a bargaining failure. That is, the two sides have been unable to reach a deal which would have spared them the costs and risks of fighting. Naturally, and as already alluded to, a belligerent's decision to fight is not independent of its expectation of how this fighting will end. One does not expect leaders to start or join a war if they think it will put them in a worse situation than before the war.

Fearon suggests several reasons why rational officials may accept war despite their awareness of its costs and risks. One possible reason is that they may have *private information* that leads them to believe that they will do better in the forthcoming conflict than their opponent gives them credit for. For instance, they may know that their military is stronger and better prepared than their opponent thinks. Or perhaps they have a secret weapon that will give them an edge on the battlefield. Naturally, leaders are wary of revealing such information to their opponent because this disclosure will give away an important advantage. Moreover, their opponent will not necessarily believe in the truthfulness of this disclosure because this counterpart may very well suspect that it is a deliberate attempt to deceive or mislead. Therefore, the well-known fact that officials often engage in *misrepresentation*—that is, to lie and bluff—can also stand in the way of reaching a deal to avoid war.

Fearon also gives another possible reason why states fight even when their leaders realize that wars are inefficient. Their failure to strike a deal to avoid war can be due to an inability to make a *credible commitment* (see also Powell 2006). How can each party be confident that its counterpart will abide by the terms of a deal if circumstances change in the future? For instance, when the other side becomes stronger in the future, what is there to prevent it from reneging on its promise to abide by the deal or from demanding further concessions? Doubts about the enforceability of a deal tomorrow obstruct its realization today. Thus, for example, fewer defense pacts will be formed if leaders doubt that their counterparts can be relied on to render assistance when war breaks out (Leeds, Long, and Mitchell 2000). The same logic argues that if officials believe that another country is implacably hostile and their own country's relative power will slip in the future, they may decide to wage war now rather than later when their country will be weaker (for preventive war, see Chan 2012b; Copeland 2000; Lemke 2003; Levy 1987; Van Evera 1999). It is difficult for officials to demonstrate that they will honor a deal even if their country gains more power in the future, and this difficulty stands in the way of reaching a deal in the first place. Even if one believes in the sincerity of these officials, what is there to bind their successors to their pledge? Naturally, credible commitment is especially difficult to make and enforce during periods of rapid power shifts, one likely reason for a higher risk of war during these times.

The commitment problem explains in part why negotiations over Iran's and North Korea's nuclear programs have involved other major powers besides the United States in an apparent effort to make a deal more credible given the involvement of these other countries such as China and Russia. Presumably, the idea is that this deal has a better chance of being implemented if other major powers have put their reputation and support behind it. Washington's subsequent withdrawal from the Joint Comprehensive Plan of Action suggests that such an arrangement may still be insufficient. Indeed, from the perspective of Tehran and Pyongyang, what is there to hold back Washington from attacking them after they have given up their nuclear weapons? They are unlikely to overlook what happened to Ukraine and Libya.

Kyiv had dismantled Soviet-era nuclear weapons installed on its territory in exchange for a security guarantee from Moscow and Washington, and Muammar Qaddafi had opened Libya to international inspection to prove that he did not have weapons of mass destruction. Once the Western countries were sure that Libya did not have these weapons, they launched an attack that ended in his death. As a counterfactual thought experiment, would Russia have attacked Ukraine if Kyiv still had nuclear weapons? We know that North Korea does have nuclear weapons and that Iran has a program that would enable it to acquire these weapons in a relatively short time. They have not been attacked. Besides Libya and Ukraine, Saddam Hussein's Iraq was attacked because he was allegedly developing weapons of mass destruction when he did not in fact have such a program.

What conclusions should onlookers draw from these different episodes? Countries must rely on themselves rather than others' promises for their security. There are great risks and severe costs when one misplaces one's trust. Conversely, it is difficult for officials to convince their counterparts that they can be trusted, and efforts to make their commitments credible can also be risky and costly (think of Qaddafi's fate). When asked what conclusion he would draw from NATO's air campaign against Serbia in 1999, an Indian general reportedly said, "Don't fight the U.S. unless you have nuclear weapons" (quoted in Chan 2008, 150). Rather than stopping nuclear proliferation, these episodes have instead encouraged incentives to acquire nuclear weapons due to the difficulties of making and enforcing commitment.

There is a third possible reason why the parties caught in a dispute are unable to reach a settlement to avoid war. It pertains to the object of their contest. Is it over something tangible that lends itself to being divided easily, such as money, territory, or fishing quotas? Or is it something intangible with high emotional salience and psychological investment, such as sovereignty, that is more difficult to divide? Even though there may be creative ways to finesse the problem of *indivisible goods* (such as those involving joint custody over minor children), disputes involving indivisible goods are more difficult to settle.

When, however, tangible assets are infused with highly charged symbolism, such as control of sacred sites like the city of Jerusalem (Goddard 2006), a dispute over them can still defy easy resolution. In sovereignty disputes like the one over the Falklands/Malvinas, proposals such as flying the United Nations flag or Britain retaining sovereignty over these islands but leasing them to the Argentinians (or vice versa) turned out to be unacceptable, infeasible, or impracticable. Similarly, the so-called One-China Consensus pertaining to relations across the Taiwan Strait has also turned out to be a temporary and fragile compromise that only conceals and defers more fundamental disagreements for the time being. As a third example, recent anti-government protests in Hong Kong impinge on the fundamental question of Chinese sovereignty. Does Beijing have the final say in matters concerning Hong Kong's governance? Any agreement that Beijing had reached with London when Britain returned this colony to

Chinese rule would not be able to trump the fundamental principle of Chinese sovereignty. This example also points to the difficulty of making a credible commitment and enforcing it. What is London to do if Beijing reneges on its pledge to maintain Hong Kong's existing political and economic arrangements for 50 years? This question has, of course, also occurred to Taipei. What if Taiwan reunifies with China under the principle of "one country, two systems" and Beijing fails to honor its promises subsequently?

Stylized Facts and Nagging Puzzles

A stylized fact is a simplified presentation of an empirical finding. "Stylized facts are broad tendencies that aim to summarize the data, offering essential truths while ignoring individual details" (https://en.wikipedia.org/wiki/Stylized_fact). Some examples of stylized facts in international relations are democratic countries do not fight each other, imperial overstretch causes hegemonic decline, second-strike capabilities stabilize the strategic relationship between two nuclear powers, and economic interdependence discourages war. These propositions refer to broad empirical patterns. One may find individual cases that deviate from these generalizations, but these are exceptions to the rule. Thus, the fact that some highly educated individuals have low earnings does not invalidate the stylized fact that "education raises lifetime income."

Quantitative research on international conflict reports one stylized fact: a small number of states are responsible for a disproportionate amount of such conflict, and they get involved in violent clashes against each other on a recurrent basis. Thus, if we are to understand the causes of international conflict, we need to come to grips with the motivations that incline these "repeat offenders" to initiate crises and fight wars. The relevant literature has characterized these contentious dyads as "enduring rivals" (Diehl 1998; Diehl and Goertz 2000; Goertz, Jones, and Diehl 2005).

Specifically, enduring rivals—the same contentious dyads—accounted for 40% of all the militarized interstate disputes and almost half of all the wars that occurred during 1816–1992, even though they represented only 1% of all possible pairs of countries in the world and only 5% of those dyads that have ever been involved in a military conflict (Stinnett and Diehl 2001). Applying a different conception of rivalry based on leaders' perceptions of threat and competition (in contrast to the identification of a rivalry based on the frequency of past militarized disputes between pairs of countries, or their "disputatiousness"), William Thompson (2001, 557) reports that rivals were involved in 58 of 75 of wars since 1816 (or 77.3%). His "strategic rivals" fought each other in 41 of 47 wars (or 87.2%) in the 20th century and 21 of 23 wars (or 91.3%) since 1945. These figures are quite extraordinary and cannot be a statistical fluke. What can explain the unusual tendency for a small number of countries to "select" themselves disproportionately and repeatedly into many conflicts that the world has experienced?

William Thompson (2001) identified a total of 174 strategic rivals during 1816–1999. As just mentioned, he identified these dyads based on the perceptions of their leaders, seeing themselves locked in a competitive relationship. They treat their counterpart as a source of serious threat and even as a mortal enemy. In contrast to this perceptual approach, another tradition defines a rivalry based on the frequency of militarized disputes between two countries. In this latter approach, a pair of countries must have six or more militarized disputes in a span of 20 years to qualify as an enduring rivalry. Based on this definition, Paul Diehl and Gary Goertz (2000) identified 63 such dyads. Other scholars, such as Scott Bennett (1997; 1998), have also relied on this approach by counting the frequency of militarized disputes. These scholars' operational definitions of a rivalry have differed on the number of militarized disputes and the length of time used to count these disputes, and these criteria for identifying a rivalry have also changed over time. These variations have produced different conclusions (W. Thompson 2001). The inventory of militarized interstate disputes used to identify rivalries has also undergone revisions over time. Yet despite their differences, two important facts stand out from the pertinent literature. A small minority of states accounts for a large portion of past armed conflicts. Moreover, these conflicts tend to recur for the same contentious dyads.

Naturally, not all these rivalrous pairs are identical. William Thompson (1995) differentiates between those countries engaging in what he calls positional rivalries and others that are participants in spatial rivalries. Positional rivals compete for leadership status in a region or globally. In contrast, spatial rivals usually quarrel over territory. These quarrels are more common, less deadly, and usually easier to settle—although not always, as we shall see later. Unlike spatial rivalries that usually characterize disputes among minor states, positional rivalries by their very nature tend to implicate major states. As Thompson points out, they require more resources and tend to be more protracted, usually terminating only when one of the contestants becomes exhausted when its resource base is depleted due to defeat in war or economic collapse. Most rivalries involve minor powers, but about a third of them involve major powers. Because they constitute a much smaller percentage of all states in the international system, major powers are therefore much more disputatious and understandably so. Finally, a rivalry can encompass elements of both the positional and spatial kinds. Thus, the current war in Ukraine and tension over Taiwan's status exemplify this combination.

People act based on their anticipation. I do not challenge a professional football player to a fight because I can anticipate its outcome. Thus, I avoid such fights. Similarly, officials presumably do not start or join a war if they think that it will end badly for them and their country. Of course, officials can make mistakes. After all, they are human. Yet, why would they repeat their mistakes, especially if they have suffered defeat in previous bouts fighting the same opponent? Why do they persist in view of their prior setbacks? Before we dismiss their behavior as crazy, might there not be a rational reason for it? Moreover, the weaker side of asymmetric conflicts often instigates a confrontation to challenge its stronger opponent. This pattern is also puzzling because its leaders can reasonably expect to be defeated on the battlefield.

The recurrent nature of these conflicts adds to the enigma. This is so because being close neighbors and having had multiple prior encounters, the leaders of these enduring rivals should know their opponent well. With each successive confrontation they acquire more information about the other side, and they should therefore be in a better position to avoid misperception and miscalculation. Presumably, South Korean leaders are in the best position to understand North Korea, and vice versa. Similarly, India's and Pakistan's officials should be most familiar with their counterparts' motivations and calculations. Yet these enduring rivals continue to "select" themselves into additional episodes of confrontation. Perhaps to them, wars are after all not inefficient. Their behavior suggests that they may in fact believe that wars can produce a positive return and that they have reason to think that they are protected against the worst risks of taking part in a war (such as losing their country, their power, and even their life). It seems that even defeat in combat is not a sufficient deterrent against these "repeat offenders."

The above stylized facts appear to be counterintuitive and challenge common sense. As suggested in the last paragraph, having been involved in repeated crises and wars, enduring rivals should have gained a better understanding of each other's concerns, interests, and perceptions. They should have therefore been better positioned to reach a settlement to avoid war because of this understanding. With each additional round of contest, they should be able to improve this understanding. Due to their many prior encounters, these disputants should have become more "knowledgeable of each other's capabilities and intentions so that they should be less likely to blunder into war out of misperception or ignorance" (Chan 2012b, 175). Yet, their record of repeated rounds of fighting belies this supposition.

For those reasons just stated, long-running feuds should be less likely to experience war, and the phenomenon of serial wars (or "streaking") should be rare (Bennett and Nordstrom 2000; Gartzke and Simon 1999)—if we assume that leaders learn their lessons from their past failures to avoid war and wish not to repeat this experience. In fact, the available data show that the probability of conflict *rises* with each additional episode (Colaresi and Thompson 2002; Goertz, Jones, and Diehl 2005; Hensel 1999; Leng 1983). Could this tendency mean that the relevant leaders have drawn from their experience lessons that differ from our supposition, namely, the assumption that they seek to avoid war because it is inefficient and dangerous? Could it be that something from their experience taught them to encourage rather than discourage war with each additional bout of conflict?

One would have expected, perhaps naively, that the longer a dispute has lasted, the greater the probability that it will be resolved, especially if one takes the view that it is dangerous to let a dispute fester lest it escalate to war. This view, however, is once again contradicted by the available data. The protracted nature of enduring rivalries indicates that they have defied any effort to settle them. This phenomenon does not at all mean that the rationalist perspective is wrong; it only suggests that wars may serve some rational purpose despite their obvious costs and risks. What can stand in the way of resolving these disputes? Can it be that at least one party to these disputes believes that it has more to gain by keeping it alive than burying it? Can third parties also prefer to see enduring rivalries persist because they see benefit from a long-running feud continuing to simmer rather than being settled? Would, for example, the United States stand to gain or lose leverage vis-à-vis China should the two sides of the Taiwan Strait come to a settlement? Would China's and Japan's strategic position become stronger or weaker if the Korean peninsula is reunited? What were Washington's and Moscow's attitudes toward the Iran–Iraq War (1980–88)? Henry Kissinger, former US national security advisor for President Nixon and subsequently his secretary of state, reportedly quipped, "it's a pity that both sides can't lose" (https://www.goodreads.com/quotes/3247581-it-s-a-pity-both-sides-can-t-lose-commenting-on-iran-iraq).

The mystery deepens when we consider that many of these protracted disputes involve asymmetric dyads (Paul 1994). The conventional rule of thumb in characterizing such conflicts as asymmetric or unequal contests is when the stronger side enjoys a three-to-one advantage over the weaker side. Fully four-fifths of enduring rivalries are characterized by this extent of lopsidedness (Klein, Goertz, and Diehl 2006). Colaresi, Rasler, and Thompson (2007) also show that interstate crises often involve highly asymmetric dyads, but this asymmetry in the contestants' capabilities does not deter these crises from escalating. For those minor-power participants involved in enduring rivalries, most of their militarized disputes reflect large capability disparities between the opposing sides (Diehl and Goertz 2000). Given the prevalence of such asymmetric conflicts, what is keeping these rivalries going?

The relative strength of the contestants is usually calculated based on the Composite Indicator of National Capabilities (CINC) of the Correlates of War (COW) Project at the University of Michigan (Singer 1987; Singer, Bremer, and Stuckey 1972; Singer and Small 1972; Small and Singer 1982; Suzuki, Krause, and Singer 2002). This measure emphasizes "hard power," such as a country's steel production, its military expenditure, and its population and territorial size. This practice has been criticized for being outdated because contemporary international competition emphasizes information and technology. Moreover, CINC overlooks the more intangible factors constituting national capability, such as morale, training, leadership, and strategy, that affect performance on the battlefield. We do not, however, have any reason to expect that these possible errors of commission or omission will introduce a consistent bias in underestimating the strength of the weaker side in the historical lineup of enduring rivalries. Importantly, although the Arab states are larger in demographic and territorial size, Israel is the stronger party in their several violent encounters, especially if we consider it to be a nuclear power (although Tel Aviv has not disclosed that it has nuclear weapons, it is widely suspected to have them). Israel also enjoys a qualitative edge in its weaponry and military training. Despite their relative weakness, however, Egypt and Syria, sometimes joined by other Arab states such as Jordan and Iraq, have been the ones initiating these wars. The most recent armed clash between Hamas and Israel in October 2023 furnishes another such example.

Our impression of many enduring rivalries suggests that these contests often involve a much more lopsided match than a ratio of three to one. Any number of objective indicators would support this impression. Conflicts such as those involving the United States and Cuba, China and Taiwan, Russia and Ukraine, Russia and Georgia, India and Pakistan, Ethiopia and Somalia, Turkey and Greece, Peru and Ecuador, and South and North Korea come easily to mind. The cases just mentioned include some dyads pairing a major power with its smaller neighbor (such as those implicating the United States, China, and Russia). These dyads are even more striking because the power gap between the relevant countries is even larger than is typically the case in rivalries between minor powers. In the past, weak states have put up a fight against much larger adversaries even when they are unlikely to receive outside help (Labs 1992).

What can account for the weaker side's continued resistance against its much stronger opponent in these major–minor power dyads? There is little realistic prospect that its disadvantage will disappear in the future. If anything, the trend often points in the other direction. That is, it can expect its bargaining position to become even weaker with the passage of time—for example, Taiwan vis-à-vis China. If so, why does it not try to reach a deal now with its stronger counterpart before its position deteriorates further? Why continue to hold out? One plausible reason comes immediately to mind: the minor power has reason to believe that another major power "has its back," an inference that in turn helps to explain why enduring rivalries persist despite the fact that they are often characterized by large power disparities. This inference also implies that outside powers sometimes have a vested interest in keeping local rivalries alive rather than terminating them. There can, of course, be other reasons that are not mutually exclusive, such as the difficulty of making and enforcing commitments to settle a conflict.

This discussion does not deny that sometimes the ostensible weaker side prevails over its stronger opponent as measured by conventional indicators such as CINC which, as already mentioned, can be misleading in gauging national power in the contemporary era (Arreguin-Toft 2005; Mack 1975; Merom 2003; Record 2007). We all know that the outcomes of war are not determined by just a country's demographic, economic, or territorial size; they are also influenced by intangible assets not captured by such indicators. Morale, training, leadership, and national will are such factors that sometimes enable the weaker party to outperform expectations based solely on objective indicators such as CINC and to produce a deadlock or stalemate on the battlefield such as in Korea, Vietnam, and Afghanistan. Israel's advantages in more intangible assets, such as morale, training, leadership, and quality of weaponry give it an edge in each war that it has fought against its Arab opponents despite its numerical inferiority. The enigma is why Israel's adversaries continue to instigate conflicts against it even knowing its relative strength. Without denying that some weaker states do sometimes end up "winning," why do other such states often challenge a stronger opponent when their leaders should know that they cannot possibly prevail militarily? One strong hint is that they do not have to win on the battlefield to achieve their political objectives—and, in fact, did not usually win in the conventional sense—as attested by the US experience in Korea, Vietnam, and Afghanistan. These wars were lost in the family rooms and around dinner tables in the United States.

The decision to initiate a war is not independent of leaders' expectations of how it will turn out. Thus, the phenomenon that asymmetric fights are often followed by foreign intervention can be due to anticipation by officials representing the weaker belligerent that significant others will get involved to assist or protect them. Naturally, officials sometimes make the mistake of overestimating their chances of victory or, conversely, underestimating their probability of defeat. For example, the Argentinian generals started the Falklands/Malvinas War in the mistaken belief that Washington would restrain the British from fighting back and that London would have to accept a fait accompli after the Argentinians had seized the islands. In contrast, the Russo-Japanese war—which was started and won by the weaker Japanese side—was a relatively rare phenomenon (Nish 1986). Significantly and unlike the Russo-Japanese War, most asymmetric wars won by the weaker side are *not* the ones they initiate.

This phenomenon is intriguing because it contradicts the general pattern that countries initiating a war *do* usually emerge as winners. This latter tendency makes intuitive sense because of the logic of selection mentioned earlier. People do not get themselves into a situation that they expect to end badly for them. Therefore, countries that start wars usually win; they pick vulnerable prey. They act strategically by selecting weak victims that they can expect to prevail over and ones that are not expected to receive assistance from allies, meaning that these conflicts tend to be limited to bilateral fights (Gartner and Siverson 1996; Smith 1996b). Significantly, the patterns just mentioned refer to war expansion and war outcome as a general class, and one can surmise that most of these conflicts are initiated by the stronger side. In this chapter, however, we have been discussing those asymmetric conflicts often started by the *weaker* side. This distinction gives us an important hint about this side's motivation. Instead of the usual incentive for the party starting a war to limit this conflict to a bilateral contest, in the subset of disputes and wars concerning this chapter, the initiator is interested in internationalizing it into a multilateral affair. This initiator also does *not* expect to win a decisive victory on the battlefield but is usually more interested in escalating a dispute to procure a political settlement more to its liking (Chan 2011).

One may, of course, debate about the definition of "win." The Afghans' resistance against the Russians and Americans and the wars in Vietnam and Korea can be considered "wins" by the weaker side which fought off and outlasted its stronger opponent, even though it did not defeat its adversary militarily in the traditional sense. Why does the weaker side in a rather substantial number of other asymmetric conflicts accept and sometimes even instigate the escalation of these conflicts when its leaders could and should have anticipated that there is little prospect for them to prevail militarily? Part of the answer is, of course, that in all these conflicts, the weaker belligerent received substantial outside aid, a phenomenon that in turn offers a hint explaining the fact that these conflicts tend to be long drawn-out struggles.

In those wars just cited, the weaker side did not defeat—and, indeed, did not expect or intend to defeat—its stronger opponent on the battlefield. The stronger side also refrained from using all the capabilities available to it. But what or who would restrain the stronger side from applying fully its coercive capability against the weaker side? Again, foreign influence appears to be a strong plausible reason. When a weaker disputant's officials anticipate that outside powers are likely to intervene to impose a ceasefire before their stronger opponent would be able to exercise maximum force against their country, this situation would limit their risk in starting or accepting an asymmetric war. This consideration was present in several bouts between Pakistan and India, Egypt/Syria and Israel, Greece and Turkey (over Cyprus), Ecuador and Peru, and Argentina and Britain (over the Falklands/Malvinas). It appears to have also been on the minds of Bosnian and Kosovan officials when they engaged in provocative actions against the stronger Serbs and the Palestinians vis-à-vis the Israelis. Sometimes another factor is involved. The prospect of counter-intervention by other great powers would have a deterrent effect. That the United States refrained from invading North Vietnam in the Vietnam War or invading China in the Korean War had surely something to do with possible Soviet reaction.

Russell Leng (2000, 221) remarks on the motivations behind the weaker side's officials:

> The diplomatic intervention [in the 1965 Kashmir or Rann of Kutch conflict] of an influential outside power [Britain], as in Sadat's strategy in 1973 [the Yom Kippur War between Egypt and Israel], became a critical component of Pakistan's success both in obtaining its limited military gains in a negotiated settlement and in keeping the fighting limited. The British cease-fire was an essential component of the success of Ayub's strategy in 1964, just as the American–Soviet sponsored cease-fire was essential to Sadat's diplomatic success in 1973. . . . Both operations prepared the ground for negotiations that adversaries had steadfastly rejected.

Leng (2000, 299) concludes, "ironically, one of the reasons that the challengers were so willing to risk the consequences of war in the Egyptian–Israeli and Indo–Pakistani rivalries is because they believed that the superpowers would intervene before the fighting reached the level of a general war." This conclusion supports strongly one of the main propositions being advanced by this chapter.

Janice Stein (1996, 145) also considers the Yom Kippur War as a clear example of the weaker side in a dispute trying to mobilize outside powers to negotiate a new settlement. Avi Shlaim (2000, 319) shares this view, stating that "the Arab aim in launching the [October 1973] war was to break the political deadlock and to provoke an international crisis that would force the superpowers to intervene and put pressure on Israel to withdraw from the territories it had captured in June 1967." Similarly, Kenneth Stein (1999, x) concludes that "Sadat unquestionably launched the October 1973 War to harness American involvement in removing Israel from the Sinai." Rather than seeking a military victory, "once across the [Suez] canal, he [Sadat] counted on American as well as Soviet diplomatic intervention to achieve a cease-fire and diplomatic discussions regarding the future of the Sinai" (Leng 2000, 179).

The preceding discussion addresses the calculations of the weaker side's leaders. There is a flip side to this story concerning the calculations of the stronger side's leaders. As mentioned just now, when these latter officials anticipate retaliation from other countries backing their weaker opponent, they will be self-restrained from escalating a war. Thus, even though the United States had made veiled threats to use nuclear weapons in the Korean War, it did not do so. It also refrained from invading North Vietnam or bombing its dams and dikes in the Red River delta for fear that these actions might trigger Chinese intervention as in the Korean War. Rumors have it also that Washington agreed to a secret deal with Moscow not to invade Cuba again in exchange for the USSR's removal of its missiles from that island after the 1962 crisis. It is thus important to recognize that local spatial rivalries are often linked to or "nested" in other rivalries of the positional type involving extra-regional great powers.

The last observation in turn addresses the seeming puzzle that given the great disparities between the capabilities of the two enduring rivals and their frequent crises and/or wars, the stronger side has often been prevented from crushing its weaker counterpart and from imposing a victor's peace on the vanquished. Arab–Israeli and Pakistani–Indian conflicts again reflect this phenomenon. What keeps these conflicts interminable, causing them to flare up time and again? Why the usual stalemate or deadlock that keeps a rivalry alive and gives it its protracted character (Fortna 2004; Goertz, Jones, and Diehl 2005; Grieco 2001; Maoz and Mor 2002)? Deng Xiaoping, China's paramount leader in the 1970s and 1980s, did not mince words when he reportedly said that for China the Taiwan issue was ultimately a US issue. The ongoing war in Ukraine can also become a protracted stalemate due to foreign assistance enabling Kyiv to hold out against its stronger neighbor.

Note, however, that threats of intervention or escalation by a third party do not always succeed in restraining the stronger party in a bilateral conflict from applying force. We can say in retrospect that President Biden's effort to deter Russia from invading Ukraine was ineffective. Similarly, China failed to dissuade North Vietnam from invading its junior partner, Cambodia, under Khmer Rouge's rule. Vietnam's invasion of Cambodia, however, led to China starting a border war with it in 1979, which in turn signified that Hanoi's hope that the USSR would deter China for undertaking such action was disappointed. We have seen a similar situation in the Greco–Turkish conflict over Cyprus. Although Washington's opposition did prevent a Turkish invasion for a while, it still happened contrary to the hope or expectation of officials in Nicosia and Athens. In these instances, we see again that a state's policy can fail even though the motivation we as analysts attribute to its leaders may still be valid. It should moreover be noted that by preventing a direct fight between Greece and Turkey, Washington's restraining influence did shield the former country from the latter country's military wrath.

In this context, it is also relevant to mention that Washington was successful in dissuading Israel from attacking Egypt and Syria in 1973 (Pressman 2008, 110–15), even though the United States did not prevent war from happening when Egypt and Syria attacked Israel in October of the same year. A situation in reverse had happened in 1956, when the United States was unable to prevent

Britain and France from attacking Egypt in the Suez Canal Crisis, although its pressure subsequently forced these countries to agree to a ceasefire and withdraw their forces. In 1967, US efforts also turned out to be inadequate to prevent Israel's preemptive strikes against its Arab adversaries in the Six Day War. Nor was the United States effective in discouraging Israel from invading Lebanon and its military operations there in 1978 and 1982. Thus, as Pressman (2008) shows, Washington has an uneven record of restraining its allies. Moreover, as Beckley (2015) shows, there are also a considerable number of occasions when US allies restrained Washington from taking more aggressive actions. This restraint has been a two-way street among allies.

Moreover, as discussed earlier in the context of strategic anticipation and the logic of self-selection, there is likely a relationship between the probability of a conflict escalating to war and the prospective belligerents' prewar expectation of foreign assistance. For instance, Ukraine's leaders might have been less inclined to compromise with Russia to avert a war because they were confident that they had strong support from the United States, a belief that might have made Russia's invasion more likely. In the case of North Vietnam's invasion of Cambodia, the failure of China's deterrence threat was not unrelated to Hanoi's belief that it had Moscow's backing (Ross 1988). Thus, security ties still had their impact, albeit in a more complicated way. In all these instances, the important factor was the perception of strong foreign support rather than the existence of a formal treaty or alliance relationship. After all, the United States and China in the above examples were not obligated by treaty commitments to come to the assistance of their respective partners in Kyiv and Phnom Penh.

Ties between the local disputants and their foreign patrons or supporters help to illuminate the phenomenon of protracted rivalries and the failure of wars to produce decisive outcomes between unequal belligerents. Even when wars result in a decisive victory for the stronger combatant on the battlefield, nearly half of them do not end in an imposed settlement (Senese and Quackenbush 2003). Put in another way, "an imposed settlement does not follow necessarily from a decisive [military] victory for one side and a devastating defeat for the other" (Maoz 1984, 230). This phenomenon again appears puzzling until we realize that foreign intervention, including that by international organizations like the United Nations to broker, monitor, and enforce a truce, often prevents the victor from dictating the terms of a peace settlement to the vanquished. This tendency has the effect of providing a "safety net" for the weaker side to start or accept an armed confrontation, creating a moral hazard for it to repeat this behavior later to initiate another round of confrontation. It also incentivizes others to follow its example, thus producing a backlash effect that encourages, rather than discourages, more conflict.

As just remarked, the final piece of the puzzle pertains to the identity of the party initiating or escalating a conflict. Naturally, there is almost always controversy surrounding the question of "who started it." Moreover, the side that fired the first shot is not necessarily the aggressor in every instance. The COW Project codes this side as the initiator of a war. The point of this discussion, however, is that the weaker side often assumes this role. It even sometimes instigates and provokes an armed clash, and despite its military disadvantage, it does not shy away from accepting and even escalating military action. Counterintuitively, minor powers have initiated more militarized interstate disputes against major powers than vice versa (Gochman and Maoz 1984). As T. V. Paul (1994, ix) has said, "Attacks by weaker powers against stronger opponents are seen as improbable [by most people] given the notion that rational decision-makers would not engage in such risky ventures that they are likely to lose." Naturally, the pertinent question is how this action compares with its alternative of inaction. As remarked earlier with respect to Japan's decision to attack Pearl Harbor, the option of doing nothing could appear even more unpalatable to the relevant officials.

Summing up the apparent paradoxes enumerated in this discussion, Goertz, Jones, and Diehl (2005, 743) observe, "empirically . . . power preponderance and victory in disputes [by the stronger side] do not seem to end many rivalries. Even in those cases in which one side has prevailed, success does not necessarily prevent the losing side from starting another dispute or war." Indeed, repeated challenges of the status quo mounted by the weaker side account for a disproportionate share of recurrent conflicts—even though this party has failed previously in similar attempts. This repetition does *not*, however, seem to be a result of this party having become stronger (Grieco 2001). If anything, a state whose power has suffered relative decline is more likely to start another round of confrontation than one that is getting stronger (Hensel 1994). This tendency suggests that when the weaker side is becoming even weaker, it is more likely to initiate another challenge after a shorter interlude following its last attempt. Paradoxically, when the power gap between the two contestants becomes wider, the next round of confrontation appears sooner after the previous one (Senese and Quackenbush 2003, 711–12). In the next section, I draw heavily from prior case studies of asymmetric conflicts (especially Chan 2010a; 2011; 2012b; Kuperman 2008; Leng 1983; 2000; Paul 1994), focusing on common themes and features that characterize the relevant leaders' decisions.

Foreign Intervention and Domestic Politics

As just indicated, even after having suffered a defeat in a previous military confrontation, this setback does not appear to deter the weaker side from initiating another round of conflict. This phenomenon may appear less puzzling if the weaker side is protected by its foreign ally so that it does not dread the prospect of being completely subjugated by its stronger opponent. Moreover, even though its opponent may enjoy an edge in overall strength, the weaker side may still command a local advantage such as in Japan's war with Russia in 1904. This consideration and a window of opportunity that confers upon the weaker side a temporary advantage in some respect also seem to have motivated Pakistan to launch its offensive in Kashmir against India in 1965 and Argentina to initiate its invasion of the Falklands/Malvinas in 1982. Similarly, the weaker side sometimes does not have to prevail over the stronger side militarily. Fighting to a draw—a limited objective—might be enough, and similarly, reducing the stronger opponent's military edge and thereby reducing one's own military limitations by choosing to fight in or near one's "home court" might also be an important consideration for a weaker belligerent, such as in the Chinese decision to enter the Korean War (Chen 1994; Whiting 1962).

Although Japanese leaders realized that they could not win a protracted war of attribution against Russia in 1904, they had good reason to believe that the United States could help them to mediate a quick end to the war and that Britain (Japan's ally) would oppose intervention by other European powers on Russia's side. Thus, Japanese leaders reasoned that they could profit from a short conflict with limited aims, imposing on Russia a fait accompli that would be difficult for St. Petersburg to reverse (Paul 1994). Alliance with Nazi Germany was an important consideration for Tokyo to protect Japan from an attack by the USSR when considering its planned attack on Pearl Harbor. "The assumption of German victory [in Europe] was a linchpin of Japan's plan for war" (Van Evera 1999, 94). Similarly, its alliance with the USSR was important in China's decision to enter the Korean War. Friendly support from China also provided an "insurance policy" for the Pakistanis in their deliberations on launching the Kashmir offensive in 1965.

When they decided to invade and seize the Falklands/Malvinas, Argentinian generals had believed that the United States would "either lean towards it in the conflict or remain strictly neutral, in either case this would have made it impossible for Britain to mount a credible military reaction" (Barnett quoted in Paul 1994, 159). Buenos Aires had served as a proxy for the United States in combatting Marxist insurgents in Central America, and it had thought of itself as Washington's "privileged ally" in Latin America. Foreign Minister Costa Mendez acknowledged after the war that Argentina had banked on the Reagan administration's support—or at least its neutrality—in the conflict and on Washington's readiness to work as a mediator to settle it before armed combat escalated. That the Argentinian leaders were mistaken in holding these beliefs does not disprove the important role that these considerations had played in their decision process.

We encounter a similar situation in the 1956 Suez War—when Israel joined Britain and France (Operation Musketeer)—to attack Egypt in the expectation that the United States would not oppose their plan. In this case again, this expectation turned out to be wrong. President Dwight Eisenhower pressured Britain and France to withdraw their forces, and he warned Israeli prime minister David Ben-Gurion that unless he agreed to a ceasefire, "there should be no expectations of American help in the event of a Soviet-assisted attack on Israel" (Sachar 1981, 114). Still, although Britain, France, and Israel had miscalculated about US support, their mistake does not nullify the importance of security ties (even if not a formal alliance in the case of Israel) in their decision processes. Israel's defense minister Moshe Dayan professed, "If it were not for the Anglo-French operation, it is doubtful whether Israel would have launched her campaign" (Levy and Gochal 2001/2002, 40). At the same time, Dayan was a leading hawk who had wanted "to force a showdown before the military balance shifted to Egypt's favor" (Shlaim 2000, 144).

Prior to the 1967 war, Egypt's president Gamal Abdel Nasser realized that his country was weaker than Israel but nevertheless closed the Straits of Tiran to Israeli shipping, thus initiating another round of confrontation (Mor 1993, 118). He had wanted to "forestall a further and perhaps disastrous decline of his prestige in the Arab world," initiating "the crisis in order to prevent an adverse change in the status quo" (Mor 1993, 126). Like some other leaders, he had counted on the United States to restrain Israel from escalating the conflict but was mistaken in this belief. Although Washington delayed Israel's preemptive war, it was not able to stop it. However, the United States did join the USSR to arrange a truce under United Nations auspices, and it put heavy pressure on Israel to accept it (Brecher and Geist 1980, 37, 145–46, 177–78, 187–88, 226–28).

As discussed above, leaders decide based on their perceptions and beliefs that sometimes turn out to be unwarranted. Thus, although they try to advance their cause, their actions may not succeed and may, in fact, backfire. That their policies can fail does not necessarily refute hypotheses regarding the motivations that had led them initially to undertake these policies. We encounter this situation in several other asymmetric conflicts in the past.

For example, Somalia had initiated repeated incursions into Ethiopia and clashed with the latter country's armed forces (in 1961, 1964, 1977, 1980, 1982, 1987). President Mohammad Siad Barre invaded his stronger neighbor in 1977, hoping to take advantage of a window of opportunity when Ethiopia was beset by domestic turmoil and when the United States was concerned about Soviet and Cuban influence in Addis Ababa. His timing was motivated by a desire to exploit Ethiopia's moment of vulnerability after Haile Selassie was overthrown by the military led by Mengistu Haile Mariam and the Eritrean People's

Liberation Front had launched a secessionist movement at about the same time. This moment appeared to be a transient chance in the context of an unfavorable long-term trend as he believed that "the longer [he] waited, the stronger Ethiopia would become" (Colaresi 2005, 76).

However, Barre's gambit failed to gain Washington's support (Colaresi 2005; Gorman 1991; Lefebvre 1991). As in the case of the Greek and Argentinian generals, his gamble turned out to be a serious mistake. His attempt to recruit US support failed as the Carter administration refused to support his aggression. His complaint about being "let down" by the Americans was rebuffed by US assistant secretary of state Richard Moose, explaining that Washington had only promised defensive weapons which "were not of such a nature that a prudent man would have mounted an offensive on the basis of them" (quoted in Farer 1979, 126).

In addition to Barre's miscalculation as well as those of the Greek and Argentinian generals, we encounter other episodes of policy failure such as the national disaster that befell Japan resulting from its leaders' gamble to attack Pearl Harbor. Still another example from the war between Iraq and Iran comes to mind (Hiro 1991; Pelletierre 1992). Saddam Hussein had started this war to claim the disputed Shatt-al-Arab waterway, seeking to exploit a window of opportunity when Tehran was weakened by domestic tumult and international isolation after it had seized the US embassy and held American diplomats as hostages. This was another instance of a war started for territorial gain in the hope of establishing a quick fait accompli. It turned out, however, to be one of the longest and costliest wars in recent history. Contrary to Saddam's expectation, outside powers did not assist Iraq to win this conflict—although they did try to prevent an Iranian victory. The war was a hard-fought stalemate (1980–88), causing Saddam to complain about the superpowers' unwillingness to compel Iran to accept a United Nations–mandated ceasefire (Chubin and Tripp 1988, 195). Thus, we see in this case again an example of policy miscalculation although the rationale attributed to the initiation of armed hostilities—the logic of exploiting a window of opportunity to achieve a quick fait accompli based on an assessment of an ostensible favorable international environment—is still valid.

Parenthetically, Iraq had to depend heavily on Saudi Arabia and Kuwait to finance its war with Iran, thus sowing the seeds for its later quarrel with them and even its invasion of Kuwait. In its war with Iran, Iraq also sought to choke off Tehran's oil revenue by attacking its oil shipments, and Tehran's subsequent retaliation led to more direct US involvement to "re-flag" Kuwaiti tankers transiting the Persian Gulf and even to attack Iranian vessels and offshore oil rigs. This US involvement finally convinced Tehran to accept a United Nations–endorsed ceasefire in July 1988.

As a final example of the influence that alliance politics or outside ties has had on officials' decision-making, the conflict between Greece and Turkey over Cyprus is illuminating. During the 1960s and 1970s, this island's Greek-dominated government had sought to alter the existing power-sharing agreement with Turkey and to revise the Cypriot constitution negotiated with Britain when the island gained its independence. These attempts culminated in a coup that installed a pro-Greek government in Nicosia and a subsequent military campaign to expand territory under its control. These actions were predicated on support from the United States, with the expectation that Washington would at least restrain Ankara from military retaliation. This expectation, however, was dashed when Turkey invaded the island, bringing about its partition into two ethnic communities (Crawford 2003; Joseph 1997; Krebs 1999). In this case again, we see anticipation of foreign reactions entering the decision processes of Greek Cypriots and their backers in Athens—even though outside intervention did not help their cause or, for that matter, end the impasse that continues to this day (Doherty 2021). In contrast to the other asymmetric conflicts mentioned in this chapter, Greece and Turkey did not come to exchanging blows directly. Theirs was a conflict by proxy waged by their compatriots in Cyprus. But this fact is itself important because it indicates that Washington's concern over NATO's unity had played an important role in restraining two of its members from going to war.

In practically all the armed conflicts mentioned thus far (e.g., the Russo-Japanese War, Japan's Pearl Harbor attack, China's intervention in the Korean War, Pakistan's Kashmir campaign, and Egypt's Sinai campaign), there was not any false hope on the part of the relevant leaders that they could achieve a decisive victory by knocking out their stronger adversary. Even in the Falklands/Malvinas War, the Argentines did not expect to defeat the British in a contest of arms. They had thought that they would be able to capitalize on their local advantage conferred by their proximity to the conflict site and get away with a limited campaign to present a fait accompli that their opponent could not easily reverse. The head of Argentina's junta, General Leopoldo Galtieri, acknowledged after the war that he would not have started it had he known that Washington would oppose Argentina and support Britain (Paul 1994, 159). Although Saddam Hussein and Mohammad Siad Barre had hoped to make territorial gains, they also did not expect that they could defeat their opponent decisively on the battlefield.

It was pointed out earlier that Japan's attack on Pearl Harbor was a desperate gamble motivated by an acute sense of urgency that its economy and war machine would face imminent collapse due to the stranglehold imposed by the Allies' economic embargo. Revealingly, a sense of urgency to seize a closing window of opportunity (resulting from a small qualitative advantage in its armament) and a foreboding sense that Pakistan was facing a deteriorating position also characterized its decision-making process leading to the Kashmir War in 1965. Pakistan's foreign minister Zulfikar Ali Bhutto expressed this view when he said, "With the passage of time, as the military and economic strength of India increases, the possibilities of its agreeing to a peaceful and reasonable settlement of our outstanding disputes with it are correspondingly reduced" (quoted in Paul 1994, 116–17).

Concern with timing and passage of time also loomed in Egypt's decision to launch the Yom Kippur War in 1973. Anwar Sadat had wanted 1971 to be the "year of decision" but had delayed any action in recognition of Egypt's military weakness, allegedly because Moscow had refused to supply it with promised armament (Paul 1994, 143). But by 1973, the USSR had equipped Egypt with air-defense missiles that would neutralize Israel's air superiority. These missiles provided cover for Egyptian forces to cross the Suez Canal and seize a narrow strip of land along it on its eastern side. Egypt did not have military superiority and was in danger of being defeated by Israel after the latter country had a chance to recover from the initial shock of an Egyptian offensive. But Egypt banked on the United States' and the USSR's intervention to force a ceasefire and to pressure Israel to the negotiation table. Cairo had a limited objective of forcing Israel to return occupied Sinai to its possession rather than entertaining any false hope of defeating Israel decisively on the battlefield. The war was intended to avert Israeli occupation of Egypt's territory from becoming perpetuated. Sadat believed that the "two super powers appeared to be reaching agreement on all subjects, including the Middle East, which made this [the Yom Kippur War] the last chance for action" (quoted in Paul 1994, 138).

Foreign intervention or the prospect of this intervention protects the downside risk for the weaker side of an asymmetric rivalry in getting into an armed confrontation with its stronger foe. Major powers often intervene before the stronger belligerent has a chance to utterly crush its weaker opponent. Moscow's and Washington's intervention to prevent Israel from annihilating the Egyptian Third Army during the Yom Kippur War comes to mind. The United States, the USSR, and Britain also played the role of peacemakers in several wars between Pakistan and India, arranging a truce before India could bring its full military power to bear on Pakistan. These actions had the practical effect of preventing a total military defeat and complete political collapse of the weaker belligerent. They also caused, intentionally or unintentionally, the continuation of an enduring rivalry by keeping the weaker side "in the game."

The role played by a strong ally in asymmetric conflict is confirmed by T. V. Paul (1994), whose study included six historical cases of a weaker party starting a war against a stronger adversary: the Russo–Japanese War of 1904, Japan's

Pearl Harbor attack in 1941, China's intervention in the Korea War in 1950, Pakistan's offensive in Kashmir in 1965, Egypt's initiation of the Yom Kippur War in 1973, and Argentina's invasion of the Falklands/Malvinas in 1982. One conclusion is strongly supported in all six cases: "the hypothesis that the anticipated support from a great power considerably influences the choice for war by the weaker challenger is strongly upheld" (Paul 1994, 171). Significantly and contrary to the usual view that alliances serve primarily a defensive purpose, this conclusion indicates that alliance ties can have the opposite effect of encouraging or at least enabling a decision to initiate war (in the next chapter, I will also address an opposite effect, namely, that alliances can also help to restrain their members from undertaking risky policies endangering peace). Paul's six cases also share another similarity: all the weaker challengers have limited aims, and they all followed a common strategy to achieve a quick fait accompli. Moreover, their decision processes tend to reflect a sense of urgency due to concerns about an unfavorable long-term trend that would further weaken their bargaining position.

Significantly, the preceding remarks on the influence of alliances refer mainly to a *permissive* condition for the weaker side to become involved in a confrontation with its stronger opponent. Protection by an ally helps to remove an obstacle that would have otherwise caused the leaders of the weaker challenger to hesitate to go to war. But this consideration does not in itself indicate the (positive) incentives that encourage these officials to initiate a violent confrontation. What motivates them to do so? In other words, what can they expect to *gain* by initiating or at least not turning away from a clash with their stronger opponent? What considerations would incline them to hold out when the ongoing trend suggests that their country is likely to become even weaker (relative to its stronger counterpart) in the future?

When a foreign patron "has its back," the weaker side's cause no longer appears to be so hopeless. Although it may continue to suffer a disadvantage, the odds are less prohibitively stacked against it. More to the point about its positive incentives to instigate, provoke, and even escalate a conflict with its stronger rival, however, is the fact that the only chance that this actor can hope to change its predicament is by internationalizing its bilateral conflict. Although there are important exceptions (e.g., China on Taiwan, Russia on Ukraine), the stronger side is usually not motivated to change the status quo that benefits it (e.g., Israel in its occupation of the Sinai, India in its control of Kashmir, Britain in its possession of the Falklands/Malvinas, Ethiopia's dominant position in the Ogaden in its territorial contest with Somalia). It usually refuses to negotiate with its weaker counterpart or to submit their dispute to international adjudication.

In order to alter the status quo perceived to be detrimental to their interest and in order to avoid this situation from becoming a permanent state of affairs, the weaker contestant is motivated to start a crisis and even war to arouse international attention and to press for foreign mediation that they hope will improve their position. Anwar Sadat's decision to launch the Yom Kippur War in 1973 and Ayub Khan's decision to start Pakistan's war with India in 1965 exemplify these considerations (Chan 2012b; Leng 1983; Paul 1994). As another example, in 1995 Ecuador started a border fight against its stronger neighbor, Peru. Quito did not expect to win the war or to gain and hold on to disputed territories by military force. Rather, its objective was to mobilize intervention by the United States and Latin America's larger countries (Argentina, Brazil, and Chile) to broker a new deal with Lima, which the latter had resisted before the armed clash (Marcella and Downes 1999; Mares 1996/1997; Simmons 1999). These outside parties eventually helped Ecuador and Peru to reach an agreement, the Brasilia Accord in October 1998, to settle their dispute. Christopher Gelpi's (1999) study of mediation efforts shows that when a great power and one that is allied with one of the disputants is involved, this situation is more likely to produce a settlement. Moreover, coercive pressure from this mediator also contributes to this success. His study includes 117 mediation attempts in international crises between 1918 and 1988.

In this and other similar cases (e.g., the Kashmir War in 1965, the Yom Kippur War in 1973), the primary motivation was to seek foreign involvement to achieve a new negotiated settlement rather than outright territorial conquest. These cases therefore differ from others such as the Russo–Japanese War, the Falklands/Malvinas War, Somalia's attacks on Ethiopia, and Iraq's invasion of Iran, where the weaker side's leaders had hoped to make territorial gains by launching a military campaign with the objective of establishing a fait accompli that would be difficult or costly for their opponent to reverse. However, in all the cases just mentioned, these leaders either had an incentive to exploit a temporary window of opportunity or were motivated to act before their country became even weaker.

These remarks should not be interpreted to suggest that the weaker side in asymmetric conflicts is always motivated by limited aims. In the 1950s, Syngman Rhee's South Korea and Chiang Kai-shek's Kuomintang regime in Taiwan had ambitions of reuniting Korea and retaking the Chinese mainland, respectively. They agitated for US support in these endeavors, which would obviously entail the risk of military escalation. Washington resisted and rebuffed repeatedly their entreaties in no uncertain terms (e.g., C. Kim; 2019; T. Kim 2011). It tried to restrain these leaders, pressuring Rhee to agree to the armistice in exchange for a security pact, which the United States subsequently used to limit the danger of entrapment by him and his successor, Park Chung-hee. Similarly, it pressured Chiang to remove troops from the Tachen (Dachen) islands in 1955, and it inserted important qualifications in its military treaty with Chiang to restrain him. The next chapter will pick up the topic of how alliances may be used to manage intra-alliance affairs, especially for the stronger partner to control the weaker partner.

But restraint and influence represent a two-way street. Allies of the United States have often sought to overcome or bypass resistance from the US executive branch by networking with the legislative branch and parts of US agencies that work closely with them (such as US aid and military missions in their country) and by cultivating and appealing to US elite and public opinion (Keohane 1971). The activities and influence of Taiwan's and Israel's lobbies in the United States have been especially well documented (Bachrach 1976; Koen 1960; Mearsheimer and Walt 2007). Thus, ostensibly weak and small allies can also influence the policies of their more powerful partners.

Returning to the idea that a country may start or escalate a conflict in the hope of recruiting third parties to broker a new deal, those states involved in repeated clashes are in fact more likely to induce foreign mediation than others that do not share this experience. Significantly, outside involvement in these enduring rivalries does not decrease the danger of yet another confrontation. In fact, it has the opposite tendency of increasing the probability of a subsequent armed confrontation and its escalation to war (Bercovitch and Diehl 1997). This paradoxical phenomenon may appear puzzling but only if we overlook the possibility that foreign intervention is more likely to happen in the more serious militarized disputes that threaten to diffuse and escalate in the first place. These tend to be also the more intractable quarrels.

Put bluntly, the weaker disputant's cause often seems hopeless without outside intervention. In this context, its leaders may deliberately provoke its stronger foe in the hope that the resulting conflict escalation and human tragedy would call attention to their cause and mobilize international sympathy—especially if their counterpart retaliates against their provocation with disproportionate force. The history of armed clashes between the Palestinians and Israelis comes to mind. The fights that the Bosnians, Kosovans, and Croats had with Serbs provide further examples. Media publicity reporting on war's horrors, such as on the plight of victims of wartime displacement and ethnic cleansing, has the effect of compelling international intervention to provide humanitarian aid and institute a truce. Other conflicts involving the plight of the Kurds in Iraq and the Syrian resistance movement against Bashar al-Assad display similar traits. As these words were being written, a war between Hamas and Israel was raging in the Gaza Strip populated by Palestinian refugees. There were horrific civilian casualties on both sides. US president Joe Biden flew to Israel in the middle of this armed conflict, but his meetings with Arab leaders were canceled because of the bombing of a hospital in Gaza that caused hundreds of casualties. We do not yet know the full details of this unfolding story, but the dynamics described in this chapter might again be operating. Hamas' initial attack on Israel could have been motivated to disrupt ongoing talks between Israel and Saudi Arabia to establish diplomatic relations and to involve Iran in a wider conflict on its behalf.

The international community is shocked by mass atrocities and humanitarian disasters. It intervenes with the best of intentions. This intervention protects the weaker side, preventing it from being annihilated by its stronger foe. But it also has the effect of encouraging this weaker actor to repeat the same behavior of instigating or provoking another round of confrontation. In other words, by not "giving war a chance" to utterly defeat the weaker side, international intervention has an important unintended consequence. It creates a moral hazard that prolongs rivalries and encourages the recurrence of violence (Benson 2012; Benson, Bentley, and Ray 2013; Benson, Meirowitz, and Ramsay 2014; Kuperman 2008). *Moral hazard* refers to a policy or action that has an unintended consequence that defeats its original intention, such as no-fault automobile insurance having the perverse effect of causing motorists to become more reckless drivers (Arrow 1963; Shavell 1979).

There is another plausible explanation for the leaders of a weaker party to hold out even when faced with a lopsided contest and even when their country's situation presages a further weakening of its bargaining position in the future. Domestic public opinion may be strongly opposed to reaching a compromise with the opposing side. Moreover, any accommodation of the other side may be criticized by the government's political opponents and critics as appeasement. Electoral incentives and partisan politics can therefore impede a deal to end a rivalry, even when leaders realize that this conflict can be a source of grave danger if it is not resolved. Therefore, leaders facing the pressure to win the next election may very well resist settling with a foreign counterpart even though they may believe privately that it will be in the best interest of their country. The more popular course of action is usually to confront a rival rather than to compromise with it. The default is to continue an existing policy because it takes political capital and courage to reverse it.

When the next election is always just around the corner, there never appears to be a good time to reconcile or conciliate with a rival. Even for leaders without elections, their political position may be vulnerable and even precarious given challenges and threats from opposing factions in the ruling coalition. Politicians tend to be risk-averse in this respect. But they may be risk-acceptant in another way. The diversionary theory of war, mentioned earlier, suggests that they may be inclined to make political hay out of demonizing and confronting a foreign enemy. Bellicosity toward foreign enemies can be employed to deflect citizens' dissatisfaction and compensate for the regime's unpopularity. It can also be used in some circumstances to appease the demands of factions within the ruling elite.

These tendencies, in addition to those foreign factors discussed above, tend to reinforce the perpetuation of rivalries.

As former US secretary of labor John Dunlop has remarked, reaching a deal with one's opposite number in the other country requires at least three agreements—one across the table and one on each side of the table (Raiffa 1982, 166). Domestic "ratification" will be required of each side's important stakeholders (Putnam 1988). That is, the negotiated deal must be approved by the respective leaders' important domestic constituents—if not receiving active endorsement from them, then at least their acquiescence or passive acceptance. Naturally, a deal across the table can only be possible if the "win sets" of the opposing sides' leaders overlap. Among other considerations, this requirement suggests that the political clocks on both sides must be in sync—that is, the windows to offer and exchange concessions must be open concurrently on both sides (Nincic 2011).

Matters can, of course, get more complicated when multiple states are involved in a dispute, such as the important role of the United States in the Russo-Ukrainian War and the Sino-Taiwanese impasse. Furthermore, the respective leaders must be politically strong and secure so that they are able to overcome any domestic opposition to a negotiated settlement. They are less likely to "stick their neck out," politically speaking, when their domestic opponents and detractors are breathing down their neck or when they have only a slight political mandate. These are demanding conditions. The stars usually do not align to produce a propitious context for all parties to a dispute to settle their longstanding conflict. This said, one should also not minimize the chances for a diplomatic breakthrough. Who would have predicted Anwar Sadat's peace overture to Israel and the Camp David accord in 1978? Of course, this overture also came with the price of his life.

Concern over the domestic consequences of failing to take decisive action was apparently an important factor in Anwar Sadat's decision to go to war in 1983. "A failure to go to war in October would almost certainly have brought the overthrow—probably by military coup—of the regime" (Burrell and Kelidar quoted in Paul 1994, 141). In view of the regime's unpopularity due to its political repression and poor economic performance, the junta in Buenos Aires also worried about the domestic consequences of inaction, "compounding the fears of an insecure military regime that time was running out for it to act" (Paul 1994, 155).

The two plausible explanations advanced above, one referring to foreign intervention and the other pointing to domestic politics, are, of course, not mutually exclusive. They are usually operating in combination to sustain conflict recidivism. These explanations also raise policy predicaments and moral dilemmas. As implied earlier, the prospect of foreign intervention—even when to arrange and supervise a ceasefire—can have the unintended effect of encouraging reckless behavior, especially emboldening the weaker side to practice military and diplomatic brinksmanship. Some people have in fact argued that we should "give war a chance." Edward Luttwak (1999, 36) has commented on the problem of "premature peacemaking":

> An unpleasant truth often overlooked is that although war is a great evil, it does have a great virtue: it can resolve political conflicts and lead to peace. This can happen when all belligerents become exhausted or when one wins decisively. Either way the key is that the fighting must continue until a resolution is reached. War brings peace only after passing a culminating phase of violence. Hopes of military success must fade for accommodation to become more attractive than further combat.

Thus significantly, even when they mean well, outside parties' intervention as peacemakers or peacekeepers creates a moral hazard. These outside parties include not only national governments but also international organizations like the United Nations and nongovernmental relief organizations. By removing the weaker belligerent's fear of the worst outcome of a war, this action emboldens it and inclines it to accept and even escalate a conflict that it would otherwise have been reluctant to undertake. "Imposed armistices . . . artificially freeze conflict and perpetuate a state of war indefinitely by shielding the weaker side from consequences of refusing to make concessions for peace" (Luttwak 1999, 37). Because nowadays "wars among lesser powers have rarely been allowed to run their natural course," they only interrupt a conflict without helping to bring it to a conclusive end by resolving its root cause. This being the case, the interlude provided by a truce only enables the parties to recuperate and regroup for another round of fighting.

Moreover, the emergent norm of "responsibility to protect" has had the effect of "raising expectations of diplomatic and military intervention to protect [vulnerable groups from genocidal violence]" and, by so doing, "unintentionally fosters rebellion by lowering its expected cost and increasing its likelihood of success" (Kuperman 2008, 49). Indeed, it even encourages incentives on the part of the rebel or secessionist groups to provoke the government in the hope that the latter's overreaction might garner international sympathy and support for them. Although the preceding remarks refer to recent episodes of armed struggles by the Bosnians and Kosovans against the stronger Serbs, they pertain equally to other situations involving the Palestinians' intifada against Israeli occupation, Muslim resistance to Indian rule in Kashmir, Uighur opposition to Chinese rule in Xinjiang, and protest movements in Iran and Myanmar. Expectations of foreign intervention can thus have the unintended consequence of causing mass violence and creating false hopes when this intervention does not occur or when it occurs too late or too ineffectively to protect the victims (Kuperman 2008).

This situation results in an ethical dilemma. The international community's commitment to prevent humanitarian tragedies and alleviate human suffering may play into the hands of those who want to see its intervention by deliberately causing such tragedies and suffering to induce or invite its involvement. This tendency makes conflicts more likely to occur and escalate, especially if others start to imitate and repeat the same unscrupulous behavior. Yet a refusal to act in the face of humanitarian tragedies and mass suffering would also be unconscionable. To avoid its good intentions from being exploited, the international community cannot possibly announce that it would "stand aside" to allow atrocities to occur. Yet, shielding the weak side from atrocities has the effect of encouraging its recklessness and of conflicts being re-enacted time and again. The international community is thus caught on the horns of an acute dilemma.

Of course, international interventions may not always be motivated by noble humanitarian reasons. As implied earlier, there may instead be Machiavellian or realpolitik incentives to support a state embroiled in an enduring rivalry to distract, wear down, or simply irritate another country that happens to be an opponent or competitor for both the intervening country and its protégé. From this perspective of a third party, keeping a rivalry alive may be an attractive policy. Foreign intervention may also be undertaken for purely symbolic reasons to deflect domestic criticism or appease international opinion. When the heat is turned up and body bags start coming home, such intervention may be terminated quickly, leaving its intended beneficiaries behind, as in the case of the hasty US withdrawal from Somalia depicted in the movie *Blackhawk Down*. This situation can be even worse such as when the Belgian troops left Rwanda, accelerating the departure of other foreigners from Kigali. By removing potential international eyewitnesses to atrocities, this action indirectly enabled the massacre of Tutsis by Hutus. The Dutch Supreme Court ruled in 2019 that Dutch peacekeeping troops were partially responsible for the deaths of hundreds of Bosnian men who were removed from a Dutch base in Srebrenica and delivered to Bosnian Serbs, despite knowing they "were in serious jeopardy of being abused and murdered" (Murphy 2022).

Preventive Motive, Gambling for Recovery, and Strategic Opportunism

The initiation, escalation, and persistence of conflicts may be due to multiple motivations. The preceding discussion shows that the weaker side in asymmetric conflicts is often the one that initiates or instigates an armed confrontation. Although in some cases the weaker party in these asymmetric conflicts has been influenced by an incentive to make gains, this phenomenon is less common than the opposite incentive to prevent or reverse a loss. Japan's attack on Russia in 1904 presents an example of the former phenomenon. That it was able to force St. Petersburg to accept a fait accompli was also unusual. The wars launched by a weaker Somalia against its stronger neighbor Ethiopia also represent an agenda for aggrandizement. Iraq's invasion of Iran in 1980 and Argentina's invasion of the Falklands/Malvinas provide still two other such examples. In the latter three cases, the aggressor states failed to achieve their territorial ambitions. In most conflicts reviewed in this chapter, however, the weaker belligerent started a war not because of greed for gain but rather from a desire to avoid loss or a fear that an unfavorable situation might deteriorate even further if they should fail to act. This preventive motivation appeared in the calculations of the Japanese officials leading to Pearl Harbor, the reasoning of Chinese leaders to enter the Korean War, and the deliberations of Egyptian and Pakistani leaders to start the Yom Kippur War and the Kashmir offensive, respectively.

Two quick caveats are in order. First, a preventive war can also be launched by a stronger country in anticipation that it will be in a weaker position in the future. Germany's decision to go to war in 1914 reflected this logic (Copeland 2000; Levy 1987). Second, a preventive war is not the same as a preemptive war. The latter kind refers to a country initiating the first blow when it sees itself in imminent danger of being attacked by its opponent such as Israel in the Six Day War in 1967. This kind of war is quite rare (Reiter 1995).

The preventive motivation was even present in the Argentinian junta's decision to seize the Falklands/Malvinas if we consider the regime's unpopularity at home. As pointed out in the preceding discussion, consideration of an unfavorable or deteriorating domestic political situation also played some role in the decisions by the Japanese, Egyptian, and Pakistani leaders. In general, these cases suggest that in their effort to explain international conflict, analysts might have assigned too much weight to the role of ambitions (or greed) to make gains compared to insecurity (or fear) over incurring losses in motivating officials' bellicosity. A country may be motivated more strongly by a sense of urgency and even desperation (such as in Japan's decision to attack Pearl Harbor and Germany's decision leading to World War I) to head off a deteriorating situation. Rather than a burning desire for acquisitive accumulations, leaders are often driven more by their strong aversion to losses. Stephen Van Evera (1999, 79) observes that "preventive motives were evident in most wars." The historian A. J. P. Taylor (1954) concurs that every war fought among great powers between 1848 and 1918 started as a preventive war and not as a war of conquest.

This phenomenon often reflects a tendency to "gamble for recovery." This tendency can be literally true when gamblers at casinos raise their betting amount after suffering a series of losses. Such behavior has a strong psychological basis. Prospect theory (Kahneman and Tversky 1979; 2000; Kahneman, Slovic, and Tversky 1982) suggests that people are more strongly motivated to avoid losses than driven to acquire gains. When people perceive themselves to be in the domain of loss, they tend to take excessive risks to prevent or reverse an actual or imagined setback (Boettcher 2005; Chan 2012b; Farnham 1994; He and Feng 2012; Levy 1996; 1997; McDermott 1998; Taliaferro 2004). People are inclined to take more risks in the domain of loss than when they are in the domain of gain. Case studies of decision processes involving Dwight Eisenhower in the U-2 affair, Lyndon Johnson in escalating the Vietnam War, and Bill Clinton's management of the Bosnian and Iraqi conflicts show that these tendencies apply to top leaders as well.

I argued that the usual behavior of the weaker side to escalate its conflict with a stronger opponent also makes sense if we consider their feuds in a broader international context. In many cases reviewed in this chapter, this party does not have a realistic prospect of forcing its counterpart to pay attention to its grievances or to prevail in an armed conflict. It is likely to lose in a war of attribution. Its best hope to even the odds against it in a conflict is to bring about outside intervention. This intervention can force its stronger adversary to the negotiation table when it would otherwise not be inclined to engage in diplomatic talk. Outside powers can also provide the weaker belligerent a "safety net" by arranging a ceasefire that prevents it from being annihilated or crushed in a war. Moreover, a foreign patron can provide the necessary assistance to keep a weaker disputant "in the game," whether it is to continue to wage a war (Ukraine, Vietnam, Korea) or hold out against the stronger side's pressure during peacetime by perpetuating its status or sustaining its survival (Taiwan, North Korea). Thus, disputes and conflicts are rarely strictly bilateral affairs because significant third parties are often lurking in the background (Chan 2012b, 185).

Although the discussion in this chapter has focused on the incentives of local disputants to involve outside parties to advance their cause, this is a two-way street because outside parties are also often interested in exploiting these local disputes to advance their own partisan agenda. Indeed, competition between the United States and the USSR during the Cold War played an important role in abetting and sustaining local disputes. When competition between these superpowers declined, it sucked "oxygen" from some local conflicts such as in the Horn of Africa and civil wars in Angola, Mozambique, and Central America with varying degrees of intervention from outside parties, including Cuba. Parties to local disputes lost their ability to exploit the competition between Washington and Moscow to support their cause, often trying to get the great powers into a bidding war to recruit local clients. The danger of Egyptian–Israeli and Pakistani–Indian armed conflicts also began to recede after the Cold War. At least to some extent, these conflicts can be traced to exogenous sources having to do with positional rivalries involving major states. As international relations are being again defined increasingly by such rivalries, we may return to the days when great powers try to advance their partisan agenda by increasing their support and sponsorship of their clients, proxies, and associates in local disputes. After switching its diplomatic recognition to Beijing and unilaterally abrogating its defense treaty with Taiwan, Washington's increased support recently for this island reflects this new turn of events.

In a televised speech from the Oval Office on October 19 shortly after his trip to Israel in the midst of a war between that country and Hamas, US President Joe Biden stated that the world is at an "inflection point" (Collinson 2023). He asked Congress to authorize an emergency package of $100 billion to fund assistance to Ukraine, Israel, and Taiwan and to provide for US border security. This request has encountered varying degrees of resistance, especially the proposed aid to Ukraine which would receive about $60 billion of this money compared to about $14 billion for border security. It signaled US priorities in foreign policy and its increasing involvement in the world's three chronic hot spots that can potentially involve Washington in an armed confrontation with Russia, Iran, and China, respectively. I will return to this discussion in the next chapter, including how loss aversion may incline outside powers to intervene in local or regional conflicts to prevent the defeat or demise of their junior partners.

Finally, outside powers sometimes actively intervene on behalf of the weaker side by directly attacking its stronger opponent such as NATO's bombing campaigns against Serbia in the Bosnian and Kosovan conflicts and the eviction of Iraqi forces from Kuwait. They have also actively intervened on the side of the rebels or insurgents by directly attacking Qaddafi's regime in Libya, Assad's regime in Syria, and Saddam Hussein's regime in Iraq. As already mentioned, the outside powers have their own agenda, and it is often more in the interest of these supposed foreign benefactors to keep local conflicts alive than to bury them. Thus, strategic opportunism characterizes both the local disputants' efforts to recruit foreign support and the outside powers' attempt to take advantage of the local disputes to embarrass, harass, and wear down their adversary or to defeat or destroy this nemesis outright. There is therefore mutual exploitation.

Indeed, foreign support is often indispensable for continued resistance by the weaker side. It has been especially important in instances such as US support for the mujahideen to fight Soviet occupation of Afghanistan and Syrian rebels opposing the Assad regime. Western countries' diplomatic recognition of Slovenia and Croatia hastened the disintegration of the former Yugoslavia, giving the Bosnians the implicit green light to follow the precedent created by the Slovaks' and Croats' declaration of independence by announcing their own secession, which in turn motivated the Kosovans to do the same—even though neither the Bosnians nor the Kosovans were initially set on that course of action (Kuperman 2008). They abandoned the idea of gaining more autonomy by negotiating within a federal framework, realizing fully well that their secession would cause Serbian retaliation which they were unable to deter or to protect their civilians from. On the contrary, they had counted on provoking Serbs' reprisals, such as ethnic cleansing, which would cause Western countries to intervene militarily to assist their cause of achieving political independence. Strategic opportunism characterized their behavior. Their gambit paid off.

Other onlookers drew similar lessons so that Kosovo in turn inspired the Georgians who had a brief war with Russia in 2008. Georgia's "Rose Revolution" (so called because protestors handed roses to government forces deployed to crack down on them) happened in 2003 over allegations of a fraudulent election. The country's longtime ruler, President Eduard Shevardnadze, was replaced by Mikheil Saakashvili. Disputes related to Georgia's breakaway regions Abkhazia and South Ossetia as well as Adjara were largely frozen until his election. Two events provided critical background for Saakashvili's push to recover these territories for Georgia.

First, NATO's summit meeting in April 2008 announced that this alliance would welcome Georgia and Ukraine to join it. Second, in February 2008 Western countries recognized Kosovo as an independent state. Russia's president Vladimir Putin reacted angrily to the first development, declaring "We view appearance of a powerful military bloc on our borders . . . as a direct threat to the security of our country. The claim that this process is not directed against Russia will not suffice. National security is not based on promises" (Toal 2017, 125). His warning foreshadowed the subsequent Russo-Georgian War in the same year and the current Russo-Ukrainian War started in February 2022. As for the second development, Vladimir Putin protested, "If someone thinks that Kosovo can be granted full independence as a state, then why should the Abkhaz or the South-Ossetian people not also have the right to statehood!" (Toal 2017, 154). Michael Kofman (2018, n.p.) writes:

> The Western recognition of Kosovo as an independent state in February [2008] was a more important factor on the road to war than typically recognized. Saakashvili's decision to open hostilities, during an escalating cycle of violence, seems reckless when considered without that context. Russia was positioning itself to recognize South Ossetia and Abkhazia as independent states in retaliation for the recognition of Kosovo.

Kofman's remarks point to the contagion phenomenon whereby people draw lessons from others' experience and follow or imitate the precedent that others have created. His observation gains further poignancy when he reports former US secretary of state Condoleezza Rice's recollection:

> "I told Georgian President Mikheil Saakashvili—privately—that the Russians would try to provoke him and that, given the circumstances on the ground, he could not count on a military response from NATO." Some of my colleagues who served in government during this time still recall their fear that warnings from the State Department wouldn't deter anyone, and that the U.S. government wasn't doing enough to get ahead of the problem. For my own part, I doubt any messaging would have been sufficient to avert war between these two countries. The August War is a cautionary tale not just about a revanchist Russia, but also the fears and ambitions of small states, and the delusions of patrons who think they can control their partners.

The Independent International Fact-Finding Mission on the Conflict in Georgia, sponsored by the Council of the European Union, blamed Georgia for starting the war (Toal 2017, 127). Saakashvili escalated the conflict even though he "was told in no uncertain terms that if he launched a war the cavalry was not coming" (Kofman 2018, n.p.). Significantly, Georgia's 2003 "Rose Revolution" that led to its war with Russia five years later had itself inspired other similar episodes such as the replacement of pro-Russian prime minister Viktor Yanukovych with Viktor Yushchenko in Ukraine's "Orange Revolution" in 2004 and the overthrow of President Askar Akayev in Kyrgyzstan's "Tulip Revolution" in 2005. These events were preceded by mass protests overthrowing President Slobodan Milosevic in Yugoslavia's "Bulldozer Revolution" in 2000, followed by the unsuccessful "Green Revolution" against the election of Iran's president Mahmoud Ahmadinejad in 2009, the "Jasmine Revolution" ousting Tunisia's president Zine El Abidine Ben Ali in 2011, and demonstrations against Syria's president Bashar al-Assad in 2011 that later became an armed insurgency. The contagion of these "color revolutions" certainly deserves the description of a chain reaction due to learning and imitation whereby the occurrence of a protest movement in one place tends to be followed by occurrences in other places.

For their part, the Russians also drew lessons from their war with Georgia, which is not unrelated to the current conflict in Ukraine. These conflicts in Russia's near abroad present important geopolitical consequences and significant historical and cultural meaning for Russia (Toal 2017), just as Kosovo resonates strongly for the Serbs and Taiwan for the Chinese for the same reasons. As just noted, we encounter a similar phenomenon of serial developments in the "color revolutions" and popular uprisings during the "Arab Spring" (when, for example, Libyan, Egyptian, and Syrian dissidents were encouraged by events in Tunisia) so that we can speak of a contagion such that a phenomenon spreads from one country to another. *Contagion* has also been used to describe the spread of a pandemic, fears about falling dominoes to communism, the collapse of communist regimes in Eastern and Central Europe in rapid succession, and the re-enactment of insurgencies and coups d'état (Li and Thompson 1975).

I have also used this term to refer to an increasing number of states joining a militarized dispute or war as discussed in the previous and next chapters. This (horizontal) contagion can combine with (vertical) escalation to enlarge a local conflict and turn it into a larger conflagration—the topic for the next chapter focusing on the idea of "chains," whereas the focus of this chapter has been on the idea of "fuses" that can sometimes be provided by local disputes or insurrections to become internationalized.

Moral Hazard and the Backlash Effect

The consequences of moral hazard can be grave when pronouncements made by Western countries create false hopes—when the expected support does not materialize or when it is withdrawn from the intended beneficiaries (e.g., the Kurds in Iraq, Afghans who resisted the Taliban). A moral hazard is created when an action or policy produces an unintended consequence that it is supposed to stop or prevent. To anticipate the discussion in the next chapter, an alliance in the 1950s committing the United States to defend South Korea and Taiwan could have this effect by making war more likely because these allies would be emboldened to behave recklessly and even provocatively to get the United States into a fight to advance their revisionist agenda. This predicament continues to this day, and it is part of the rationale for Washington's policy of strategic ambiguity toward Taiwan. Obviously, if Washington commits itself to Taiwan's defense, this policy can have the effect of encouraging Taipei to declare independence, which will cause China to attack—an event that the United States wants to deter and prevent in the first place.

I will discuss in the next chapter the role of alliances and informal security ties in influencing the expansion or containment of conflicts. Although alliances are usually thought of as legal arrangements to aggregate their member states' capabilities, they also serve the important purpose of providing mutual restraint between the contracting parties, thus having an effect in limiting the spread or escalation of conflict (Pressman 2008; G. Snyder 1997; Tierney 2011; Walt 1987). Paul Schroeder (1976) has described this effect of alliances as *pacta de contrahendo*.

Returning to the focus of this chapter, a declared policy to support democratic change abroad and undertake humanitarian missions may perversely cause a backlash effect in the sense of backfiring or causing pushback. This policy abets rebellion and insurrection domestically and armed conflicts internationally. It gives hope to the weaker side that outside assistance will enable it to turn the tables on its stronger foe. As Kuperman (2008) has shown, it can even incentivize the weaker side to deliberately provoke its opponent to overreact by committing atrocities such as ethnic cleansing so that it can galvanize international sympathy and support for its cause. It is also imaginable for the weaker side in an international rivalry to engage in similar action to draw a foreign power into its dispute. Foreign intervention to enforce a ceasefire, provide humanitarian aid, and support pro-democracy protesters can have the unintended consequence of encouraging copycats, thus unwittingly causing further conflicts and insurrections. Such policy can therefore backfire by producing a backlash effect.

For instance, as alluded to earlier, during the 1950s US officials talked about "leashing" their allies in South Korea and Taiwan, because they were wary of Syngman Rhee and Chiang Kai-shek trying to get Washington into a war against their respective nemeses. Taiwan's then Kuomintang government sought confrontation with its communist opponent on the Chinese mainland rather than retrenchment. It did not shirk from this confrontation but instead welcomed it (C. Kim 2019; Stolper 1995). Embroiling Washington in a direct fight with Beijing appeared to be the only feasible way that it could hope to recapture the mainland. Dean Acheson, US secretary of state during President Harry Truman's administration, spoke plainly when he remarked in 1958 that Chiang Kai-shek intended "to embroil the United States with his enemies, the [Chinese] Communists" (quoted in Benson 2012, 152). More recently, Barry Posen (2013, 122) warns that "U.S. security guarantees . . . encourage plucky allies to challenge more powerful states, confident that Washington will save them in the end—a classic case of moral hazard."

This phenomenon points to the concern of entrapment on the part of the stronger party in an alliance, a topic for the next chapter. Of course, the weaker party in this relationship has the opposite fear of abandonment (e.g., Cha 2016; Mandelbaum 1988; Schroeder 1976; G. Snyder 1984; 1997). Smaller states can also fear entrapment. They must balance the danger of abandonment with the risk of (reversed) entrapment (T. Kim 2011).

Support for an ally can have two seemingly opposite effects. Instead of emboldening a junior partner like Taiwan, could the reassurance of US support and protection have the reverse effect of making it feel more secure and hence *less* likely to provoke a crisis? Would removing the ambiguity in US policy toward Taiwan have the effect of deterring China more effectively or the opposite effect of provoking it? The debate in Washington continues about whether to remove ambiguity in US policy toward Taiwan and make a firm commitment to its defense (e.g., Carpenter 2005; B. Glaser 2020; Mazarr 2020). The issues of moral hazard and unintended consequences have not disappeared.

In an insightful study, Brett Benson (2012, 6) shows that contrary to the popular belief that deterrence threats must be firm, costly, and irrevocable in order to be credible to the target state, ambiguous commitments are quite common, and "the uncertainty generated by ambiguity has a positive, though counterintuitive, effect on international peace." I will return to this topic in the next chapter when discussing whether alliances have a general effect on entangling or entrapping states in an unwanted conflict (e.g., Beckley 2015; Benson 2012; Christensen 1997; Christensen and Snyder 1990; C. Kim 2019; T. Kim 2011; Pressman 2008; Priebe et al 2021; G. Snyder 1984; 1997; Tierney 2011).

As just stated, entrapment refers to a deliberate attempt by a weaker disputant to initiate a crisis to gain or shore up support from a stronger ally. Although the weaker party in asymmetric conflicts has often pursued this approach in the past, it is nevertheless a risky proposition because the expected help may not materialize, as, for example, already mentioned in past episodes involving Cyprus, Somalia, and Argentina. One important statistic would urge caution on the part of weaker contestants seeking outside help by provoking an armed confrontation or war. States honor their treaty obligations on only 75% of occasions when war breaks out (Leeds, Long, and Mitchell 2000), meaning that there is one chance in four that help will not be forthcoming from an ally. Others have reported an even more sobering figure of allies honoring their commitments only about 25% of the time (Sabrosky 1980; Siverson and King 1980), although this figure is more questionable after improvements were made in the more recent study by Leeds, Long, and Mitchell (2000). This is an astonishing figure considering that states select themselves into alliances based on their expectation of giving and receiving assistance from each other—even though it is also true that states with allies are still much more likely to receive foreign assistance than those without allies when they are attacked (e.g., Bueno de Mesquita 1981; Huth and Russett 1988). As discussed later, the danger of conflict instigation by a weak contestant is less likely when it enjoys a tight relationship with an ally (that is, when it is confident that it has support from this ally) or when it lacks any realistic prospect of gaining support from a major power. There is therefore a curvilinear association whereby the most likely states to engage in this behavior are the ones that have some good reason to expect outside intervention and would like to secure greater involvement, assistance, and commitment from this outside source.

Conclusion

There is strong empirical evidence to support the proposition that a very small minority of countries accounts for a very large majority of interstate disputes and wars. These enduring rivals get repeatedly into violent encounters even though many of these pairs are characterized by contestants with lopsided capabilities. They engage in long-running feuds that seem to be interminable. Given their pronounced dispute- and war-proneness, the conduct and motivations of these enduring rivals should be especially relevant to informing efforts to promote peace and avoid instability. Because their feuds represent such a large portion of interstate violence, these dyads should also enable us to gain a better understanding of the genesis, dynamics, and evolution of international conflicts in general.

This chapter has argued that, whether warranted or not, the prospect of foreign intervention has inclined participants in local conflicts, especially the weaker contestants, to take more risks and engage in more reckless behavior than they would otherwise have done. By protecting the weaker side by stopping a war prematurely and thus preventing its utter defeat, foreign intervention and alliance ties that sometimes ensure such intervention tend to embolden this side, making an armed conflict more likely to occur and recur. At the same time, looking at the situation from the weaker side's perspective, it is always concerned about the danger of being abandoned by its foreign ally or patron. It needs to shore up support from this source, and precipitating a crisis or conflict may be one way to get this outside power to recommit and perhaps even increase its support.

Although the focus of this chapter is on interstate conflicts, it has also referred occasionally to domestic strife and civil wars. Domestic conflicts share important similarities with the interstate kind. The logic presented in this chapter applies equally well to domestic conflicts. Political dissidents, insurgents, and secessionists consider and anticipate how powerful outsiders might act on their behalf in their challenges to incumbent governments. When they perceive and expect strong foreign support, they are more likely to mount these challenges (Kuperman 2008; Thyne 2006). Naturally, the moral dilemma and political predicament raised in the context of asymmetric interstate conflicts are also pertinent to these domestic conflicts. Just as with interstate conflicts, foreign powers often have a partisan interest in promoting or sustaining domestic contests. Foreign statements of support tend to encourage Syrian and Kurdish rebels, Iranian and Egyptian protesters, and dissidents in Hong Kong and Xinjiang but may also give them false hope if the expected support does not materialize. Conversely, as explained earlier, domestic groups such as Bosnian and Kosovan secessionists and Libyan insurgents also try to recruit and manipulate foreign intervention to advance their own partisan cause. An especially glaring example from Beijing's perspective of foreign interference perpetuating a domestic conflict is, of course, Taiwan's separation from China, a legacy of the Chinese Civil War and a result of US support for the government in Taipei.

Notwithstanding the proposition that expectation of international intervention can abet and encourage war and insurgency, it is important to acknowledge that this intervention can also contribute to enabling belligerents in civil wars to overcome their mutual mistrust, to broker truce, to protect civilians, and to enforce conflict settlement so that postwar reconstruction can begin. Therefore, it has had a positive impact on limiting casualties and restoring peace (e.g., Fortna 2004; Walter 2002; Werner 1999; Werner and Yuen 2005). Impartial foreign observers and a settlement reached with the help and assurance of powerful outside parties can help to mitigate the commitment problem discussed earlier. Therefore, international intervention can have a double-edged quality.

Support and guarantee from a strong ally can also alleviate concerns about an unfavorable trend portending a weaker position in the future, one of the reasons sometimes motivating one side of an enduring rivalry to initiate a confrontation now rather than wait till later. For example, the United States played a critical role in the Camp David Accords bringing about a peace agreement between Egypt and Israel. It practically committed itself to Israel's defense in future security crises. Yet, as already mentioned, the involvement of outside parties can ironically also encourage conflict initiation and escalation in the first place by lowering the anticipated costs of fighting and raising its prospective gains, thus making war easier to contemplate. Therefore, paradoxically, "foreign intervention can help to conclude internecine conflicts but also abet repeated challenges to the status quo" (Chan 2010a, 182). In the next chapter, I will try to sort out the circumstances under which one or the other tendency is more likely to prevail.

I would be remiss if I failed to recognize the phenomenon of "the dog that did not bark." Not all enduring rivalries have an equal potential to spread and escalate. In fact, some of the most contentious ones—between East and West Germany, North and South Korea, and China and Taiwan—have managed to avoid war even though they were and, for the latter two dyads, continue to be chronic hot spots in international relations. To anticipate the discussion in the next chapter, security or alliance ties appear to have a nonlinear relationship with the potential for a local bilateral dispute to spread and escalate. When the weaker side cannot threaten credibly to shift its alliance affiliation, when it is confident of the support it will receive from its foreign patron, or when both sides of a dispute are allied with the same foreign power, an armed conflict is more likely to be short, limited, defused, or prevented from happening in the first place. Conversely, when one of the disputants believes that it can count on all the great powers to support it or when its sense of insecurity leads it to attempt to shore up its foreign support, the corresponding danger is higher (Chan 2010a).

We can think of several preventive wars that could have but did not happen. The first of these non-events was the failure of a joint Anglo–French attack on Germany in the interwar years. French officials "would have gone to war with Germany, probably in 1936 and almost certainly in 1938 if they had been able to secure British support" (Ripsman and Levy 2007, 62). This quote supports again the importance of the alliance factor. The second non-event was that, contrary to realism's expectation, the USSR accepted its demise without mounting a desperate gambit to fight for its survival. It did not undertake a preventive war in large part because Moscow's possession of nuclear weapons continued to provide it with a large margin of safety from an overt, direct foreign attack. Another reason, however, was that it did not have any allies to join it in this effort. As a third example, despite tension in their relations, Athens and Ankara did not go to war—again largely because of Washington's restraining influence exercised through its alliance ties with both antagonists. Finally, the United States considered bombing Chinese and North Korean nuclear facilities but decided not to follow through on its plan of attack (Burr and Richelson 2000/2001; Levy 2008). It also decided to pull back from attacking Soviet missiles in Cuba during the 1962 crisis (Allison 1971). Alliance considerations did not appear to have been involved in these US decisions.

Finally, except for the Korean War, there has not been a large, multilateral war involving great powers since 1945. There has, in fact, been a historically unprecedented "long peace" among the great powers (Gaddis 1986). One can also question whether China qualified as a great power when it intervened in the Korean War. As acknowledged at the outset of this chapter, this conflict also did not follow the pathway for contagion and escalation described in this chapter. It was not a war started by a weaker side in the hope of involving outside powers. Thus, we have been fortunate that the mechanisms and processes described in this chapter to potentially cause a local conflict to spread and escalate have thus far not produced the feared outcome of a direct armed conflict between great powers after 1945. The Cuban Missile Crisis in 1962, the closest that the world came to this catastrophe, also does not fit the profile of asymmetric conflicts instigated or provoked by the weaker side of a conflict—even though its origin could be traced to the failed Bay of Pigs invasion in 1961 organized by Washington which, according to Moscow, motivated the USSR to install missiles in Cuba to deter the United States from repeating its aggression.

So why much ado about nothing? In other words, why should we be concerned about local rivalries escalating to a military confrontation and even systemic war between great powers, since this phenomenon has yet to materialize in more than seven decades after World War II? Because the danger is there. The ongoing Russo–Ukrainian War and Sino–American tension over Taiwan are two hot spots that can potentially spread and escalate. Although it appears that the danger of an Egyptian–Israeli war leading to intervention and counter-intervention by the United States and Russia has receded, there is still the potential for other areas in the Middle East, such as Syria, Iran, Iraq, Lebanon, Yemen, Saudi Arabia, and the Palestinian territories, to in one way or another trigger a multilateral conflict that involves one or more of them, Israel, the United States, and Russia. Moreover, the Indian subcontinent and the Korean peninsula can similarly produce armed involvement by Russia, China, and the United States. Attempts to resolve some enduring rivalries, such as those between Greek and Turkish Cypriots and between Pakistan and India over Kashmir, have encountered failures despite international mediation (Doherty 2021; Happymon 2021). The border dispute between India and China also remains unsettled. Therefore, even though the world has not seen a replay of the dynamics of multiple, intersecting rivalries reminiscent of that which set off by Sarajevo, the danger of a local feud starting a larger, more intense, multilateral war has not entirely disappeared.

Chapter 3
Alliances as Balls and Chains on Conflict Contagion

Overview

This chapter discusses the influence of alliances on interstate conflicts. Alliances have served as the main transmission mechanism to cause conflicts to spread and escalate. But they can also dampen such processes. Various conditions can affect these different outcomes, including the relative standing and policy outlook of the states involved, the balance of defensive and offensive capabilities, and the evolving structure of the international system. This being the case, dogmatic assertions about alliances' impact on war and peace would be unwarranted. Like many other things in life, this impact is contingent.

The *Merriam-Webster Dictionary* defines *balls* and *chains* as "something that limits one's freedom or ability to do things." I use these terms to describe the effects of alliances—and formal and informal security ties more generally—in this chapter. *Balls* is intended to mean tying down something or someone. When chained to a heavy ball, a person's movement is severely restricted. When the word *chain* is used alone without a *ball* attached, it means tying one person to another as in a chain gang. This can cause a chain reaction such as when one person falls, it causes others also to fall. In the context of a formal alliance or an informal security partnership, *balls* refers to restraining a confederate's actions, whereas *chains*—or *chain-ganging*—refers to pulling a confederate along in lockstep to wage war. Christensen and Snyder (1990) have used *chain-ganging* to describe the process whereby allies of Austria–Hungary and Serbia became involved in their feud, thus causing the diffusion and escalation of the conflict that we now call World War I.

In my usage, *chains* can also refer to parts of a physical, social, and even cognitive system that are closely coupled to present a pathway or process whereby "one thing leads to another." Thus, for example, in the "steps to war" model (Senese and Vasquez 2008), territorial disputes produce diplomatic tension, which in turn leads to an arms race and recurrent crises; and these latter phenomena in turn arouse emotions such as suspicion, fear, and anger that elevate the danger of war. The spiral model of conflict, whereby adversaries engage in a series of escalating tits for tats, provides another example of chain reaction.

Fuses, Chains, and Backlashes. Steve Chan, Oxford University Press. © Oxford University Press (2025).
DOI: 10.1093/9780197812907.003.0003

To anticipate the following discussion, *chain-ganging* is sometimes used to refer specifically to a situation when one ally joins another in a fight because it is fearful of the prospects of its partner defecting or being defeated (e.g., Tierney 2011). Moreover, the danger of entangling alliances can be defined to mean being influenced to join a dispute contrary to a country's national interests (e.g., Beckley 2015). Others have defined "entanglement as a situation in which a state enters a conflict because of the presence of a security relationship. The key criterion here is that the state must support the ally because of the security relationship rather than only because of its own intrinsic interests in the dispute" (Priebe et al. 2021, 9). This criterion asks, would a state have intervened in a dispute involving its partner had it not been for the existence of a security relationship? This question, of course, requires counterfactual reasoning, asking how a country would have acted in the absence of a security relationship (T. Kim 2011, 355).

Readers will also encounter in this chapter the term *entrapment*. According to Glenn Snyder (1984, 467), this concept "means being dragged into a conflict over an ally's interest that one does not share, or shares only partially." Entrapment is encompassed in the broader concept of entanglement; it therefore represents a subset of entanglement events. Entrapment is caused by a security partner adopting "a *risky or offensive* policy not specified in the alliance agreement," pulling its counterpart into a conflict that would not have occurred if it were not for the existence of their security partnership (T. Kim 2011, 355, italics in original). Entrapment is thought to be relatively rare (T. Kim 2011; Priebe et al. 2021), although more research is needed to study its origin and frequency. Even if entrapment does not happen very often, this conclusion does not necessarily mean that attempts at entrapment have been uncommon. They may be often attempted even though they have usually met resistance and failure. That alliances may embolden a partner (e.g., Benson 2012; G. Snyder 1997), as suggested in the last chapter, is related to concerns about entrapment, although naturally it does not have to end in entrapment.

In the following discussion, *chains* is used to refer to formal or informal security partnerships (including alliances) as transmission belts or mechanisms for conflicts to diffuse and spread. This phenomenon can be due to chain-ganging, entanglement, or entrapment. My focus is on the phenomenon of conflict contagion rather than the specific reasons for leaders' decisions. I mentioned in Chapter 1 that monocausal explanations are rarely adequate for international relations phenomena, which tend to be the outcome of a confluence of factors. Multiple considerations and motivations are also usually involved in deciding foreign policy, thus making it difficult to attribute these decisions exclusively to any one of them. Did the United States act in a particular situation to protect its reputation to stand by its allies, to preserve a balance of power, to protect its commercial interests, to appease its domestic interest groups, to respond to international opinion, to demonstrate its commitment to its basic values and principles, or for some other plausible reasons or a combination of them? There can be more than one reason. Moreover, reasonable people can and do disagree about what is or should be the national interest.

The role of endogeneity is also relevant in the following discussion. For example, allied states act jointly in a conflict situation believing that it is in their national interest to do so, but the convergence of their interests could very well have caused them to become allies in the first place. Similarly, that allied states are more likely to become involved in belligerencies than unallied ones can reflect the tendency for states anticipating a conflict to join security arrangements in the first place.

As another example, officials are certainly not unaware of the danger of entrapment (Cha 2016; B. Glaser 2020; C. Kim 2019; Mazarr 2020; Pressman 2008). Anticipating this risk, they can introduce conditions in treaty provisions to minimize it (Cha 2009/2010; T. Kim 2011; Priebe et al. 2021). This anticipatory step then has a nullifying effect on possible future attempts by one ally to entrap another. Such attempts or fears of such attempts can come from either a stronger or a weaker partner in a security relationship. The United States has deliberately pursued "asymmetric alliance designed to exert maximum control over ally's actions" vis-à-vis Taiwan, South Korea, and Japan (Cha 2009/2010, 158).

According to Benson's (2012) analysis, however, even conditional alliances can still create entrapment and moral hazard, for reasons explained later. Strategic ambiguity may provide a way to avoid entrapment and moral hazard by shifting the risk from one ally to another. "The persisten[t] use of ambiguity in deterrence situations suggests that there may be some advantages to ambiguity that cannot be achieved with conditionality" (Benson 2012, 11). For instance, an ally must be able to observe whether a condition has been fulfilled for conditionality to work (such as when an attack on its partner is unprovoked), but it may often be difficult, even impossible, to establish "who started it" in the "fog of war." As an example, the proximity of the offshore islands of Quemoy and Matsu, controlled by the Nationalists, to the Chinese coast makes it difficult for the United States to monitor and judge "what started it." This difficulty in observing a protégé's conduct makes the enforcement of conditional alliances more difficult, inclining the senior ally to rely on probabilistic commitments instead (that is, deliberately creating uncertainty in the protégé's mind whether its ally will come to its aid).

There is an additional consideration pertaining to the issues of self-selection and self-nullification. Naturally, more vulnerable states are more interested in seeking the protection and support of allies, thus "selecting" themselves into security arrangements including alliances. Switzerland does not seek such relationships because it does not expect to be attacked. Therefore, those countries that join security partnerships are more conflict-prone to begin with. Two offsetting tendencies, however, are also in play. Precisely because some states are more likely to get into conflict (e.g., Israel, Taiwan), others are more reluctant to commit formally to their defense. Moreover, to the extent that alliances contribute to deterring war in the first place (Benson 2011; Benson, Bentley, and Ray 2013; Benson, Meirowitz, and Ramsay 2014; Johnson and Leeds 2011; Kenwick, Vasquez, and Powers 2015; Leeds 2003; Leeds, Long, and Mitchell 2000; Leeds and Johnson 2016), those occasions when chain-ganging or entanglement happens constitute a biased sample because they do not include instances when conflict was prevented due to an alliance's deterrence effect. The latter instances are non-events, and as such they are not recorded by chroniclers and not usually studied by scholars. Besides this deterrence effect, there is some evidence indicating that a disputant is more likely to accept suggestions from an ally to settle a conflict (Fang, Johnson, and Leeds 2014).

Before turning to a review of the pertinent literature, I should also repeat several observations. Belligerents who fight on the same side of a war are not always formal allies. Even though they have not signed or ratified a security pact, some countries can still become embroiled in a spreading conflict. The Korean War offers a prime example of a large multilateral war occurring even though outsiders intervening in this conflict did not have formal treaty obligations to fight for one or the other party involved in the original quarrel, namely, the North and South Koreans. Thus, in addition to formal alliances, I have deliberately included informal security partnerships in my discussion.

As mentioned previously, the United States is not formally allied with Ukraine, Taiwan, or Israel; but it can conceivably become militarily involved in their armed disputes. Indeed, the United States fought two long, costly wars in Korea and Vietnam even though it was not bound to its partners in these conflicts by treaty obligations, nor for that matter in the two world wars with respect to Britain and France. Countries that end up fighting on the same side do not have to be bound by treaty obligations before they become for all practical purpose allies, such as when the USSR joined Britain and France in their struggle against Nazi Germany after having been attacked by it. Conversely, although Italy was nominally a member of the Triple Alliance, it stayed neutral after World War I started. In fact, it signed the secret Treaty of London, switching sides to support Britain, France, and Russia in exchange for their promise to back its territorial claims at the expense of Austria–Hungary. These comments are important because an exclusive focus on alliances as formal legal agreements among states to assist one another in the event of a military contingency can be seriously misleading because it omits an important phenomenon, as suggested by these examples.

There can be a variety of treaties, such as those that entail the contracting parties to assist each other in a war, to stay neutral in a war, or not to fight each other. The Correlates of War Project differentiates three types of alliances: defense pact, neutrality or non-aggression treaty, and entente (Singer and Small 1977). A defense pact suggests the highest level of commitment, requiring its members to provide military support if one of them comes under attack. A neutrality or non-aggression agreement pledges that the signatories will not support a war launched by another country against one of them. An entente entails the least amount of commitment. The contracting parties only pledge that they will consult each other when a crisis heightens the danger of war. Studies on the danger of chain-ganging whereby allies are pulled into a conflict have naturally focused on defense pacts, which, despite their name, can involve their members in starting offensive campaigns.

Some treaties leave open the identity of a common enemy, whereas others designate it even if not naming this country specifically. Moreover, there can be unilateral pledges, such as the Taiwan Relations Act passed by the US Congress, declaring Washington's intention to assist this island's defense. In this situation, a patron power promises to protect its junior partner without demanding reciprocity from the latter. Of course, this also means that the United States is free to withdraw its pledge, which does not have the same legal effect as a treaty committing it to act. As explained later, the "chain" effects of alliances in drawing their members into a conflict can occur both when these countries are relatively equal in their capabilities and when their relationship is characterized by large asymmetries in capabilities (that is, both stronger and weaker allies can get their partners into a conflict involving them). Naturally, the effects of "balls" to limit or restrain a partner's freedom of action are more likely when the stronger country in a coalition seeks to influence its weaker counterpart in situations characterized by lopsided capabilities between the two. But this generalization does not deny the possibility that the weaker member can also want to restrain its stronger partner from undertaking aggressive actions. The three types of accords just described reflect different degrees of "tightness" among their members. The discussion below is most pertinent to tight or tightening alliances. Naturally, an alliance's tightness is related to the idea of a system's "slack," or how closely its components are coupled, as discussed in Chapter 1. This tightness is one of the key conditions conducive to chain-ganging resulting in conflict contagion.

Different types of treaties should, and in fact do, have different effects on interstate peace and stability. For instance, neutrality and entente agreements do not require their contracting parties to render military assistance to one another should war happen. If we lump these agreements with defense pacts, our conclusion will be mistaken such as on whether allies will honor their commitments to provide military assistance to a confederate in war (Leeds, Long, and Mitchell 2000). This is so because neutrality and entente agreements do not require such action. Moreover, despite its name, defense pacts may be designed by the contracting parties for offensive or defensive purposes (Benson 2011); and they may or may not stipulate conditions under which its provisions would be activated. We need to recognize these differences when trying to determine whether these accords tend to embolden or entrap allies and whether they are likely to create a moral hazard, as discussed in the last chapter (Benson 2012).

Finally, as in the last chapter, I will combine in the following discussion two different types of scholarship on alliances and security relationships in general. I engage quantitative analyses based on large samples of alliances to discern statistical patterns and at the same time seek to understand better these patterns by consulting scholarship on detailed case studies relying on process tracing and historical documentation.

The Double Effects of Security Partnerships

President Woodrow Wilson was famous for professing his belief that entangling alliances were the chief cause of World War I. Whether alliances have this effect, the opposite effect, or an indeterminate effect continues to be a subject of research and debate among international relations scholars (e.g., Beckley 2015; Pressman 2008; Schroeder 1976; Tierney 2011; Weitsman 2004).

As for so many other issues pertinent to scholars' efforts to explain the war phenomenon, World War I is a paradigmatic case for those studying and debating about the effects of alliances on conflict contagion (referring here to the phenomenon whereby countries not initially involved in a dispute join a fracas). Germany's leaders felt that they could not let down their ally Austria–Hungary lest their country become further isolated and weakened by an expected change in the European distribution of power (Copeland 2000; Van Evera 1984; 1999). At the same time, French leaders were obsessed with the nightmare scenario of having to fight Germany alone. They were therefore also fully committed to supporting their ally Russia in a possible showdown. France became involved in war because it was allied with another country (Russia) which was allied with yet another country (Serbia) that was Austria–Hungary's enemy. For its part, Russia was determined to stand its ground in the July crisis of 1914. Having been humiliated in previous crises in the Balkans, it felt that further concessions would jeopardize its standing as a great power and its influence in that region (Levy and Mulligan 2017). Germany's intention to invade and knock out France at the outset of a conflict before turning to Russia ensured Britain's involvement in war because its Schlieffen plan called for this attack to be conducted through neutral Belgium (Tuchman 1962). German control of Belgium would threaten Britain's security. Moreover, London did not want to see the European continent dominated by any power. Britain became embroiled in the conflict because it had wanted to bolster France to prevent Germany from dominating the continent.

The account just given offers a popular rendition of the dynamics of chain-ganging (Christensen and Snyder 1990). It is necessary, however, to take several steps back to round out the picture and add important details and caveats to this account. To start, some scholars see the chain-ganging process being predicated on the existence of a multipolar system whereby the international balance of power is distributed relatively evenly among several great powers. It is difficult for them to imagine this process in either a unipolar or bipolar system. When one superpower is vastly more powerful than the rest of the pack, it is hard to see how minor states can influence this preponderant state to get into a war against its immediate interests. Similarly, the two dominant powers in a bipolar system do not depend on the support of minor states to confront and contain their opponent. Neither the defeat nor the defection of an associate would threaten their dominant position, which, by definition, does not require the support of minor states (even though one can imagine that such a development may have a reputation or symbolic cost to it). In both unipolar and bipolar systems, the dominant countries are so strong that their security does not depend on other countries. Therefore, there would be no compelling reasons for these countries to be swayed by the pleas of minor powers to join a war that they would otherwise not be predisposed to fight. If anything, they are the more likely ones to draw their junior cohort into a war.

This line of reasoning would cast doubts on the discussion in the previous chapter, where I mentioned the possibility of Taiwan and South Korea undertaking actions in the 1950s that might somehow maneuver the United States into fighting for their revisionist agenda. The danger of entrapment should be low for Washington because Taipei and Seoul must have realized that they would be taking a serious risk if they were to pursue this dangerous course of action—especially given the historical evidence reported earlier that allies have often failed to honor their treaty obligation in a significant portion of past wars (Leeds, Long, and Mitchell 2000; Sabrosky 1980; Siverson and King 1980). The United States might abandon them if they were to engage in such provocation, leaving them to fight alone in a war that they had started. After all, as a superpower it would not need Taiwan's or South Korea's support for its security, whereas the reverse would not be true. Without US support, the security situation for Taiwan and South Korea would have become precarious, but Taiwan and South Korea were hardly essential for US security. Of course, despite this fact, Washington may still decide to intervene on their behalf due to domestic politics—such as when an administration is concerned about being accused of being "soft on communism" by right-wing politicians like Joseph McCarthy—but this decision would not be because it believed that these allies were indispensable for its national security.

The above discussion suggests that alliances are formed not necessarily or exclusively for the purpose of aggregating their members' capabilities. Rather, their intended purpose can be for their members to restrain one another or for the dominant member to restrain its junior partner—thus, in such cases, alliances are supposed to work as "balls." Paul Schroeder (1976, 230) argues, "Alliances in some measure functioned as pacts of restraint (*pacta de contrahendo*), restraining or controlling the actions of the partners in the alliance themselves. Frequently, the desire to exercise such control over an ally's policy was the main reason that one power, or both, entered into the alliance." He points to the Holy Alliance among Austria, Russia, and Prussia in 1815 as a prime example. Similarly, the Congress of Vienna was as much about thwarting French aggression as checking mutual ambitions on the part of the coalition members that defeated Napoleon. Indeed, sometimes such agreements are intended in the first place to manage the danger of armed hostilities among the allies against each other (Weitsman 2004). Neutrality agreements or non-aggression accords, such as those signed by the USSR with Nazi Germany and Japan before World War II, had this intent.

According to Dominic Tierney (2011), the logic of chain-ganging comes into play when a state feels compelled to support an ally or partner because it worries that its own security would be seriously jeopardized if this confederate should abandon it or be defeated by the opposition. This view suggests that the relevance of chain-ganging depends, among other things, critically on whether we live in a multipolar world or are theorizing about such a world. This dynamic comes into play when leaders believe that their ally or partner is indispensable for their country's security. Seen in this context, chain-ganging happens when a country's leaders are motivated by loss aversion; that is, it joins a war because it fears the consequences of losing an ally or partner.

What if a preponderant country starts a war without any fear of losing its ally or partner, and this associate joins the fray out of a concern over losing the preponderant country's favor? Do we still consider this situation as an instance of chain-ganging? What if this associate is motivated to "bandwagon"—that is, to join the aggressor state in the expectation of profiting from its gains from conquest (Schweller 1994; 1997)? The conduct and consequence of these alternative scenarios can be the same. In all these situations, a conflict expands beyond the original disputants to involve additional states, even though different motivations may be operating for different belligerents. Indeed, even an aggressor state might have acted due to a preventive motive as Germany did in starting World War I (Copeland 2000; Van Evera 1999). Moreover, alliances (or security partnerships) are postulated to be the common transmission mechanism for bringing about the observed phenomenon, namely, the tendency for a conflict to spread beyond its original contestants. Equifinality, introduced in Chapter 1, suggests that different causes or pathways can produce the same outcome. Chain-ganging describes the phenomenon of conflict diffusion and contagion, even though it might have been produced by different motivations, such as the desire for gain rather than fear of loss.

This perspective, however, has a strong implication. It entails that we abandon the argument that the phenomenon of chain-ganging is limited to a multipolar system. It now becomes conceivable that follower states may join a leading state's bandwagon, being influenced by it to join a conflict. This conduct and motivation can, for example, characterize members of the "coalition of the willing" led by the United States to invade Iraq and to fight in the Korean War. Naturally in this case, instead of a patron power being pulled into a conflict involuntarily or reluctantly by its junior associate, as discussed in the last chapter, we have the opposite situation of the patron power recruiting followers to join a crusade. States may join a fight not necessarily out of a concern for their security. Those sending troops to join the US-led coalition would not be directly or seriously threatened should Iraq or North Korea prevail in these conflicts. Moreover, although anticipation of allies' reactions would have been a factor in Washington's decisions to fight in these conflicts, it was hardly the decisive one.

The preceding discussion has implied another requirement or at least an important condition for chain-ganging to occur. The alliance or partnership in question must be reasonably tight, and the pertinent allies or partners must have a broad convergence of strategic interests. On the eve of World War I, leaders of Germany and Austria–Hungary believed that their security was mutually dependent and deeply interlocked. The same beliefs pervaded in French and Russian official circles. Their leaders dreaded the thought of having to confront a powerful Germany alone. In the absence of their interrelated strategic concerns and nested security ties, it would have been much less likely for Sarajevo to trigger a large conflagration.

As mentioned in Chapter 1, when the parts of a system or network are closely integrated or tightly coupled, an occurrence anywhere would have ramifications elsewhere. Naturally, this observation in turn raises the question, how tight or integrated are the alignments in today's world? Obviously, NATO provides such an example as its members have committed themselves to come to each other's defense should one of them come under attack. Biden's warning to Putin not to invade Ukraine was ineffective precisely because it did not have the same deterrence credibility compared to Washington's announced intention to protect and defend its NATO partners. Compared to NATO and US security treaties with Japan and South Korea, the Sino–Russian rapprochement thus far is much looser, thus implying far less of a prospect for the dynamics of chain-ganging to apply to this dyad. This perspective also suggests that, except possibly for North Korea, Beijing's ties with other countries friendly to it (such as Pakistan and Myanmar) are not sufficiently tight or intimate to raise the prospect of chain-ganging.

Similarly, in the absence of a formal defense treaty and tangible actions such as stationing US troops on its soil, Washington's commitment to defend Taiwan is much less credible compared to its pledges to fight for Japan and South Korea. James Morrow (1994) and Alastair Smith (1995) have argued that alliances provide important signals to potential adversaries, communicating their members' intention to defend one another. For extended deterrence (that is, threats to fight for an ally if it is attacked) to be believable, the country making the deterrence threat must undertake costly actions (Fearon 1997). Signing a formal defense treaty is one example. There are other possibilities such as agreeing to share sensitive intelligence information, creating a joint military command, and positioning one's armed forces in a forward position in an allied country to provide a tripwire should an enemy attack. "Tighter alliances tend to produce greater deterrence and a higher probability of intervention" (Morrow 1994, 294). Such alliances also entail greater peacetime costs, which contribute to enhancing the credibility of deterrence threat and to establishing the infrastructure necessary to support an ally if intervention should become necessary. Fearon describes these actions as tantamount to "sinking costs" to convince the target of one's deterrence that one's threat to fight is serious and not a bluff.

Tight alliances cut both ways; they can facilitate both restraint and chain-ganging, and the prospects for the former outcome are greater when the dominant ally or partner is dovish (meaning an anti-war predisposition). Tierney (2011, 285) argues that the phenomenon of allies exercising restraint on their confederates is more prevalent than the opposite situation of propelling these partners to war; the phenomenon of chain-ganging causing conflict contagion does not happen very often in his view. "In tight alliance systems, restraint is inherently more probable than chain-ganging" (Tierney 2011, 288). When an alliance or security relationship is tight, this implies that the hawkish state (one that has a pro-war predisposition) is less able to credibly threaten defection to get the dovish state to come around to its view because their tightness suggests that their security is highly interdependent and interconnected in the first place. In fact, when a state threatens to defect, it means that the alliance or security relationship is already in trouble—it is getting looser or disintegrating. Moreover, a state that is dependent on a powerful ally for its security usually does not have anyone else to turn to for this protection. Lacking the option of finding another patron, its threat to defect is not credible. Indeed, its threat to defect would be inconsistent with its preference to fight the opposition as its hawkishness would suggest. Parenthetically, hawkishness does not necessarily mean being revisionist—a state may go to war in order to protect rather than upend the status quo.

Doves, Hawks, and Relative Capabilities

An alliance's tightness has a double effect. This factor can increase the danger of chain-ganging, but it can also provide greater opportunity for one ally to restrain another from taking risky policies that increase the danger of war and the momentum to rush to it. As Tierney (2011) has pointed out, whether the dominant ally is dovish or hawkish is an important determinant of whether one tendency will prevail over the other. This proposition implies that two variables—namely, the relative power of the allies and the extent to which their interests and preferences converge—should be considered. Of course, the very existence of an alliance or security relationship implies that there must be some preexisting convergence of interests and preferences or else the parties would not have entered into these agreements or arrangements in the first place. This convergence can cause a conflict to spread, but the consequent contagion would not necessarily be the result of one country pulling another into a war even when the latter country has serious reservations about the wisdom of this course of action.

In Tierney's view, the idea of chain-ganging refers to one ally being pressured by another to get into war. It implies a relationship consisting of a dove and a hawk—that is, when the two allies have different preferences on an immediate conflict even though their broader strategic interests tend to converge. The dove prefers to remain in peace, whereas the hawk wants to pursue a more bellicose course of action that is tantamount to war or that greatly increases the risk of war. According to Tierney, chain-ganging occurs when the hawk persuades the dove to adopt its position notwithstanding the latter's peaceful predisposition. The dove goes along with the hawk reluctantly for fear of losing it as an ally. Of course, both countries can be hawkish. In this case, the bellicosity of each one reinforces the other. This situation makes a war even more likely than if an alliance had not existed. It characterized the interactions between Berlin and Vienna in July 1914.

When would a dove concede to a hawk? This behavior is more likely when the hawkish ally is stronger or at least as strong as the dovish one. Alternatively, the hawkish ally's contribution to mutual security is greater than that of the dovish one so that the latter country is unable or unwilling to resist the entreaties of its hawkish counterpart. The dovish partner prefers to fight a war compared to being left alone to fend for itself. When a hawk enjoys preponderant power in a security relationship, it would not need a dove's support to go to war, such as when the United States invaded Iraq and Afghanistan. A large "coalition of the willing" was desirable for symbolic reasons, but Washington did not need other states' material support to fight these wars. Minor states that do not have a direct stake in a war's outcome nevertheless often contribute, sometimes even overcontribute, to a joint mission because they want to demonstrate to the coalition leader their worthiness as a partner (Gannon and Kent 2021).

Imagine the situation is reversed so that the dovish state is stronger and indispensable to the survival of the hawkish one. Their relationship would then have the opposite effect of chain-ganging. The dove will in this case be able to restrain the hawk, limiting the danger of a conflict from spreading and escalating. The greater the hawk's dependency on the dove, the greater the dove's veto power. This situation suggests that alliances can serve the purpose of restraining a confederate or, in other words, for intra-alliance control by the stronger partner to manage its weaker confederate. Washington's hub-and-spoke alliances in East Asia, as exemplified by its bilateral security relations with Taiwan, South Korea, and Japan, have been designed to serve this purpose (Cha 2009/2010; 2016; C. Kim 2019; T. Kim 2011). Instead of emboldening Taipei and Seoul to behave recklessly in the 1950s, as discussed earlier, these alliances gave Washington greater access and leverage to influence their behavior and thus to reduce the danger of unwanted confrontation. Although not directly supporting this proposition, evidence from international mediation leans in this direction. When a mediator is a great power and allied with one of the disputants, its mediation effort is more likely to succeed (Gelpi 1999). Washington's bilateral alliances in East Asia are in sharp contrast to its security ties with its European partners. NATO is a multilateral pact created more for the purpose of aggregating its member states' capabilities to oppose the USSR (Hemmer and Katzenstein 2002) rather than for the purpose of managing and controlling the behavior of US allies.

Do Alliances Create Their Own Interest?

I have already mentioned Tierney's (2011) view that we should use *chain-ganging* to describe a situation only if an ally decides to wage war because of its partner's pressure or entreaty, even though it would not have reached this decision on its own—that is, when a hawkish partner's preference prevails over that of a dovish one. This condition sets a very high bar for designating a situation to be an instance of chain-ganging. However, it is not necessary for me because I use this term to describe a situation when an initial bilateral conflict has widened to include more participants. When leaders of two countries agree to act jointly, including their decision to fight together, this fact does not preclude my usage of this term. Their interactions could have the effect of inciting each other's emotions, reinforcing their respective views, and hardening their mutual resolve, thus making it more likely for both to choose war. In the case of the Austro-German dyad and Franco-Russian dyad in July 1914, these interactions had the effect of fostering a greater inclination to wage war and hence chain-ganging in my usage.

In contrast to my view, Tierney would not use *chain-ganging* to describe a situation when both allies prefer war to peace because "the coalition is already favorably disposed to war" (Tierney 2011, 292). Nevertheless, whether we call it chain-ganging or not, this phenomenon still indicates conflict contagion, an outcome that would have been less likely if these countries were not allied. Tierney questioned whether World War I presented support for the chain-ganging proposition because Berlin's and Vienna's strategic views, interests, and preferences became aligned in the July crisis. Neither of them was dovish. Both were disposed to fight. Even though both parties had veto power to stop the other from going to war, Tierney argues that neither exercised it. Instead of holding Vienna back, he sees Berlin pressing it to fight—notwithstanding German chancellor Theobald von Bethmann Hollweg's two telegrams on the night of July 29–30 urging Vienna to negotiate. Germany's issuance of a "blank check" to Austria-Hungary suggested that their views, interests, and preferences had merged. Both allies preferred war as Germany wanted to forestall an emergent Russia and crush France once and for all, and Austria-Hungary intended to destroy Serbia. Therefore, they marched to war in coordination. This characterization by Tierney and his proposition that the Central Powers preferred war to peace in 1914 and that they deliberately chose war rather than blundering into it are shared by other scholars (e.g., Fischer 1967; Hamilton and Herwig 2004; Lieber 2007; J. Snyder and Lieber 2008). In short, the alliance between Germany and Austria-Hungary was turned into an offensive pact.

My own inclination is to use *chain-ganging* to refer to allies' influence on one another having the effect of increasing their willingness to fight, consequently expanding the number of belligerents in a conflict. My perspective entails us to think counterfactually. How much less likely would their officials have favored war had it not been for the existence of their security relationship? Do alliances have a separate and independent additional impact, and how much, beyond the initial convergence of interests and preferences that has led these countries to enter this security relationship? Thus, the proposition of chain-gaining in my mind corresponds more to what Michael Beckley (2015) has called the entangling effects of alliances. Does the formation of a security relationship expand further the convergence of its members' interests and preferences beyond those that had motivated them to initiate this relationship in the first place? Does the existence of an alliance create additional interests that would incline states to act jointly?

In other words, does participation in an alliance produce more shared interests? Do allies begin to adopt the views and even identities of their associates because of the interaction opportunities and socialization experience provided by their alliance? Does their coordination to prepare for war produce stakeholders and vested interests that increase their bellicosity? The idea of entangling alliances has been used to call attention to a tendency for states to fight to protect their reputation for honoring their treaty obligations and standing by their associates. In this way, upholding alliance commitments becomes a national interest rather than having national interest to decide whether to take on these commitments in the first place. I will return to this topic later.

Balance between Offense and Defense

Tierney (2011) has argued that chain-ganging is more likely when there is a multipolar international system, when there is a tight relationship among allies or security partners, and when the more hawkish member of this coalition is stronger and more indispensable to the dovish member. Christensen and Snyder's (1990) analysis introduced another variable: the balance between offense and defense—or, rather, perceptions or misperceptions about whether offense or defense has the upper hand. When the advantage is seen to go to offense, states are more disposed to make the first move in starting armed hostilities. The cult of offense—shared by Germany, France, and Russia—before World War I had this effect. Moreover, belief in the superiority of offense raises the specter that one's ally or partner can be defeated quickly, thus leaving one alone to fight the aggressor state. Tierney (2011, 286) acknowledges that "chain-ganging . . . can play a role in escalating conflicts, as alliance ties draw actors in the defending coalition into the fray."

Prior to war's onset in 1914, German military planners exaggerated France's offensive capabilities and their own offensive capabilities. They thought that a war in eastern Europe (such as in the Balkans) could quickly escalate into a Franco–German fight. Their Schlieffen plan entailed that at the first sign of war, Germany should take the initiative, concentrating its forces in a quick thrust to conquer France via Belgium. In the meantime, Austria–Hungary was to hold off Russia on the eastern front until Germany could redirect its forces to this front after defeating France. This planned course of action suggested Germany's dependence on Austria–Hungary despite the power disparity between them. Similar reasoning characterized French leaders' thinking. They needed Russia to tie down German forces, presenting Berlin with the specter of having to fight on two fronts. For their part, Russian leaders had doubts about France's ability to withstand Germany's assault. The cult of offense also led France and Russia to initiate offense against their foes once armed hostilities had commenced, resulting in Russia's crushing defeat by Germany at Tannenberg.

Thus, beliefs in first-mover advantage and the perceived vulnerability of an associate gave impetus to chain-ganging in World War I. There was a certain quality of self-fulfilling prophecy such that these countries' actions caused an initial crisis in the Balkans to become a large multilateral war. Sarajevo led to rapid military mobilization by the belligerent countries in quick succession, causing the conflict to spiral. Germany's kaiser was unable to modify the Schlieffen plan to order only a partial mobilization directed against Russia. He was told that rail schedules to move troops and supplies had been planned to the last detail, and it was impossible to improvise at the last minute (Tuchman 1962). In its attempt to seize the strategic initiative, Germany went to war against France even though Paris was not directly implicated in the Sarajevo crisis.

When defense is seen to be dominant, officials feel less need to initiate conflict. However, in this situation we are likely to encounter another pathology. Instead of chain-ganging, states have an incentive to engage in buck-passing, that is, shifting the burden of defense against aggression on to other states, for example, those frontline states that are the immediate neighbors of an aggressor state. Defense being dominant, those states that are more removed or distant from the immediate source of threat do not see the urgency of balancing against this menace, and they would rather let others do the heavy lifting. This situation creates an incentive for the more distant countries to be free riders, causing this tendency that bedevils collective action (Olson 1965; 1982). This situation explains in part Washington's tardy entry into both world wars.

In contrast to Hans Morgenthau (1985), who sees balance of power resulting from officials' policies, Kenneth Waltz stresses systemic pressure accounting for this phenomenon, stating "Morgenthau's understanding of balances of power differs fundamentally from mine. For Morgenthau, balances are intended and must be sought by the statesmen who produce them. For me, balances are produced whether intended or not" (Waltz 1997, 914). In either case, buck-passing would be an anomaly for both Morgenthau and Waltz. John Mearsheimer, a proponent of offensive realism in contrast to Waltz's structural realism or defensive realism, sees "the actual choice in a realist world is between balancing and buck-passing, and threatened states prefer buck-passing to balancing whenever possible" (Mearsheimer 2001, 140). Both he and Waltz believe that bandwagoning is self-defeating and should rarely occur.

Returning from this slight digression to the topic on hand, prior to World War II Winston Churchill and Joseph Stalin tried to deflect Germany's threat to their country by redirecting it to the other country. Both Britain and Russia thought defense had an advantage, and thus France would be able to hold off Germany. Instead, France's vaunted Maginot Line turned out to be a source of false hope. Its quick defeat by Germany came as a shock to British, Soviet, and other European leaders, as Christensen and Snyder (1990) have argued. In both world wars, the United States joined the fray late after the other belligerents had already spilled much blood and suffered great destruction. Had it not been for the Japanese attack on Pearl Harbor, its entry into World War II would have been delayed even further.

Christensen and Snyder (1990) point to the different dynamics operating before the two world wars. In 1914, offense was believed to have an advantage over defense in different European capitals (Van Evera 1984), although this popular belief turned out to be wrong. Nevertheless, the misperceptions had the effect of expanding and escalating a local conflict quickly, causing Europe's great powers to rush to war. Thus, chain-ganging led to World War I. In contrast, defense was thought to dominate over offense before World War II. This situation encouraged an incentive to pass the buck, producing a situation of tardy and inadequate balancing against the increasing danger of war coming from Nazi Germany (Schweller 1998; 2006). This phenomenon gives an aggressor state the opportunity to "run the table" on its intended victims, picking them off one by one. There was misperception again in the lead-up to World War II. Offense turned out to have an advantage such that Germany's *Blitzkrieg* was able to quickly defeat its neighbors. Berlin was able to exploit the buck-passing tendency of its adversaries by undertaking piecemeal aggression.

Thus, there is some truth to the adage that generals make plans to fight the last war. From the experience of the two world wars, it also appears that when the military dominated a country's policy processes, offensive strategic thinking was likely to gain the upper hand; and, conversely, civilian domination of policy processes tended to produce more defense-oriented strategic thinking. Christensen (1997) introduced an additional variable—leaders' perceptions of the balance of power among the prospective belligerents—to explain the two world wars as well as two other armed conflicts, the Austro–Prussian War (1866) and the Franco–Prussian War (1870). He argues that buck-passing is more likely to happen in a multipolar system when a frontline state is perceived to be strong enough to withstand an initial assault from its neighboring aggressor state.

In another informative analysis, James Morrow (1993) explains that armament and alliances can both contribute to enhancing a country's security and, in this sense, that they are substitutable. Depending on a country's domestic politics and the state of military technology, one or the other approach may be more effective and less costly. Given the trade-offs involved (such as alliances can add to a country's security more quickly, but an ally may be unreliable; alliances may not require immediate expenditures but may entail sacrificing some national autonomy and interests and may even risk entrapment; military spending and conscription may face stiff domestic opposition even though they may provide a more reliable source of support for national security in the long run), leaders seek to achieve an optimal combination of the two approaches. Morrow explains that because armament appeared more attractive, or less difficult, than alliance to Austria and France, they did not join hands in the 1860s to defeat Prussia.

Parenthetically, in a unipolar or bipolar system the dominant powers cannot pass the buck because there is no other state that they can pass it to. Minor states cannot possibly check the opposing dominant power in a bipolar system, and there is just one dominant power in a unipolar system. Realists believe that states, at least major ones, do not depend on others for their security or survival, even though they in fact do even for very capable ones such as Germany and Japan today.

Evidence from Historical Cases and Quantitative Studies

Do states get involved in others' disputes out of a concern to maintain their reputation for reliability and steadfastness in supporting their security partners? On the eve of World War I, leaders in Berlin, Vienna, Paris, and St. Petersburg saw their own country's security to be closely tied to their allies' security, and maintaining their alliance relationships became an overriding concern for them, being critical in their eyes for their respective national interest. Tierney's perspective suggests that chain-ganging did not apply in the narrow sense that the events in July 1914 did not correspond to a situation whereby a reluctant dove was overruled by a more hawkish partner.

But the broad phenomenon of alliances facilitating their members' coordination to proceed to war is still accurate, and hence the proposition that these bonds play a key role in the diffusion of conflict. Of course, Tierney recognizes that the idea of chain-ganging need not be limited to launching offensive campaigns. When states fight back in defense and their collective effort causes a conflict to expand to other areas or countries, alliances or security ties can still have contributed to the spreading of a conflict. If *chain-ganging* is used to refer to the tit-for-tat pattern of action begetting reaction and the tight coupling in the security reasonings of the leaders of Europe's great powers in 1914, then it is still reasonable to see this phenomenon as both the manifestation and the cause of conflict contagion. It provides an apt description of the almost mechanical way in which Europe's leaders responded to one another's moves in July 1914, as captured by Waltz's (1979, 167) description:

> If Austria–Hungary marched, Germany had to follow: the dissolution of the Austro–Hungarian Empire would have left Germany alone in the middle of Europe. If France marched, Russia had to follow; a German victory over France would be a defeat for Russia. And so it was all around the vicious circle. Because the defeat or the defection of a major ally would have shaken the balance, each state was constrained to adjust its strategy and the use of its forces to the aims and fears of its partners.

Christensen (1997, 67) offers a similar description: "in 1914, when Austria mobilized for war, so did Germany. When Russia mobilized for war, so did France." The strong influence that a decision made by the officials in one country had on those reached by their counterparts in other countries was evident. It is therefore reasonable to describe the result of this tight connection as a chain reaction.

Reciprocal causality was operating in another way: "[The] emergence of hardened coalitions may be symptomatic of a conflict environment" (Tierney 2011, 302). This observation is in accord with the view that the bifurcation of states' alignments into two exclusive and opposing camps augurs a more combustible environment for war to happen. Naturally, the process of self-selection and the issue of endogeneity are involved here. States join security pacts, and these associations become tighter when they expect and prepare for an impending conflict. Thus, a hardened coalition can increase the danger of conflict, but the danger of conflict can produce a hardened coalition in the first place.

Previous empirical research has concluded that war initiation and participation tend to be influenced by a process of infectious contagion and that alliances have been "an agent" in this process (Davis, Duncan, and Siverson 1978; Siverson and King 1980). Countries that are members of alliances are more likely to become involved in war. However, as just mentioned, this phenomenon does not necessarily mean that alliances fail to deter war. It can also mean that countries join alliances in anticipation of war. One indirect clue that tends to support this last remark is that states are more apt to join their allies in a war when their alliance is relatively new (Siverson and King 1980). The analytical challenge is then to determine whether alliances per se have a separate and independent influence on war initiation and participation besides leaders' anticipatory effect.

How often do security partners get entangled in their confederates' disputes, even though their national interests are not directly involved or when their perceptions of their national interests become merged or even identified with their partners' interests due to socialization? Miranda Priebe et al. (2021, v) summarize the existing literature in these words: "entanglement dynamics contributed to, but were not the only cause of, U.S. involvement in wars in Korea, Vietnam, Libya and in two conflicts short of war in the Taiwan Strait [in 1954–55 and 1995–96]." They refer to Michael Beckley, who defines entanglement as an instance "when a state is dragged into a military conflict by one, or more, of its alliances" (Beckley 2015, 12). In these cases, entanglement was deemed to have occurred because US involvement was interpretated as being motivated by a desire to uphold its credibility to support allies and maintain its general reputation for honoring its commitments. Other reasons, such as being socialized to identify a security partner's interests as US interests, were not considered. Of course, what leaders really thought to be US interests in a particular case is not always easy to determine (even though leaders routinely declare various national interests being involved in a situation, we cannot just rely on their words), and people can disagree strongly about what they should be.

Although the United States has intervened on many occasions on behalf of its security partners, Beckley (2015, 10) concludes that "in most cases, however, U.S. actions were driven by alignment of interests between the United States and its allies, not by alliance obligations." Naturally, as remarked earlier, there is a chicken-and-egg question involved here with alignment of interests producing a security partnership in the first place, and this partnership can also in itself cause the partners' interests to converge further subsequently. Regarding Tierney's (2011) observation that alliances can also enable their members to restrain each other, Beckley found four cases in which allies have prevented US escalation of a conflict and seven cases in which the United States reneged on a security commitment or restrained an ally from attacking another country. For example, Washington had pressured Britain and France to withdraw their troops after they attacked Egypt in 1956, although its objection did not prevent this attack in the first place. Sometimes, the United States exercises dual restraint or pivotal deterrence, when it seeks to prevent two of its allies getting into a fight such as tension between Athens and Ankara over Cyprus (Crawford 2003).

As already mentioned, a survey of the relevant literature found entanglement dynamics being present in five cases of US intervention, but other factors could also have contributed to Washington's decisions (Priebe et al. 2021, 58–59). However, "scholars have not identified any cases of U.S. *entrapment* in war, in which the United States fought to defend an ally or partner that risked conflict because a U.S. commitment emboldened it to behave aggressively" (Priebe et al. 2021, vi, italic in original). This conclusion agrees with Tongji Kim's (2011) assertion that although alliances may entangle, they rarely, if ever, entrap.

Although entrapment might have been often attempted, it always fails. Chapter 2 reports several cases in which a country instigating conflict had hoped for US support which, however, did not materialize. Although the United States did not prevent a war or crisis from happening in some cases, its subsequent intervention helped to limit a conflict's scope and duration.

NATO's attacks on Serbia after Bosnia's and Kosovo's secession were not considered to be successful entrapment by Beckley (2015) and Priebe et al. (2021), as Kuperman (2008) would have concluded. Their omission of these two cases and the bombing of Libya leading to Qaddafi's demise suggests that these actions were undertaken on Western countries' own volition and not due to their reaction to the rebels' actions in these cases (the Libyan case was determined to be an example of entanglement by Priebe et al. 2021). These rebels were, of course, not US allies or security partners; and, as such, the omission of these cases is understandable. Priebe et al. (2021) point out that all the defense treaties that Washington has agreed to take part in are conditional alliances with important qualifications and caveats written into them. Concerns with entanglement (or rather entrapment?) affected its treaty negotiations in three cases: Taiwan, South Korea, and West Germany, according to Priebe et al. (2021, 23–25).

Because of their conditional nature, US partners in alliances have been less likely to initiate a conflict, but it is not clear whether this phenomenon is because they feel more secure with the United States as an ally or because they are more subject to Washington's restraint. A related question on selection is also pertinent. Are countries selected by the United States to become its allies—such as the original members of NATO and those countries located in the Western Hemisphere—precisely because they are the "safer" ones that are not expected to provoke war or come under foreign attack?

It is also important to recognize that not all alliances are alike. Leeds' (2003) study is rather informative. She concludes that defensive pacts that commit states to intervene on behalf of potential targets of aggression reduce the probability that a militarized interstate dispute will occur. However, agreements that promise support for a potential challenger or nonintervention in a conflict have the reverse effect of raising the probability of such a dispute occurring. Thus, different kinds of alliances convey different information to international audiences, and they have different effects on the occurrence of militarized disputes—and understandably so.

In terms of this chapter's metaphor, the United States in its security relationships has often assumed the role of a "ball" or ballast to stabilize a situation that can otherwise be volatile. We do not, however, know the frequency of those non-events when it had restrained an ally's bellicosity (thus preventing a conflict from starting) compared to the frequency of occasions when an associate or even non-ally has started a conflict in the hope of receiving its support (such as when Saddam Hussein attacked Iran). As with alliances, international interventions can paradoxically have two opposing effects. The prospect of outside intervention can motivate weaker challengers to instigate and provoke a conflict to get outsiders to "pull out their chestnuts." But as discussed in the last chapter, international interventions can also have a pacifying effect by brokering and enforcing ceasefires in local conflicts. Alliance ties may make this intervention to prevent or contain a conflict more effective, even though they might have also motivated leaders to instigate or provoke a conflict in the first place. Note, however, formal alliance ties are not necessary for an actor to precipitate a crisis or initiate a war, as suggested by the example of the Iraq–Iran War. Nor are these ties necessary for outside intervention to occur. The United States and the USSR did not have treaty obligations with Israel and Egypt, respectively, to intervene in their wars. Yet they would have had less influence over the latter two countries were it not for the strong informal security ties that had existed between them. Christopher Gelpi's (1999) study of 171 past mediation attempts bears out this view.

Tension between Deterrence and Restraint

Alliances are intended to signal to potential adversaries the strength and resolve of the contracting parties to fight back if one of them is attacked. They also serve the purpose of restraining one's alliesr. These dual purposes of deterrence and restraint present a predicament. How can a country communicate its determination to stand by its ally without emboldening the latter to escalate a conflict? In a nutshell, "How can leaders deter enemies while restraining allies?" (Benson 2012, 3). This "deterrence-versus-restraint dilemma" (G. Snyder and Diesing 1977, 432) points to the problem of moral hazard discussed in Chapter 2. Washington's declared policy of strategic ambiguity on relations across the Taiwan Strait exemplifies an attempt to finesse this problem. It seeks to deter Beijing from attacking Taiwan and, at the same time, restrain Taipei from taking advantage of the US support to provoke Beijing, such as by declaring independence which will cause Beijing to attack. In cases such as this one, moral hazard requires adroit diplomacy to balance the desiderata of deterrence and restraint simultaneously. Benson (2012, 3) describes the problem in these words: "A third-party defender wishing to protect a protégé can best deter an adversary's challenges to the protégé by forming a maximally credible and firm commitment, but such commitments risk emboldening protégés not only to resist the adversary's challenges but also to provoke the adversary in an attempt to gain concessions."

Several studies cited in the last section conclude that entrapment rarely—if ever—happens (Beckley 2015; T. Kim 2011; Priebe et al. 2021). These studies, however, focus on only US alliance commitments since 1945, relying on qualitative judgments. In contrast, Benson's (2012) statistical analyses of all alliances between 1816 and 2000 show significant evidence of emboldenment, entrapment, and moral hazard. His study includes 259 alliances seeking to deter an attack on an ally; "74 [of them] promised to defend the ally no matter what [i.e., these are unconditional alliances], 139 conditioned third-party intervention on the initiation of conflict by a non-alliance member, and 46 were 'ambiguous' in that signatories did not have automatic contractual obligations to intervene on behalf of fellow alliance members in war" (Benson 2012, 1–2). He finds evidence that emboldenment, entrapment, and moral hazard exist even for conditional alliances designed for defensive or deterrence purposes and that these tendencies are (understandably) even stronger for unconditional offensive alliances. Two important causal mechanisms are especially important for explaining this phenomenon, considerations that have not been given sufficient attention heretofore.

First, protection by an ally, especially a powerful ally, emboldens the protégé to drive a harder bargain with its adversary. Believing that the ally has its back, this protégé is likely to demand more concessions from its adversary to settle a dispute, and it is likely to turn down offers of settlement from its adversary that it would have otherwise accepted in the absence of its alliance. Furthermore, it is likely to hold out for a better deal, thus making a dispute more protracted. Finally, it becomes more willing to risk war because it believes that an ally now has its back. Naturally, the threat of intervention by a powerful ally helps to discourage an adversary from attacking the protégé. Therefore, alliances are often seen to have this deterrence effect (Morrow 1994; Smith 1995; Yuen 2009). The attribution of this deterrence effect, however, requires counterfactual reasoning. Would an enemy (say, the USSR) have attacked but for the presence of an alliance (for example, NATO). Danilovic (2001, 97, italic in original) quotes former US secretary of state Henry Kissinger:

> Since deterrence can only be tested negatively, by events that do *not* take place, and since it is never possible to demonstrate why something has not occurred, it became especially difficult to assess whether the existing policy was the best possible policy or a just barely effective one. Perhaps deterrence was even unnecessary because it was impossible to prove whether the adversary ever intended to attack in the first place.

The putative deterrence effect of alliances is likely to be offset by the protégé's greater risk propensity and its demand for larger concessions from its adversary, thus making a deal to avoid conflict more difficult to reach and its escalation more likely. If we do not account for these processes, we would end up dismissing signs of this subtler and more indirect form of entrapment—even though it does not involve deliberate attempts to instigate a conflict or provoke an adversary to embroil an ally in an unwanted confrontation. By protecting the protégé from the adverse consequences of failing to reach a settlement, alliance with a powerful country emboldens it to be more aggressive in its bargaining with this adversary, thus raising the probability of a stalemate and even war.

Second, it is in practice difficult to limit a strong ally's support for an opportunistic protégé. Entrapment happens when these two allies do not have identical interests. Consider, for example, the senior ally that prefers that its junior partner keep 10% of the land under dispute with an adversary. The junior partner, however, wants to take over 100% of the disputed land. When negotiation breaks down and war ensues, it is difficult as a practical matter for the senior ally to transfer just enough resources to its protégé to keep 10% of the disputed land—and no more. This phenomenon is important because in this case entrapment does not entail a protégé dragging its patron ally into an involuntary war. "Rather, the conditions of war are often such that the third party [i.e., the senior ally] has no choice but to supply the protégé with a great deal more than it would prefer" (Benson 2012, 70). To some extent, Washington's recent public spat with Tel Aviv in the latter's conduct of war in Gaza exemplifies this predicament.

The senior ally's threat to limit its participation in the conflict is not credible because once troops are on the move and armed hostility has commenced, its interests may very well change. Benson refers to this as the time-consistency problem, such that the senior ally's prewar preference has now become outdated and new goals present themselves. What is its priority after the outbreak of war? Does it care about the specter of the protégé's defeat or demise to such an extent that this interest overrides its reluctance to give maximum support to the protégé to prevail in the war, which was not its first choice before the war's onset? Put differently, does it dislike the dissolution of alliance more intensely than its dislike for fighting a war? Is winning with the protégé preferable to suffering defeat at the hands of the adversary and facing the prospect of losing the protégé? Winning a war was not this country's "first best" outcome, which was before the war's onset for the protégé to hold on to 10% of the disputed territory.

The protégé exploits this grim choice forced onto its stronger ally, knowing as well that mission creep is a common phenomenon. It is difficult for the senior ally to fine-tune its transfers of resources to the protégé as such transfers tend to be lumpy, "discontinuous jumps," and open-ended. Protecting its reputation for resolve and steadfastness and protecting its sunk investments ("honoring those who have made the ultimate sacrifice") become part of the senior ally's goal set.

The adversary now also acquires a vote in deciding how and when to end the war. The stronger the senior partner in its ability to determine the war's outcome, the greater the temptation for the protégé to exploit it. Benson (2012, 50) frames the issue in these words:

> Difficulty [in] fine-tuning the amount of assistance transferred in war results in coarse decision alternatives for leaders when forming promises and delivering assistance to fight wars. Often the boundaries of war are beyond the control of third parties [i.e., allies], and a promise to become involved in any part of the war sometimes results in a fight for all of it. When incentives of war cause third parties to be all in or all out, then the moral hazard problem is especially acute.

Benson (2012, 51–52) goes on to explain:

> Limiting intervention to defense and finely specifying the level of a limited transfer of assistance can be complicated by factors beyond the third party's control. The main problem is that promises of assistance are realized only if there is war, and the third party's interests after war has begun may be different than before it breaks out. Therefore, even if it was possible to specify a limited transfer *ex ante* [i.e., written into a treaty's provision before war happens], practical features of war might impose time-consistency constraints. That is, there may be a gap between what a third party wants prior to war versus what it wants during war. The reason is that in many wars winners gain the entire pie, and losers get nothing. . . . [D]ecisions about whether to intervene often clump coarsely into categorical choices between no assistance at all and massive amounts of assistance. The coarsening of options can undermine the credibility of the third party to limit its intervention once the fight has begun.

Naturally, the third-party ally's inability to limit its support for the protégé can be considered a form of entrapment because the latter country realizes that once it is in war, its ally may come under considerable pressure to extend more assistance than it would ideally prefer prior to the war's onset (Benson 2012, 55). Indeed, the source of this pressure need not be limited to the adversary. The ally's domestic politics can also come into the picture. The ally's wartime objectives can expand, turning from defense to offense—such as in General Douglas MacArthur's decision to cross the 38th parallel in attempting to reunify Korea under a pro-American regime, thus triggering the massive Chinese counter-intervention. Importantly, the ally's entrapment in this case is not due to the protégé "drag[ging] it into a war. It becomes entrapped when it intervenes in a broader war than it would ideally prefer to fight, and losing to the adversary is worse than winning for the protégé" (Benson 2012, 55).

Although they did not share membership with the United States or other Western countries in a formal alliance, Bosnia's and Kosovo's campaigns for independence provide the closest illustration of the first causal mechanism discussed by Benson. Their leaders abandoned negotiation within a federal framework and pursued secession, accepting the risk of Serbian retaliation in the hope that they would receive outside intervention in their bid for independence. As discussed in the last chapter, their conduct supports the case of moral hazard (Kuperman 2008). Although their gambit paid off, other leaders expecting or hoping for support from outside powers (which may or may not be their formal allies) fared less well. Somalia's Mohammad Siad Barre (in the Ogaden War of 1977), Argentina's Leopoldo Galtieri (in the invasion of the Falklands/Malvinas in 1982), Iraq's Saddam Hussein (in his attack on Iran in 1980), and Georgia's Mikhail Saakashvili (in the 2008 war against Russia) took the same gamble but failed to gain US support in their respective conflicts. Their decision processes suggest how an expectation of or hope for support from a formal or informal ally had emboldened them to be more risk-acceptant as described by Benson's first causal mechanism.

Consideration of alliance ties was present to varying degrees in other cases discussed in the last chapter, such as China's decision to enter the Korean War, Japan's initiation of war with Russia in 1904, and again its attack on Pearl Harbor in 1941. In the last case, Tokyo's non-aggression pact with the USSR alleviated its concern of a security threat coming from its north, and its alliance with Germany also eased its concern of stiff resistance from European countries because they were tied down or already defeated by Hitler. Benson (2012, 67) offers another example, referring to Russia's provision of arms to Armenia, its establishment of military bases in that country, and the signing of an official alliance committing military assistance. This support emboldened Armenia, disposing it to launch attacks on Azerbaijan in February and March 1998. In late 2020, however, it suffered a devastating defeat, in part due to the withdrawal of Russia's support. Benson also shows a similar tendency by the Kuomintang in the Chinese Civil War; support from the United States encouraged Chiang Kai-shek to be more intransigent and less interested in negotiating a compromise with his communist opponent. In general, with support from a third party, leaders are more inclined to make greater demands on their adversary to settle a dispute or to turn down an offer from this adversary that they would otherwise have accepted in the absence of an alliance. When these tendencies are not matched by an adversary's greater willingness to make concessions (or, in other words, when these disputants have discrepant views on how the alliance has affected their relative bargaining position), negotiation to reach a settlement is more likely to break down.

As for Benson's second causal mechanism, the problem caused by time inconsistency tends to work against a third-party ally's attempt to limit its commitment in the event of war, and that country's goals and interests may change once it finds itself or its protégé in war. Washington's changing objective from preventing the North Koreans from overrunning the South to its decision to cross the 38th parallel to reunify the peninsula under a pro-US government offers an example. Benson (2012, 59) also illustrates Washington's deliberations in the final stages of the Chinese Civil War. Should it pursue a policy of partitioning China, leaving the communists to rule north of the Yangtze River but sustaining its ally, Chiang Kai-shek's regime, in the south? In the end, it decided not to pursue this option because it would be difficult to limit the extent of US support. This conflict forces a binary decision of all in or all out. Both sides of the Chinese Civil War insisted on carrying on their struggle until final victory over the entire country.

After Chiang's withdrawal to his last bastion in Taiwan, the United States sought to alleviate the danger of moral hazard and limit its vulnerability to becoming involved in an unwanted war against China by stipulating in its military alliance with the Chinese Nationalists that its commitment would only apply to the defense of the Pescadores and Taiwan. This provision omits any reference to the offshore islands of Quemoy and Matsu, garrisoned by Chiang's troops and located within a few miles from the mainland under communist control. By this exclusion, Washington sought to qualify the extent of its alliance commitment.

Understandably, offensive alliances and unconditional compellent alliances have the greatest effect in encouraging their members to initiate conflict (Benson 2011; Leeds 2003). When revisionist states are given unconditional deterrent commitments, they are also more disposed to initiate militarized disputes than unallied states (Benson, Bentley, and Ray 2013). Whether a state has a revisionist agenda appears to have the greatest influence on its propensity to initiate conflict. However, even alliances providing only conditional deterrent commitments suggest a greater proclivity on the part of their revisionist members to exhibit this behavior, albeit to a more modest extent than the unconditional type (Benson 2012, 84–85). Notwithstanding these differences pertaining to different types of alliances, it appears that members of "any type of alliance promising military assistance in a conflict are more likely to be aggressive and initiate challenges against states targeted by that alliance than protégés not holding any kind of alliance at all" (Benson 2012, 81). Disaggregating the entire sample of alliances, however, shows that "conditional deterrent alliances clearly decrease the likelihood that nonrevisionist states holding them will initiate militarized conflicts with non-alliance members" (Benson 2012, 85).

Future research can benefit from specific steps to account for the possible influence of self-selection and endogeneity, such as whether nonrevisionist states are more likely to join conditional deterrent alliances to begin with and whether revisionist states anticipating conflict are conversely more likely to join unconditional compellent alliances. Moreover, are those countries seeking an alliance with a major power likely to be the ones whose security is facing the greatest threat, which encourages them to look for protection from a powerful ally? If so, could the involvement of a major power in an asymmetric alliance be a clue or indicator of an increased danger of conflict escalation—even though one may also hypothesize that the involvement of this major power should have a deterrent effect on the adversary. But does this major power also have a restraining effect on its junior partner's recklessness or aggressiveness? It seems that regardless of whether an alliance entails conditional or unconditional deterrent commitments, the participation of a major power in an alliance is likely to embolden the other contracting parties. Regardless of whether the deterrent commitments provided by a treaty are conditional or unconditional, they "may open the door for reckless and aggressive behavior even though they are clearly designed to deter conflict" (Benson 2012, 88).

That even conditional deterrent commitments may still engender the risk of moral hazard does not, of course, preclude allies from undertaking precautionary steps to limit their vulnerability to becoming involved in an unwanted conflict. We encounter subtle and not too subtle attempts by the United States to control and restrain its allies. One used to hear that the US–Japanese alliance serves the purpose of "tethering" the latter country (Weitsman 2004), therefore alleviating concerns on the part of its neighbors such as China and the Koreas about the specter of its remilitarization (Kawasaki 2007). According to this perspective, the United States performs the function of a "cork" that plugs the revival of Japanese militarism. Referring to the US–Japanese security relationship, former US secretary of state John Foster Dulles remarks, "the thing that is designed to be inhibited is not [Japan's] participation in collective security, but [its] recreation of a distinctive national force" and, moreover, "We are absolutely confident that if Japan is basically committed to the free world and accepts U.S. troops in and about its territories we will have complete control over any rearmament plans Japan may adopt" (quoted in Cha 2007, 117).

Victor Cha (1999; 2007; 2009/2010; 2016) and Claudia Kim (2019) have commented on how Washington has deployed its hub-and-spokes security arrangements in East Asia to prevent its partners from instigating conflicts that can threaten its interests. In return for a commitment to defend Taiwan, Washington demanded that Taipei's use of force be subject to "joint agreement" and that it would refrain from using arms provided by the United States without Washington's "prior consent" (Cha 2007, 112–13). As just mentioned,

Washington also deliberately limited its defense commitment to Taiwan and the Pescadores, while excluding Quemoy and Matsu under the control of the Chinese Nationalists.

Similarly, the US–ROK Mutual Defense Treaty has carefully limited its scope to "an armed attack in the Pacific area on either of the parties in territories now under their respective administrative control, or hereafter recognized by one of the parties as lawfully brought under the administrative control of the other," thereby releasing the United States from any obligation to help Seoul should it attack North Korea (Murata 2007, 142). During the Cold War, Washington had occasionally threatened Beijing and Pyongyang that it would "unleash" their respective foes in Taipei and Seoul. In sharp contrast to Washington's alliance relations with its European partners which have taken a multilateral form, US security ties with its East Asian allies have been primarily bilateral in the past (Hemmer and Katzenstein 2002)—although this tendency is changing in view of more recent developments such as the trilateral summit meeting held in Washington in August 2023 among US, Japanese, and South Korean leaders and the Quadrilateral Security Dialogue consisting of the United States, Australia, India, and Japan.

There tends to be an imbalance in discussions of restraint among security partners. The preceding discussion is typical in this respect because it emphasizes the influence of a stronger partner on weaker ones, preventing the latter from engaging in reckless or aggressive behavior. Less attention has been paid to instances of weaker partners trying to restrain the stronger one such as when France and Germany sought but failed to discourage the United States from invading Iraq in 2003 without United Nations authorization or when Washington's European allies tried to delay and moderate US attacks on Serbia in 1999. As Tongji Kim (2011, 357, 361) notes, US allies fear the danger of being entrapped by Washington's bellicosity in these episodes, and Seoul has also been understandably concerned about the possibility of a preventive US strike against North Korea's nuclear facilities, an action that can embroil it in a war against Pyongyang. Moreover, Seoul and Tokyo recognize the danger of entrapment in a contingency involving Taiwan, possibly putting them involuntarily on a collision course with Beijing if Washington uses its military installations and armed forces stationed in their country to confront or fight China. Japan had a similar concern of being involuntarily involved in a conflict on the Korean peninsula. The revised 1997 Guidelines for U.S.–Japan Defense Cooperation stipulated that "the two Governments will take appropriate measures . . . in response to situations in areas surrounding Japan"—an elastic clause deliberately left vague to allow for Washington's desire for greater Japanese military contribution and Tokyo's desire to avoid firm commitment in a possible war in Korea or over Taiwan (Murata 2007, 140).

Significantly, just as with my earlier reference to President Joe Biden's public statements on whether the United States would come to Taiwan's defense in case of a war, South Korean and Japanese pronouncements have also undergone evolution. Although it has repeated in the past that maintaining peace across the Taiwan Strait is important to its security, Tokyo has inched closer to a position of openly opposing and challenging a possible resort to arms by Beijing. Similarly, South Korea's president Yoon Suk-yeol has shifted away from the signal sent by his predecessor former president Roh Moon-hyun's statement (March 25, 2005) that "we will not be embroiled in any conflict in Northeast Asia against our will. This is an absolutely firm principle we cannot yield under any circumstances" (quoted in S. Snyder 2007, 249). The United States has also altered its position now to committing itself to support Japan should there be an escalation in Tokyo's dispute with Beijing over the Senkaku/Diaoyutai islands, a change from its earlier statement that "the U.S.–Japan treaty did *not* apply in this case" (Green 2001, 87, italic in original). There has also been a recent shift in US policy to commit itself more explicitly to the defense of the Philippines, which contests China's sovereignty claims in the South China Sea.

Fears of entrapment apply to both the senior and junior partners of a security relationship, and arguably this danger is greater for the latter countries because they are less able to resist the former: "the United States has more power to entrap its allies, and other states have more reason to accept entrapment in order to avoid abandonment by the sole super-ally" (T. Kim 2011, 377). Despite pervasive American concerns about the dangers of entanglement and entrapment due to Washington's security relationships with other countries, studies by Beckley (2015) and Priebe et al. (2021) show that its partners have restrained it from reckless or aggressive actions more often than the reverse. This tendency has the effect of limiting Washington's interventionist impulses, reducing its propensity to get into foreign conflicts—rather than the opposite situation of the United States being dragged by its partners into an unwanted conflict.

These last remarks, however, should not be interpreted to mean that Washington's concerns about entrapment are unwarranted. Besides the obvious cases of Taiwan and South Korea in the 1950s and more recent episodes involving Bosnia, Kosovo, and Georgia, other US friends and quasi-allies have tried to exploit opportunities to advance their cause. Citing an article by Bergman and Mazzetti (2021), Priebe et al. (2021, 1) report that "Former U.S. Ambassador to Israel, Daniel B. Shapiro, disclosed that during negotiations over Iran's nuclear program, the Obama administration was concerned that Israel would take unilateral action against Iran, which 'could force the United States' hand to be supportive or to come in behind Israel and assist.'"

The Biden administration has been clearly concerned about the danger of conflict contagion in Israel's recent (2024) fighting against Hamas and its attack on Iranian assets such as the bombing of Tehran's consulate in Damascus, killing several of its top generals. Iran reportedly interpreted the latter action as an attempt by Benjamin Netanyahu to finesse Israel's rift with the United States over its war in Gaza and to involve Washington in a wider war with Tehran. On April 13, Iran retaliated by launching drones and missiles to attack Israel. The day after this attack, the White House leaked Biden's phone conversation with Netanyahu, indicating that the United States would not participate in any Israeli retaliation against Iran.

Of course, we face even greater difficulties in accessing information about policy debates and decision processes in Moscow and Beijing. Our understanding of the possible danger of entanglement, entrapment, and moral hazard caused by alliances has been largely based on the experience of the United States, even though these concerns should also apply to Russia and China. Russia's support for Armenia could have emboldened it in its armed conflicts with Azerbaijan, and conversely, the withdrawal of this support might have caused its defeat in 2020. Although there is a large body of studies on North Korea's nuclear program, there is less attention to how China has tried to balance its relations with its only formal ally—that is, how Beijing has tried to protect this buffer state important to Chinese security and at the same time to restrain its reckless conduct (e.g., Benson 2012, 184–89). It is not out of the realm of possibilities that a desperate Pyongyang may seek to provoke a crisis in the hope of bolstering support from Beijing and Moscow. Just as in Washington's management of its relations with Taiwan, Beijing's policy needs to serve the dual purposes of deterring an attack by the United States on North Korea's nuclear facilities and, at the same time, to check or moderate Pyongyang's nuclear ambitions. It also needs to guard against the danger of entrapment and moral hazard.

The Demand and Supply of Protection

Chapter 2 has argued that weaker contestants in asymmetric local conflicts have often instigated or provoked armed confrontations in the hope of receiving foreign support and protection to advance their agenda. This proposition naturally raises the question of which kinds of states are likely to engage in such conduct and under what circumstances. Obviously not all weaker disputants undertake such escalatory behavior. Thus, although there were repeated crises involving the status of Berlin during the Cold War, East Germany did not engage in this type of conduct, nor did other member states of the Warsaw Pact. There is, of course, also a "supply" side to the weaker contestants' "demand" for support and protection by going to war or the brink of war. Why do great powers want to get involved in local disputes and under what circumstances? Questions about possible entanglement, entrapment, and moral hazard concern the interaction effects between demand and supply.

In a bipolar world, countries located in the core areas or "home regions" of the leading powers can reasonably expect that they will be protected by their patron ally. East Germany did not have to undertake a crisis to secure Moscow's protection. Due to the nature of bipolar politics, it could be confident of this protection. At the same time, any reckless behavior on its part would be restrained by Moscow. Therefore, a weaker ally in this situation will not have the motivation or ability to behave in a reckless manner. It has neither the "willingness" nor the "opportunity," according to Most and Starr's (1989) framing. The same logic argues that countries located in the world's periphery, such as large parts of sub-Saharan Africa, will not pursue policies seeking to entangle or entrap a foreign ally by practicing diplomatic or military brinksmanship because they realize their lack of strategic or economic importance to the two leading powers, which will be reluctant to invest resources or reputation to support or protect them. Lacking such importance, these countries' appeal for foreign assistance has therefore been largely framed in terms of humanitarian causes. Even when they have intervened occasionally, such as in Angola, Mozambique, Namibia, Sudan, Somalia, and Ethiopia, outside powers' engagement tends to be limited and short-lived. Other peripheral states face an even grimmer plight of being ignored by the rest of the world—out of sight, out of mind.

The world's semi-periphery consists of areas where the superpowers competed for influence. Countries located in these areas, such as the Middle East and the Indian subcontinent, have not been "locked up;" and they are of sufficient strategic or economic value to attract the attention of the leaders of the bipolar world. Therefore, the phenomenon of weaker states instigating or provoking a crisis to seek foreign support and intervention is most likely in this intermediate zone. Those states engaging in such behavior also tended to be intermediate in the sense that they could not be entirely confident of outside protection of their security, and at the same time, the prospect of such support was not so low that it would not justify taking the risk of starting an armed conflict that could end badly for them. Therefore, there tends to be a curvilinear relationship such that those states that can confidently count on foreign protection and others that cannot realistically expect such protection will refrain from the behavior described in Chapter 2. Countries positioned in the middle of these two ends of the spectrum are the ones entertaining the expectation that their conflict escalation can succeed in recruiting foreign assistance to their benefit.

The leaders of such countries may also believe, and not unreasonably, that they may be able to exploit the superpowers' rivalry to secure outside support. The "demand" for outside intervention is most likely to come from them—those countries that feel insecure and yet lack firm commitment from others to protect them. Moreover, the "supply" of such intervention is also more likely to be forthcoming for them. The security of a superpower's core allies is rarely challenged by its counterpart. Thus, this superpower does not have an "opportunity" to intervene precisely because its "willingness" to intervene is not doubted and hence deters challenges in the first place.

There is, of course, a paradox. Although outside powers are more likely to intervene in the intermediate zone compared to countries for which they feel less need to do so because of a lack of strategic or economic value, there is a greater reticence to make firm commitments to them precisely because of the perception that those located in this zone are more war-prone and because, compared to their allies in the core regions, these countries affect only their secondary interests. Moreover, because these countries are not firmly in their respective camps and feature tight relations with them, superpowers also face greater difficulty in restraining their leaders. Because fights involving these countries do not entail the same high stakes and great risks involving those pertaining to the superpowers' core interests, they are more likely to occur and recur.

We would expect different incentives and dynamics to operate in a unipolar world. Attempts to get competing superpowers into a bidding war to support regional rivals will disappear. Naturally, the unipolar power should also have less incentive to placate its allies as there will be no alternative source of support for them to turn to. The danger of entrapment for it should recede. Of course, the preponderant state in a unipolar system should be in a stronger position to impose settlements on local conflicts; enforce contracts; and, if it is so inclined, offer important side payments to the disputants to resolve their differences. Thus, in contrast to a bipolar system, we are far less likely to encounter the phenomena of chain-ganging, entanglement, and entrapment in a unipolar world.

As implied in the discussion on alliance dynamics prior to World War I, in a multipolar world the focus shifts to relations among the great powers themselves rather than their relations with their respective junior partners or local clients. Of course, this remark does not deny the importance of the latter type of relations. After all, it was Russia's support for Serbia and Austria–Hungary's hostility toward Serbia that provided the original source of tension that later led to a chain reaction of escalating conflict in 1914. Discussions on the phenomenon of chain-ganging, however, have been largely limited to the effects that alliances among the great powers, especially the German–Austrian dyad and the Franco–Russian dyad, had in enlarging the 1914 conflict. Less attention has been paid to the role of a minor power, such as Serbia, in starting the chain reaction in the first place. Depending on those factors discussed by Christensen and Snyder (1990) and Tierney (2011)—such as perceptions of whether the offense or the defense has an advantage and the relative power of dovish and hawkish members of a coalition—opposite tendencies of emboldening or restraining an ally may prevail. We may even have a concert among the great powers to jointly enforce rules and provide order. Outside mediation and the intervention or nonintervention of other great powers can still be important considerations in a multipolar world, as in the case of the Russo–Japanese War. Tokyo had counted on its ally Britain to prevent intervention by other European states on Russia's behalf and on the United States to help it reach a settlement with St. Petersburg to avoid a protracted contract.

This discussion emphasizes the interactions between the local contestants' incentives and the motivations of their actual or potential patrons. The outside powers' strategic interests and their influence are layered over the local states' rivalry. As the interstate balance of power evolves and the system's polarity changes, we would expect different incentives and dynamics to take over. Even when the interstate system at the global level may be unipolar, bipolar, or multipolar, there can be important local or regional variations to engender different incentives and dynamics.

To assist the differentiation of cases of asymmetric conflicts such as those discussed in Chapter 2, there are firstly situations of *pivotal patronage*, approximating what Timothy Crawford (2003) has called pivotal deterrence. In these situations, both local disputants are allied with the same extra-regional power enjoying a preponderant position. Neither of these disputants has a plausible alternative source of support from another great power. Therefore, defection is not a realistic option for them. Consequently, the "patron" state has strong leverage over both disputants, and it is in a strong position to discourage their conflict from escalating and, if war should still happen, to prevent its escalation. This "patron" state is in a good position to mediate the dispute, broker a settlement, and enforce this settlement, providing side payments if necessary to get the disputants to agree to a deal. In the extreme case, this state can threaten to stand aside to let the disputants fight it out or to punish the recalcitrant party. Given these factors, this powerful state is least likely to run the risk of entrapment or moral hazard. Wars among its junior partners should be rare because it can more effectively restrain them, and those wars that do happen tend to be limited and brief. Examples of pivotal patronage include the Ecuador–Peru, Greece–Turkey, and Argentina–Britain conflicts discussed earlier.

In situations of *balanced patronage*, the local disputants are firmly committed to their respective patrons or senior allies—and vice versa. These disputants also cannot credibly threaten defection, and they can expect their loyalty to be reciprocated by their respective coalitions' leaders, and they thus have a high degree of confidence that their security will be protected. These disputants therefore are not motivated to start a crisis to shore up support from their patron or ally, and the latter countries will also check any reckless, aggressive behavior on the part of their junior partners. To be sure, there can be recurrent crises involving these states—such as between East and West Germany and North and South Korea during the Cold War. These crises, however, were not motivated by a sense of insecurity and a desire to seek outside intervention characterizing those asymmetric conflicts discussed in Chapter 2. When they do happen, these crises are likely to be closely watched and managed by the patron allies to avoid the risk of inadvertent escalation.

As just implied, bipolarity and tight alliances have a restraining influence in these cases, which are more likely to occur in contested regions than traditional spheres of control by the two superpowers. While entanglement is possible and even likely, entrapment is less probable. Since insecurity motivates a weaker disputant to start or escalate a crisis or confrontation in the hope of shoring up support from a patron, the occurrence of such a crisis or confrontation indicates that an alliance or security relationship is becoming looser or even facing the danger of dissolution. Provocations such as North Korea's sinking of the South Korean corvette *Cheonan* in 2010 may be an example of this phenomenon.

Of course, great powers can and do disagree about the boundaries of one another's "home turf" or sphere of influence, thus producing especially protracted wars in their immediate neighborhoods, such as in Korea, Vietnam, and Afghanistan—as well as the missile crisis over Cuba in 1962 and other "close calls" when wars were avoided in several confrontations over the status of Taiwan and Berlin during the Cold War and several Balkan crises preceding World War I. Moreover, balanced patronage whereby Beijing supported its client in Phnom Penh and Moscow supported its ally in Hanoi did not prevent Vietnam's invasion of Cambodia, nor China's subsequent border war with Vietnam in 1979.

A weaker party to an asymmetric local contest may be motivated by opportunism to extract advantages by encouraging competitive bidding by outside powers in pursuit of extra-regional influence. Pakistan (vis-à-vis support from the United States and China), Egypt, and Somalia (vis-à-vis competition between the United States and the USSR during the Cold War) in their respective struggles with their neighbors (India, Israel, and Ethiopia) come to mind. These states' behavior encourages conflict recidivism and abets the danger of entrapment. The pertinent dynamics may be described as *competitive patronage*.

The attempts by the local disputants in these situations to get outside powers involved in their conflicts do not always succeed, but that does not prevent them from trying. Moreover, when outside powers do intervene, they often prevent wars from escalating and arrange truces to protect the weaker contestants from the most catastrophic consequences of starting a war. Those cases described by competitive patronage naturally point to situations where the states' alignments are more fluid and the probability for the local disputants to defect or switch sides is real, which is the reason they think they can exploit outside powers to advance their cause. Shifting alignment and power tend to alter relationships such as Israeli and Egyptian ties with Washington which have evolved over time, making the United States the pivotal patron by the time when the Camp David Accords were reached. In contrast, Moscow's influence over Cairo receded so that a situation of balanced patronage no longer applied.

Mohammad Siad Barre's repeated incursions or invasions of contested territory in Somalia's wars with Ethiopia over the Ogaden also exhibit some features of competitive patronage. He tried to exploit a window of opportunity when Addis Ababa was weakened by political instability and secessionist challenges. He tried unsuccessfully to get Moscow and Washington into a bidding war to gain his support, switching his allegiance from the former to the latter. His attempt, however, turned out to be a failure, when President Jimmy Carter refused to support his invasion of the Ogaden. As the Cold War wound down, both Moscow and Washington disengaged from the Horn of Africa as well as conflicts elsewhere in Africa such as the Congo and Sudan. When outside powers lose their interest in competing for influence, local disputants' leverage to gain outside help also disappears.

Finally, there is *one-sided patronage*, describing situations where all the outside major powers gang up against one of the local disputants, or at least when one of these disputants lacks an effective supporter for its cause. This situation is most likely to embolden reckless, aggressive behavior by a revisionist state, encouraging it to take risks to start a war of aggression against a stronger opponent, especially when this opponent is temporarily vulnerable due to its domestic turmoil or international isolation. Saddam Hussein's decision to break Iraq's agreement with Iran on the division of the Shatt al-Arab waterway and to launch an attack against Iran offers perhaps the best example of this opportunism. He wanted to exploit a window of opportunity when Tehran was isolated because of its seizure of US diplomats as hostages and when all the major powers of the world were opposing the regime headed by Ayatollah Khomeini. His belief that he could leverage foreign support for his cause turned out to be mistaken. Although outside powers, especially the United States, prevented Iranian victory, they did not support him to win an Iraqi victory. His decision resulted in the longest and bloodiest war since Vietnam. Still, Iraq's attacks on Iran's oil shipments provoked the latter country to retaliate by attacking tankers operated by Kuwait, Iraq's ally, which in turn caused the United States to extend military protection to Kuwait by reflagging its tankers and thus changing their nationality to the US and subsequently to attack Iran's offshore oil facilities in 1986. These US actions finally pressured Tehran to accept a United Nations–mandated ceasefire.

Other possible examples pertain to North Korea's initial invasion of South Korea after US secretary of state Dean Acheson had publicly excluded the Korean peninsula from the US defense perimeter, and possibly when the USSR approached the United States to explore the possibility of initiating a joint attack on China's nuclear facilities at Lop Nor when it was beset by its Cultural Revolution and was isolated internationally. As discussed earlier, the campaigns by Bosnia and Kosovo to gain independence also suggest their emboldenment due to Serbia's isolation and the enfeeblement of its chief sponsor, Russia. Their experiences and the demise of Libya's Qaddafi also indicate that the effective removal of Russia as a potential obstacle encouraged NATO countries' aggressive resort to force. Therefore, emboldenment can happen for the local disputants as well as outside interveners.

As alluded to earlier, relations between the great powers often determine the evolution of their ties with local clients. From the time Beijing and Washington established formal diplomatic relations in 1979 until the last several years, the United States trimmed its support for Taiwan, and the danger of a crisis in Sino–American relations over Taiwan's status receded to the background. It has recently re-emerged as a source of tension between these two countries. Here is an example that also involves an outside power (namely, the United States) exploiting or leveraging its ties with a local client to pressure or antagonize its adversary (China). Similarly, conflicts between Russia and its neighbors Ukraine and Georgia cannot but reflect and create tension between Moscow and Washington. These hot spots are located right on Russia's and China's borders. Prior conflicts featuring this geographic proximity to these countries, such as those in Korea, Vietnam, and Afghanistan, tend to be protracted and costly wars. These wars, however, differ from those discussed in asymmetric conflicts discussed in Chapter 2 as they reflect more the tendency of self-entrapment (a topic for the next chapter) than entrapment by others.

This discussion suggests that power shifts at both the regional and global levels have implications for the dynamics of local disputes to escalate into more serious and dangerous confrontations. Pivotal patronage, which stems from power concentration and unipolarity at least at the regional level, tends to curtail the danger of conflict escalation and moral hazard. Yet paradoxically, one-sided patronage is also buttressed by power concentration, and the apparent lack of a strong opposition or restraint has produced excessive, even unrestrained, use of force in NATO's bombings of Libya and Serbia and the US-led invasion of Iraq and Afghanistan. In the latter episodes of long, costly, and ultimately unsuccessful wars, self-entrapment is perhaps a better description. Opportunism can characterize both the local disputants and outside interveners in instances involving one-sided patronage.

By comparison, balanced patronage appears to produce the most stabilizing influence and engender the least danger of entrapment or moral hazard. China's rise thus far has not yet created a situation of competitive patronage whereby Beijing and Washington become involved in a bidding race to recruit local clients or followers. Beijing has so far refrained from challenging US dominance in its traditional bailiwick in Latin America and western Europe, although there are signs that some countries in the Middle East, including traditional US allies Saudi Arabia and the United Arab Emirates, may be in the process of realigning themselves. If Beijing gains more power, we may encounter more frequently situations reminiscent of competitive patronage during the Cold War, situations that are more likely to abet entanglement, entrapment, and moral hazard. Should Beijing manage to carve out a sphere of influence—which is by no means inevitable, or even likely—this development may engender situations of balanced patronage which, according to the logic presented earlier, would tend to have a more stabilizing effect.

Conclusion

States join alliances to communicate to their potential adversaries their collective strength and resolve. Most alliances are contracts of conditional defensive commitments intended to deter the target state(s) in question from attacking; but some treaties exchange mutual unconditional support for their partners, and a small number are intended for offensive purposes with or without conditions. Still some others are probabilistic promises with hedges, such as leaving future actions up to the contracting parties' legislatures. As mentioned earlier, some treaties are non-aggression or neutrality pacts pledging that the states involved will not attack each other or will remain neutral in the event of a war involving one of the signatories, and others are ententes requiring them only to engage in consultation. Given their different nature, lumping all these different types of security treaties in research, such as when we ask whether alliances in general induce chain-ganging, entanglement, or entrapment or whether they help to preserve peace, will produce misleading results. As we have seen in the previous discussion, various factors and conditions intervene to mediate their effects raised by questions such as these. Moreover, the danger of chain-ganging, entanglement, or entrapment exists for security partners even in the absence of a formal treaty between them—such as in situations involving the United States and its security partners Israel, Taiwan, and Ukraine.

Naturally, issues of endogeneity and self-selection are pertinent. Alliances tend to form when states anticipate war; thus, their formation may be a precursor to war as well as a cause of war. Moreover, states join alliances because their leaders feel insecure. Of course, there can also be a reverse tendency such that states may be more guarded in making firm commitments to defend those others that are seen to be most likely to become involved in a war. There is something to the saying that banks are most ready to extend loans and credit to people who are financially secure and thus least in need of this money, whereas those who are most needy have more difficulty in accessing such funding. For the same reasons, states may be most willing to extend defense commitments to countries that are least expected to cash the promissory notes of military assistance. As for most things in life, however, there is also an opposite tendency such that those states whose security faces the greatest danger are more likely to seek formal or informal relationships with other countries to protect themselves. If so, those states that join alliances are more likely to get into war than others that are unallied. We thus need to disaggregate and distinguish the effects of these opposing tendencies and to distinguish those circumstances under which one or the other is likely to prevail. Factors affecting the demand and supply for alliances interact in multiple ways, and analysts have yet to disentangle the relevant processes and to determine their relative frequency and importance.

Although debates and research continue, there is considerable evidence to suggest that alliances can affect their member states' decision processes after discounting these preexisting tendencies. Alliances can in themselves create additional shared interests, and allies take on their counterparts' views and preferences due to their interactions and socialization. Moreover, coordination and joint preparation for war can in themselves produce institutional and personal stakes and vested interests, thus giving alliances an importance beyond their original purposes. As mentioned earlier, protecting a country's reputation to meet its alliance commitments can acquire an importance in influencing policy decisions. This consideration can itself become a national interest—even though national interest should dictate whether to take on these commitments in the first place. In the next chapter I will discuss further how a determination to protect or enhance a country's reputation for resolve and firmness can in some circumstances actually weaken its ability to fend off challenges from its adversaries.

We also need more rigorous, well-designed studies to take up counterfactual questions about how states would have acted in the absence of alliances. Do these treaties encourage a state to negotiate more aggressively with an adversary and to incline it to reject settlement proposals from this adversary that it would have accepted were it not for the existence of an alliance? Do states become more risk-acceptant because expected support from allies makes the prospect of war less intimidating? Does the time-inconsistency problem encourage opportunism, inclining minor states to exploit their stronger backers in the expectation or belief that it is difficult for the latter countries to limit or withhold support once they are in war? Furthermore, can communications among allies on the eve of war have an effect in reinforcing their shared biases, increasing their mutual confidence, and fortifying their reciprocal resolve to produce increased odds of a decision in favor of going to war? Additionally, can concerns about one's reputation to abide by treaty commitments and support partners in need acquire a large influence in making policy decisions, a consideration that would not have existed in the absence of a security relationship?

Finally, can minor members of an alliance—and even for non-members motivated to demonstrate their loyalty to a coalition's leader and seek favors from it—flock to a war even when their security is not directly at stake? Alliances as well as more informal but nevertheless tangible security relationships such as those between the United States and its informal allies (e.g., Israel, Taiwan, Ukraine) can have the effect of pulling more states into a conflict than otherwise. Chain-ganging, entanglement, entrapment, and moral hazard do not necessarily have to implicate a state taking deliberate actions to get its partner(s) into an unwanted war. There are less obvious ways in which alliances can have these effects. Case studies of asymmetric conflicts and alliances suggest that entrapment has often been attempted but usually fails in the way that it is usually defined—that is, a confederate committing aggression deliberately to provoke war and crisis in order to get its alliance partner(s) into an involuntary conflict to assist its agenda. However, as Benson (2012) suggests, alliances can have subtler and indirect effects. Allies can be entrapped in a conflict because their confederate may become more intransigent and risk-acceptant in bargaining with its adversary and because of the time-inconsistency problem. Considering these factors, entrapment can be more common than usually acknowledged.

The risk of entrapment and moral hazard is the greatest when several conditions exist and especially when they are all present. When an alliance leader is much more powerful than its protégé and when its participation can influence the outcome of a war decisively, the protégé can expect the greatest return by involving its senior partner in a conflict. When the preferences of the senior partner and its protégé diverge significantly, the former is also at greater risk of being exploited by the latter. Moreover, when the senior ally is unable to monitor and observe the protégé's actions, the risk of entrapment and moral hazard is also greater. These intuitions receive empirical support from Benson's (2012) analysis. As already mentioned, this risk does not have to originate from the protégé's deliberate attempt to drag its patron into a war, although this possibility exists. Instead, it can stem from incentivizing the protégé to drive a harder bargain with its adversary and to be more willing to risk bargaining failure because its ally's support mitigates a war's deadly consequences should it happen. In addition, the ally faces the time-inconsistency problem so that once war has started, prewar preferences are likely to undergo change. Even though war might have been distasteful, the choice now becomes winning with the protégé versus losing to the adversary.

Significantly, these remarks pertain to asymmetric conflicts, involving a powerful patron and a vulnerable dependent in a situation of extended deterrence. Entanglement, entrapment, and moral hazard can also operate in reverse, such that minor allies become involved in wars started by their stronger partners. Naturally, these situations involving asymmetric relations are fundamentally different from those characterizing the interactions among Europe's great powers on the eve of World War I. That world of 1914 was multipolar, and the post-1945 world was first marked by bipolarity and since 1989 by unipolarity, although China's recent rise may yet return us to an era of bipolarity. These differences in systemic structure create different conditions and dynamics for the possibilities of entanglement and entrapment. The greater danger, however, is self-entanglement and self-entrapment, as discussed in the next chapter.

Chapter 4
The Backlash Effects of Self-Defeating Policies

Overview

Thucydides, a historian and general who lived in ancient Athens, wrote about the Peloponnesian War that had devastated the Greek world some 2,500 years ago. His classic text *The History of the Peloponnesian War* (Balot, Forsdyke, and Foster 2017; Jaffe 2017; Kagan 1969; Mynott 2013; Strassler 1998) has had great influence on students of history and war throughout the ages. His aphorism that the original cause of the Peloponnesian War could be found in the rise of Athens and the fear that this development had engendered in Sparta has been in vogue in recent years because of Graham Allison's (2017) popularization of this observation, calling it *Thucydides' Trap* to warn about its contemporary relevance to the danger of a possible war between a rising China and a declining United States.

Less well known is Thucydides' reference to the warning by Athenian leader Pericles to his fellow citizens "not to extend your empire at the same time as you are fighting the war [in Sicily] and not to add self-imposed dangers, for I am more afraid of our own mistakes than the strategy of our opponents" (quoted in Kagan 1969, 192). Thucydides did not attribute any moral superiority to his own polis Athens, a supposed democracy by the standards of its time, remarking that it had established a "tyrannical empire." He told his fellow Athenians, "Nor can you now give [the empire] over for already your government is in the nature of a tyranny, which is both unjust for you to take up and unsafe to lay down" (quoted in Platias and Trigkas 2021, 229).

This chapter turns to the third leg of the triad—fuses, chains, and backlashes—that abets war. As remarked in Chapter 1, the term *overreach* has also been used to describe this element. It can have two connotations. First, it can refer to a mismatch between ends and means so that a country's ambitions outstrip its available resources. Second, it can refer to a country's conduct causing negative reactions from other countries, resulting in its self-isolation and self-encirclement. Thus, a country's actions can backfire (hence, the reference to backlash), causing harm to itself. As I have addressed the first topic elsewhere (Chan 2024a), I will focus on the second one in this chapter, which is more

Fuses, Chains, and Backlashes. Steve Chan, Oxford University Press. © Oxford University Press (2025).
DOI: 10.1093/9780197812907.003.0004

directly relevant to the issue of conflict escalation and contagion as the discussion later will show. But before turning to that discussion, a brief review of the main propositions and conclusions presented by studies on the first meaning of overreach is warranted.

In his book *The Rise and Fall of the Great Powers*, historian Paul Kennedy (1987) used "imperial overstretch" to describe the recurrent phenomenon whereby a great power's foreign policy goals and commitments exceed its more limited capabilities, leading to its eventual exhaustion and downfall. In this case, a country's own policies can produce serious consequences to the detriment of its basic, long-term interests. These consequences are self-inflicted. There is a rather large body of studies seeking to determine whether there is a "defense–growth trade-off." Does a country's defense spending come at the expense of its economic performance by hurting, for example, its capital formation and thereby depressing its investment to foster leading industries, export competitiveness, human capital, physical infrastructure, and technological innovation? In the view of those who see military expenditures as a wasted asset, defense vigilance comes with a heavy price tag in slower economic growth and even stagnation and decline. Since the pioneering study by Bruce Russett (1970), analysts have asked whether military expenditures have come at the expense of investment, private consumption, and future economic growth. They have also asked whether there is a "defense–welfare trade-off," such as whether military expenditures tend to reduce other kinds of government spending for housing, education, health, unemployment benefits, old-age care, and other kinds of welfare support for the needy. Recent reviews of this literature suggest that considerable divergence and uncertainty continue to characterize researchers' conclusions (Chan 2024a; Rooney, Johnson, and Priebe 2021). Problems with data and methodology continue to challenge their inquiry.

Mandatory spending, such as for entitlement programs like Social Security and Medicare, takes up about two-thirds of the US federal budget. Discretionary spending constitutes just over a quarter of this budget, with the remaining 8% going to interest payment on the federal debt. About one-sixth of the federal budget is spent on defense. In 2022, $750 billion or about 45% of the discretionary spending went to defense outlays, leaving 55% for other kinds of spending. Thus, if one wishes to reduce the federal deficit while leaving defense spending intact, budgetary cuts will have to come from a relatively small slice (about 14%) of the federal budget. Because there are sharp disagreements over which of these programs should bear the brunt of these reductions, the usual tendency is to finance the gap between expenditures and revenues by borrowing. Although defense spending appears to have a short-term impact on stimulating economic growth, its effects on reducing investment in infrastructure and expanding national debt are likely to be deleterious to long-term economic growth (Rooney, Johnson, and Priebe 2021). We will see in the following discussion that resource constraint is important and relevant to states' misguided attempts to protect their reputation, thereby contributing to self-inflicted injuries, albeit not exactly in the way that a heavy defense burden can impose on the economy and society as just discussed.

Concerns over the defense–growth trade-off and defense–welfare trade-off as well as the risks of entanglement and entrapment due to Washington's alliances and security relationships with other countries have motivated and become embedded in a larger debate about US foreign policy posture. Should the United States maintain its current, extensive presence abroad, or should it retrench and "come home"? On the one side are those who express concerns that the United States is in danger of imperial overstretch and that its foreign security partnerships are not only burdensome but also dangerous because they can entangle or entrap it in unwanted conflicts and distract it from more urgent and important needs at home.

Barry Posen is one of the more influential and eloquent voices advancing this argument. Referring to Washington's support for the Philippines and Vietnam in their maritime quarrels with China, he warns "Not only do these disputes make it harder for Washington to cooperate with Beijing on issues of global importance; they also risk roping the United States into conflicts over strategically marginal territory" (Posen 2013, 122). Christopher Layne, another vocal proponent for trimming US commitments and profile abroad shares this concern, remarking "America's alliances are transmission belts for war that ensure that the U.S. would be embroiled in Eurasian wars" (Layne 2006, 169). Others such as Paul MacDonald and Joseph Parent (2011; 2018a; 2018b) have written about the feasibility and desirability of retrenchment. A strong and vibrant domestic economy is indispensable for funding effective foreign policy. Conversely, sagging economic performance will inevitably jeopardize a country's national security and weaken its international competitiveness (Chan 2024a).

Other scholars have also taken this side of the debate, urging Washington to trim its foreign obligations and adopt a more restrained policy posture, calling the United States "to come home" to give greater attention and priority to its pressing domestic needs. They argue for less US commitment abroad and a grand strategy relying more on offshore balancing (e.g., Gholz, Press, and Sapolsk 1997; J. Glaser, Preble, and Thrall 2019; Mearsheimer and Walt 2016a; 2016b; Posen 2014). In opposition are others who take the side arguing that Washington should maintain its active and extensive international presence. These scholars argue that world peace and stability depend on Washington's continued involvement and engagement abroad, which is also indispensable for US security itself (Brands 2015; Brands and Feaver 2016; Brooks, Ikenberry, and Wohlforth 2012/2013). They tend to see the arguments presented by those calling for US retrenchment to pose a false choice, contending that US activism and influence abroad and its domestic goals need not be mutually exclusive. In their eyes, the United States can have both.

We do not have comparable studies or debates by Chinese scholars on these subjects. Beijing has but one formal ally, North Korea, although its relations with Pyongyang are fraught with the risks of entanglement, entrapment, and moral hazard, as discussed in the last chapter. Beijing spends on its military about only half as much as the United States relative to its gross domestic product. As it faces a more difficult economic future as its population ages and its foreign economic ties encounter decoupling by the United States, the burden of defense spending on its economy is likely to become more serious.

What States Have versus What They Do

I now turn to the second meaning of overreach, referring to how a state's policies can backfire on it. Susan Shirk (2023) uses the term in this way, describing how Beijing's policies during Xi Jinping's administration have produced deleterious effects for China both abroad and at home. As already mentioned, I use the term *backlash* to describe this phenomenon but limit it to how a country's foreign policies can cause pushback by other countries, causing or aggravating its isolation, arousing others' suspicion about and hostility toward it, and encouraging the formation of a coalition to oppose it. Thus, I do not use this term to describe errors of domestic policy, even though it can obviously also apply to excesses such as Mao Zedong's Great Leap Forward campaign and the Cultural Revolution that had devastated China's economy and society. Moreover, unlike Shirk, my focus is not just on China as I am interested in using backlash as a generic term for policy failures by different states at different times. For readers who have come thus far, this interest in making comparisons and generalizations across countries and over time should not come as a surprise. As I have said, I want to embed my study of China and Sino–American relations in the broad context of international relations scholarship.

My specific concern in this chapter pertains to the phenomenon of conflict contagion and escalation brought about by states' own policy or conduct, reflecting Pericles' remark that "I am more afraid of our own mistakes than the strategy of our opponents"—that is, states' unforced errors. Therefore, my emphasis is on what a state does in contrast to what it has or is. This distinction is important. Many leading theories in international relations are predicated on what states are or have rather than what they do. For example, power-transition theory and Thucydides' Trap both emphasize states' changing power (Allison 2017;

Gilpin 1981; 1987; Organski and Kugler 1980). The focus of these theories is on structure rather than agency, giving analytic priority to systemic structure rather than government conduct in determining international peace and stability. In fact, their premise is often that people never learn and tend to therefore repeat the same mistakes, being trapped by their circumstances so that structural conditions always trump officials' attempts to overcome or transcend them.

This being the case, China's rising power is often construed as the principal cause for concerns about Sino–American competition and the key determinant of outcomes such as the maintenance of international peace and the outbreak of war. John Mearsheimer argues that China's rise will not be peaceful. He predicts that China will follow the US example to install itself as a regional hegemon and "come up with its own version of the Monroe Doctrine, as Japan did in the 1930s" (Mearsheimer 2006, 162). He is clear that this expectation is not about China per se; any country in China's position is expected to behave in this way.

I cite these scholars to call attention to the distinction between what a state is or has and what it does. In the above example, it is China's—and, for that matter, any country's—power and not its conduct that is given analytical priority. Why should this matter? Transferred to the discourse on the origin of the Peloponnesian War, was Sparta alarmed by the rise of Athenian *power* or Athens' *policy* of imperial expansion that had increased its power? James Lee (2019) argues that scholars who emphasize Athens' power rather than its conduct have misinterpreted Thucydides, thus questioning whether Thucydides himself would have agreed with the contemporary rendition of Thucydides' Trap. This is not a trivial matter because it is one thing to speak of Athens' rising power and another to point to its imperial expansion. Where did Athens derive its power from? Most scholars engaging in the discourse on China's rise overlook this question. So what?

Ascendance to the elite group of great powers in the past has been almost invariably associated with the outcomes of wars and conquests—at least in the modern era (usually dated from the end of the Napoleonic Wars in 1815). Think of Athens and Sparta, Rome and Carthage, Venice and Genoa, Tang and Ming China, the Ottoman Empire, Portugal, the Netherlands, Habsburg Spain, France of the Bourbons and Bonapartes, Prussia/Germany, Russia/the USSR, imperial Japan and Britain, and the United States. Perhaps one can argue that Venice, Genoa, and Portugal did not rise on the basis of wars and that France was already a great power before the Bourbons and Bonapartes. But these countries did wage war before they made their appearance as the world's premier powers. When I refer to wars, I have in mind also civil wars or wars of national unification, whose conclusion assisted the ascent of Germany, the United States, Italy, and the USSR to the front ranks of interstate hierarchy. Contemporary China stands out, presenting us with the only instance in the modern era that a country's rise has been due to domestic economic growth rather than foreign conquest. To be sure, China had fought the Korean War (1950–53) and two border wars with India (1962) and Vietnam (1979). But these wars had preceded China's recent rise and could not have been responsible for its rise. I point to this phenomenon in order to distinguish China's experience from those of the Europeans, Americans, and Japanese who had undertaken territorial expansion and quest for foreign colonies *when they were a rising power*.

China's recent rise has been due exclusively to its domestic economic expansion. In view of this fact, it is sometimes ironic to hear Western narratives of a "China threat" while overlooking the histories of expansionism, imperialism, and colonialism of previous hegemons and would-be hegemons. There has never been any hostile Chinese soldier setting foot on British, French, Japanese, or US soil—but we cannot make the reverse claim. Naturally, focusing on just a country's power rather than its conduct is also problematic because this emphasis suggests that, short of asking countries not to grow their power, even if this power stems from their domestic economic growth, the world is destined to suffer recurrent wars and instability. Moreover, which leaders would want to have less rather than more power for their country? Accordingly, in this chapter I attend to a country's use of its power rather than its power per se. It is the former, not the latter, that can cause a conflict to spread and escalate. Wanton and reckless use of power has often been the undoing of great powers in the past.

Aggressor States' Self-Encirclement

Neorealism, pioneered by Kenneth Waltz's (1979) classic study, has been influential among international relations scholars. Predicated on the view that systemic anarchy requires states to engage in self-help to ensure their survival, Waltz (1979, 127) avers that "secondary states, if they are free to choose, flock to the weaker side, for it is the stronger side that threatens them. On the weaker side, they are both more appreciated and safer, provided, of course, that the coalition they form achieves enough defensive or deterrent strength to dissuade adversaries from attacking." Other realists, such as John Mearsheimer (2001), agree that states pursue a balance of power to deter aggression from a more powerful state. In their view, buck-passing behavior is myopic and dangerous. *Bandwagoning*—meaning to join and support a powerful state—would be even more so, and we should rarely see such behavior. Instead, weaker states are expected to band together to deter and if deterrence fails, to fight the most powerful country among them. States' dominant mode of response to potential and actual threat to their security is to balance against it. Because the most powerful country poses the greatest threat to them, neorealism expects other countries to balance against it.

Even though many scholars, who share the view that an actual or potential power transition between the world's top two states elevates the danger of a systemic war, consider themselves realists, they in fact stand the traditional realist tenet on the imperative of balancing power to preserve international stability on its head. This is so because they see an approaching power parity, such as when China and Germany catch up to established leading states Britain and the United States, respectively, as a destabilizing rather than stabilizing factor. Beijing's efforts to balance against US preponderance are thus seen as a threat not only to US security but also to the stability of the entire interstate system.

Ambitious rulers—Charles V, Philip IV, Louis XIV, Napoleon Bonaparte, Wilhelm II, and Adolf Hitler—had made repeated bids for mastery of Europe in the modern era. As neorealism would expect, these would-be hegemons were eventually defeated. But contrary to neorealism's expectation, the processes leading to their demise did not follow its script. Consider Hitler as an example. His *Wehrmacht* carried out a successful campaign of *Blitzkrieg*, conquering Germany's neighbors, including France, in quick succession in the opening stages of World War II. He then turned his attention to the invasion of Britain, and in the Battle of Britain his *Luftwaffe* was stymied. Instead of seeing this campaign to a successful conclusion, he ordered Operation Barbarossa to invade the Soviet Union in June 1941—thus subjecting Germany to a two-front war. His actions brought together an anti-German coalition that Winston Churchill and Joseph Stalin would not have been able to achieve on their own. To compound Germany's strategic predicament, he declared war on the United States shortly after the Japanese attack on Pearl Harbor.

Hideki Tojo, Japan's prime minister, also took the fateful gamble of attacking the United States when his army was already bogged down in China. Moreover, his campaign to seize British, French, and Dutch colonies in Southeast Asia also forced these countries off the fence to join China in its fight against Japan. Significantly, although Germany and Japan were formal allies, they never coordinated their military operations and thus fought for all practical purposes alone in World War II. The defeat of Germany and Japan in that conflict was due to these strategic blunders to a significant extent. Their ambitions and recklessness brought about a powerful alliance against them, such that the outcome of the war was never in doubt. Although it is true that a countervailing coalition did eventually form against these aggressor states, it emerged only after their attacks left their victims no choice but to join hands to fight back.

Prior to the war, Germany was the strongest country in Europe. Contrary to neorealism's expectation, its neighbors did not try to balance against it. British and French response to the emergent threat from Germany was tardy and lethargic (Schweller 2006). Their domestic politics caused them to underbalance this threat. Instead of joining hands to oppose Hitler, Britain and the USSR were wary of each other, seeking to deflect Hitler's hostility to the other country. Moscow in fact signed a non-aggression treaty (the Molotov–Ribbentrop pact) with Berlin. Instead of balancing against Germany, Italy bandwagoned with it. Rome signed the "Pact of Steel" with Berlin, seeking to profit from the spoils of Germany's conquests. At the Munich conference in September 1938, British and French leaders Neville Chamberlain and Edouard Daladier pressured Czechoslovakia to concede territory (the Sudetenland) to Germany so that peace might be preserved, an agreement that later became the symbol of appeasement. All in all, these events contradicted neorealism's expectations.

The dynamics of the Napoleonic Wars also belied neorealism's expectations. Although France was indisputably the strongest military power posing a threat to other countries, its neighbors failed to rally against it. Rather, the opposite phenomenon tended to prevail. Paul Schroeder (1994b, 121) writes,

> Napoleon was able to organize most of Europe for war against a single isolated foe (Britain in 1803 and 1807, Prussia in 1806, Spain in 1808, Austria in 1809, Russia in 1812). In short, the main response to Napoleonic hegemony and imperialism by European states, large and small alike, was not balancing but either hiding or bandwagoning. . . . Besides the smaller, weaker states who bandwagoned as Napoleon's satellites, many of them willingly and profitably, every major power in Europe except Great Britain—Prussia, Austria, Russia, Spain—bandwagoned as France's active ally for a considerable period. Wars continued to break out mainly not because European states tried to balance against France as a hegemonic power, but because Napoleon's ambition and lawless conduct frustrated their repeated efforts to hide or bandwagon.

Anti-French coalitions were created repeatedly, but just as repeatedly they disintegrated when French military victory caused one or more countries to abandon these coalitions. Joining a united front to resist French aggression was not their first choice but tended to be their last resort. More to the point of this chapter's focus, Napoleon's insatiable appetite for aggression eventually brought together a coalition that defeated him at Waterloo. By repeatedly lashing out against other countries, Napoleon's aggression forced them to fight back. His recklessness caused his victims to band together—something that British diplomacy had failed to achieve. Napoleon's own actions caused his self-encirclement and eventual demise.

We saw a similar pattern earlier when France under Louis XIV waged wars of aggression. All countries except Spain sought to appease or bandwagon with him. Schroeder (1994b, 135) remarks, "States . . . did not balance against France as a response to French hegemony in accordance with the constraints of structural anarchy. Rather, they tried to hide or bandwagon, and failed because France would not let their efforts succeed; they resisted because France kept on attacking them." French policies were thus responsible for other countries eventually turning against it—because Louis XIV did not know when to declare victory, quit fighting while he was ahead, and accept advantageous offers from his opponents to settle conflict. Overweening ambition and a wish to have it all created in the end resistance and backlash against him from multiple quarters.

Schroeder (1994b, 117–18) argues that bandwagoning—jumping to the stronger or winning side—has been historically more common than balancing, especially for the smaller powers. Balancing policies tend to be rare and often occur only as a fallback option and last resort. Thus, the fact that states sometimes unite to fight back *after* being attacked does not constitute persuasive proof supporting the neorealist logic on balance of power. A countervailing coalition came about belatedly because the aggressor states would not leave their neighbors alone.

The tendency for countries often to join the stronger side rather than balancing against it was again evident during the Cold War and continues to this day. The USSR and the Warsaw Pact it led never reached the strength of the United States and NATO. The communist camp probably never reached two-thirds of the collective strength of the Western countries—especially in the aftermath of the Sino–Soviet split. More recently, the United States and its coalition partners are again overwhelmingly stronger than any conceivable challenger, even in view of China's recent rise. As just one example, the United States alone spent on its defense more than the *combined* total of military expenditures by the next 10 or 11 highest countries, as mentioned earlier. With the exceptions of China and Russia, all the other countries on this list with the world's highest military expenditures are formal, informal, or quasi allies of the United States. They include the other member states of the G7 group (Canada, Britain, France, Germany, Italy, and Japan), as well as Australia, India, Saudi Arabia, and South Korea. In view of this phenomenon of countries often joining the stronger side in contradiction to Waltz's (1979) prediction, Stephen Walt (1985; 1987) has introduced the "balance of threat" theory to salvage neorealism. He argues that states balance against the greatest *perceived* threat facing them rather than the country with the most power. But perception is such a large fudge factor that almost any conduct can be explained by it—or by its opposite, misperception.

Why do interstate conflicts spread and escalate, evolving into intense, multilateral struggles? A large portion of the answer pertains to the decisions of megalomaniac leaders who commit serial aggression. Most countries are not initially disposed to rally against a perceived threat from them but are often practically forced to join forces due to their repeated attacks. Self-encirclement is responsible for these would-be hegemons' exhaustion and their eventual downfall. This is the backlash effect that I address in this chapter. It is perhaps also on Joseph Nye's mind when he says, "If a rising China throws its weight around, it drives neighbors to seek to balance its power. In that sense, only China can contain China" (Nye 2015, n.p.).

Although Wilhelmine Germany did not wage serial wars in the manner of Louis XIV, Napoleon, and Hitler, its brusque diplomacy alienated other European powers and its naval buildup alarmed especially Britain (Murray 2010; 2019), causing Berlin to be tethered to a weak Austria–Hungary and an unreliable Italy. As mentioned earlier, Germany went to war in 1914 to forestall a rising Russia as a future threat (Copeland 2000; Van Evera 1999). This preventive motivation distinguished it from the aggressions of Louis XIV, Napoleon, and Hitler. Loss aversion rather than greed for gains was also a more powerful motivation in Japanese leaders' desperate gamble to attack Pearl Harbor to extricate their country from the resource stranglehold on it caused by the embargoes imposed by the United States and its allies (Barnhart 1987; Ike 1967; Russett 1969). As mentioned earlier, Germany's invasion of Belgium ensured that Britain would join the fight against it in World War I, just as Japan's attack on Pearl Harbor guaranteed US participation in a multilateral war against it in World War II. As already mentioned, after going to war against France and Britain, Hitler turned to invading the USSR. The aggressor states' actions were self-defeating, causing their wars to spread and escalate even further. By taking on these formidable opponents in addition to those that were already fighting them, they had practically sealed their own fate.

This common phenomenon describes the backlash effect, whereby a country's aggressive conduct causes other countries to rally against it even though some of them were initially inclined to accommodate it and even bandwagon with it (such as the USSR, which had joined Nazi Germany to partition Poland). The backlash phenomenon therefore describes another mechanism by which an initial bilateral conflict can become multilateral.

Why do states engage in self-injurious behavior? Some leaders (e.g., Napoleon, Hitler) might be megalomaniacs motivated by an insatiable desire for gains, while others (e.g., Tojo) might have acted out of an acute sense of insecurity. Still others, such as Spain's Philip III and Philip IV (discussed in the next section), might be motivated to demonstrate their resolve to fight all challengers. Domestic politics could also play a role, such as the iron-and-rye coalition in Wilhelmine Germany and logrolling by militarists, industrialists, and ultranationalists in imperial Japan in these countries' respective aggressive conduct (J.

Snyder 1991). Still other examples of domestic politics, such as Mao Zedong's disastrous Leap Forward campaign and Cultural Revolution and Joseph Stalin's purge of Red Army officers, come to mind. An extended discussion of this topic, however, would require another book.

Fighting for Reputation

It was mentioned in the last chapter that states care about their reputation for meeting their treaty commitments. Diplomatic communication is helped by a reputation for honesty (Sartori 2003). How to make signals credible to foreign counterparts has been an important research question for international relations scholars since James Fearon's (1997) influential work. That a reputation for resolve is important for effective foreign policy has been an article of faith for officials, with the 1938 Munich Agreement serving as an emblematic lesson that warns officials about the follies of appeasement. As conventional wisdom has it, one should stand one's ground lest an adversary concludes that one is irresolute in opposing its encroachment, a perception that will embolden this opponent as well as imitators in the future to demand further concessions. According to Don Baltasar de Zúñiga, who served as senior minister to Philip III of Spain, "a monarchy that has lost its *reputación*, even if it has lost no territory, is a sky without light, a sun without rays, a body without soul" (quoted in Treisman 2004, 366). His logic argues that reputation is worth fighting for.

In contrast to Louis XIV, Napoleon, and Hitler who were motivated by greed for gains, Philip IV, who ruled Spain during the Thirty Years' War, was driven more by concerns over losses. Presiding over a declining Spain, he fought wars on several fronts, often simultaneously. As Daniel Treisman (2004) reconstructs the foreign policy of his reign, his court's overriding concern was to establish a reputation for resolve and firmness in the belief that this stance would deter other challenges. Yet, ironically, by taking on all challengers and fighting on all fronts, the Spanish monarch's policy depleted his country's resources—thus, it had the contrary effect of encouraging more internal rebels and external foes against him.

It was believed that weakness in any part of Philip IV's vast domain would jeopardize his control of other parts in a manner of a series of falling dominoes. Thus, according to Count-Duke Olivares (Gaspar de Guzmán y Pimentel), who served as Philip IV's prime minister, "the first and most fundamental dangers threaten Milan, Flanders and Germany. Any blow against these would be fatal to this monarchy; and if any one of them were to go, the rest of the monarchy would follow, for Germany would be followed by Italy and Flanders, Flanders by the Indies, and Milan by Naples and Sicily" (quoted in Treisman 2004, 366). This thinking led to Madrid's wars in Bohemia and Flanders as well as against England and France. There were also rebellions in Catalonia, Portugal, Naples, and Sicily. Continuous warfare eventually exhausted Spain's treasury, accelerating its decline.

Philip IV's determination to take on all challengers in the belief that he would thus establish a reputation for resolve and firmness, in fact, backfired. It might have been unnecessary because it is questionable whether one's reputation in one situation is transferable to another, because adversaries realize that these two situations are not comparable. It might also be counterproductive, when any reputational gain would not be sufficient to offset the loss of resources in fighting. For a country with limited resources and multiple enemies like Spain, it might have been better to practice selective appeasement, conserving resources so that it would be in a better position to deter or fight the next challenger.

Spain's policy turned out to be self-defeating. "In large part, the country's failure appears the result of misguided preoccupation with the need always to fight to preserve reputation. . . . Rather than increasing its security . . . Spain's aggressive responses to challenges united all powers against it, while provoking internal rebellions and eroding public finances" (Treisman 2004, 366). When the stakes are low and the costs of fighting are high, appeasement would have made more sense. By taking on all challengers, Philip IV reduced Spain's resource base, and this weakness in turn emboldened further challenges. Treisman concludes that for states with limited resources and multiple adversaries, selective appeasement may be rational.

As with Spain, imperial Britain faced multiple challenges. Its peak years were clearly behind it by the late 1800s when the United States had reached parity, if not having already overtaken it, at least in the size of their respective economy. London had come to the realization that US ascendance was inevitable (Bourne 1967; Friedberg 1988). Its chance to prevent the emergence of a powerful United States had already come and gone. British Prime Minister Robert Salisbury lamented, "It is very sad, but I am afraid America is bound to forge ahead and nothing can restore the equality between us. If we had interfered in the Confederate Wars [on behalf on the South] it was then possible for us to reduce the power of the United States to manageable proportions. But two such chances are not given to a nation in the course of its career" (quoted in MacMillan 2013, 38).

British leaders, however, were farsighted and understood Prussia and later Germany's Chancellor Otto von Bismark's aphorism, "The statesman's task is to hear God's footsteps marching through history, and to try and catch on to His coattails as He marches past" (https://www.goodreads.com/quotes/217967-the-statesman-s-task-is-to-hear-god-s-footsteps-marching-through). Instead of trying to check the rise of the United States, they sought to accommodate and even befriend it—and in the process gained an indispensable ally when World War I came.

There were several occasions when Britain and the United States came close to blows (Chan 2023a; Layne 1994). On each occasion, London decided to make concessions to defuse it. It agreed to arbitration on US terms to end the border dispute between Venezuela and British Guiana in 1895. It succumbed to US pressure and withdrew its objection to the construction of the Panama Canal in 1898–99. And it backed down again in the border dispute between Alaska and British Canada in 1902, agreeing to settle this dispute on US terms. As Treisman (2004, 363) points out, these disputes involved relatively low stakes for Britain, whereas the costs of fighting would be high. Despite arguments from some quarters that Britain should take a hard line to preserve its reputation, London decided to appease—realizing that its decisions in these cases involving low stakes and high costs for fighting would not be interpreted by other countries as a sign of weak resolve and embolden them to challenge Britain in other situations where the stakes and costs would be different. Importantly, accommodating the United States was only part of the British grand strategy. London also settled its differences with France, conciliated with Russia, and even reached out to Japan to form an alliance in the Asia-Pacific (Vasquez 1996; 2009a). It practiced selective appeasement to conserve its resources so that it could concentrate on the nearby threat coming from Germany.

China's relations with Japan and several Southeast Asian countries (Brunei, Malaysia, the Philippines, and Vietnam) have been contentious in part because of their competing sovereignty claims over islets in the East China Sea and South China Sea, respectively. The resulting tension contributes to the danger of self-encirclement facing Beijing. In contrast to these maritime disputes, Beijing has settled almost all its land boundaries—with the major exception of its continuing border disputes with India and three small Himalayan states (Bhutan, Nepal, and Sikkim) whose border demarcations are intertwined with the Sino–Indian border dispute. In contrast to its ongoing dispute with India and its maritime claims, China has often settled its land boundaries amicably and often on terms more favorable to its counterparts (Fravel 2007a; 2007b; 2008; 2012). It has made concessions without any apparent fear that its compromises may be seen by other countries as a sign of weakness. According to Taylor Fravel (2008, 310), Beijing "repeatedly pursued compromise without any apparent concern for the effect that its concessions would have on its reputation or for appearing weak to other states. This suggests that, under some conditions, states may seek to create reputations for cooperation instead of toughness." Beijing's conduct also suggests that a reputation for either toughness or niceness is not easily generalizable, that is, transferable from one case or situation to another.

Naturally, this discussion has contemporary relevance for the United States with its interests and commitments spanning the globe. Unless a country has infinite resources, a determination to fight every threat can be self-defeating as it will stretch and even exhaust its available assets. Indeed, a refusal to differentiate the varying amounts of stakes involved in different disputes and to acknowledge the potential costs of fighting will not improve Washington's reputation but would rather call into question its judgments. Adversaries cannot necessarily infer its resolve to fight in Korea should there be a war on that peninsula from its withdrawal, say, from Afghanistan. Nor can one necessarily conclude that just because Washington had taken a hard line in the 1962 Cuban Missile Crisis it would necessarily intervene militarily in a contingency involving Taiwan. Withdrawing from or refusing to intervene in the first place in conflicts with low stakes should not entail a high cost to a state's reputation—as other leaders can imagine themselves making the same call. Likewise, when the costs of fighting are high such as for the United States in Vietnam, a refusal to intervene or a decision to withdraw should also have only limited costs to a country's credibility. "The higher are the resource costs of intervening, the lower the reputational costs of withdrawing" (Treisman 2004, 368).

These remarks suggest that establishing a general reputation for resolve is elusive, although prior experience in interacting with specific others may have an influence on subsequent episodes. Paul Huth (1988, 81) explains, "The potential attacker did not seem to draw conclusions about the future behavior of the defender based on the defender's behavior in disputes with other states. Rather, the past behavior of the defender was taken as an indicator of behavior in the current conflict only when the potential attacker has been directly involved in past confrontations with the defender."

Interestingly, beliefs in the importance of having a reputation for resolve and firmness appear also to be held by leaders in domestic politics. Why do some governments accommodate separatist movements but others do not? It appears that one pertinent factor is whether officials expect other separatist challenges in the future (Walter 2003; 2006). When they have this expectation, they are more inclined to invest in their reputation for resolve and firmness by fighting in the belief that this behavior will discourage future challenges.

Reputational effects depend on interdependency across events and actors. That is, they hinge on the expectation that what X does or does not do today will affect what Y will or will not do tomorrow. It is not clear that this expectation receives strong empirical support. There is even the possibility that knowledge about the other party's prior behavior can turn out to be self-invalidating. Say that a player's bluff in a poker game has been called. What should I conclude? Is he or she likely to bluff again, or was the initial bluff a deliberate ploy to set me up for entrapment the next time he or she has a strong hand? Prior to the Yom

Kippur War, Egypt and Syria had conducted repeated military exercises as a ruse to disguise their plan to eventually attack Israel. Consider another example from Europe in July 1914. After observing that St. Petersburg had backed down in previous Balkan crises, should leaders in Berlin and Vienna expect Russia to repeat this behavior or to be more determined not to yield again (Levy and Mulligan 2017)? The czar chose the latter path.

If I care for my reputation, why should my counterpart not care about his or hers? We tend to see more reputational damage to our own actions than others' behavior to theirs. For example, why should the US withdrawal from Afghanistan do more damage to its reputation than the USSR's withdrawal from the same country? Can one think of any greater reputational damage than Mikhail Gorbachev's decision not to call out the Red Army and thereby to let communist regimes in Central and Eastern Europe, including that of his own country, fall in quick succession? If the United States wants to uphold its reputation to protect its formal or informal allies, it must also consider that China's reputation is engaged in disputes involving North Korea and Taiwan. Thomas Schelling (1966, 125) calls attention to this reciprocal relationship. In a bilateral confrontation, it is "equally important . . . to help to decouple an adversary's prestige and reputation from a dispute; if we cannot afford to back down we must hope that he can, and if necessary, help him [to do so]." This is perhaps part of the reasoning behind President John Kennedy's reported instruction to his subordinates not to gloat after Nikita Khrushchev decided to withdraw Soviet missiles from Cuba in 1962.

Our current analyses on reputation often fail to capture the subtleties and complexities of states' interactions. For instance, should we expect a state with a strong reputation for having fought challengers in the past to bluff more often in the expectation that it will more likely be able to get away with its bluff? Do states with a record of having backed down on previous occasions, such as Russia in July 1914, feel a strong need to convince others that it will fight *this time*? In a similar vein, having backed down in previous confrontations over Taiwan, how should we interpret a decision by Beijing to initiate yet another round of confrontation? Does it mean that this time it is even more confident or optimistic about the outcome or more resolved to have its way—or else why would it want to repeat its prior setback?

States that have an obviously high stake in a dispute do not need to bluff because it is evident to others that their reputation is engaged in this dispute. Conversely, states with obviously a low stake in a dispute are likely to eschew bluffing because others are likely to call their bluff. Accordingly, states with an intermediate range of interests are more likely to bluff, especially when matched against others with about equal capabilities. Strong states are more tempted and likely to bluff and get away with bluffing because they realize that weaker states are reluctant to call their bluff. Even if they are caught in bluffing, they can more afford this damage to their reputation because their strength means that they will still have to be reckoned with. Weaker states are reluctant to call their bluff because of the serious consequences if their call is mistaken, and of course, they are themselves less likely to bluff because they will also pay a heavy penalty if their bluff is called. Therefore, when weak states stand their ground and declare their intention to resist a stronger adversary—such as when Beijing threatened to intervene in the Korean War in 1950—they should be taken seriously because they are less likely to be bluffing (Chan 2016, 74–76, 117–18).

Applying a social psychological perspective, Jonathan Mercer (1996; 2007) argues that states tend to exaggerate the importance of reputation. Attribution theory suggests that we tend to explain another person's unfriendly (or unfavorable) behavior in terms of his or her disposition (or his or her inherent character) and attribute his or her friendly (or favorable) behavior to his or her circumstances. Accordingly, when a country assists an ally, this behavior will not enhance its reputation in the eyes of its ally because it is likely to interpret this behavior as the result of the defending country's circumstances and not as an indication of its disposition (such as its reliability). When this country fails to support its ally, which would be a favorable development from the perspective of an adversary, it will likewise attribute this behavior to the defender's circumstances and not its disposition (that it has become nicer to the adversary). Of course, unfavorable or unfriendly behavior will likely be seen by the defending country's ally and adversary alike as a sign of its character flaw (such as its inherent unreliability or hostility) or its malevolent intention. Such dispositional attributions, however, are a necessary but insufficient condition for acquiring reputation, which requires actors to use their interpretation of the current case to make predictions about future behavior. Yet, if the defending country's actions are seen to be the result of its circumstances, its conduct could very well be different next time when the circumstances change, thus implying any such reputation will be fragile. That people tend to apply different logic to explain their own conduct versus that of others shows up in many situations.

A Second Look at Bandwagoning and Self-Encirclement

There is a seeming tension, even contradiction, in the discussion thus far. On the one hand, I have argued that bandwagoning—that is, joining a stronger country or coalition, even an aggressive one—is more common than balancing against it. On the other hand, I have pointed out that strong, aggressor states have often produced self-encirclement by bringing about a countervailing coalition due to their reckless behavior of lashing out repeatedly against other countries. How can the tendency for states to bandwagon with a strong, aggressor state be reconciled with the phenomenon of this latter country's self-encirclement?

Charles V and Philip IV of Spain, Louis XIV and Napoleon Bonaparte of France, Wilhelm II and Adolf Hitler of Germany, and Hideki Tojo of Japan had indisputably the strongest military in their respective region. They were therefore able to defeat their opponents individually and often sequentially in quick succession—until their campaigns began to falter. Their neighbors would quite naturally prefer to be on the winning rather than the losing side. This motivation explains in large part their bandwagoning behavior.

At the same time, to openly challenge and defy these stronger countries is dangerous because, as the Japanese say, "the nail that sticks out gets hammered down." In the recent past, leaders have learned that it is hazardous to come into the US strategic crosshairs. It is safer to "hide," "transcend," and even bandwagon. The fates of Saddam Hussein, Muammar Qaddafi, and Manuel Noriega serve as objective lessons for those daring to openly antagonize the United States. Such troublemakers are vulnerable to being picked off by Washington. Therefore, it is difficult for an anti-hegemonic coalition to form—but if it were to form, it would form quickly, for there is safety in numbers (Pape 2005, 17). The formation of such a countervailing coalition requires states to overcome the problem of collective action. One important prerequisite for such a coalition to form is that there must be a country that can be a credible candidate to serve as the core or anchor of this countervailing partnership, such as the role Britain had played in organizing the opposition to Napoleon. This view also explains in part why China has come under Washington's strategic headlight.

Although weaker states tend to bandwagon with a stronger, even aggressor, state, they are also quick to abandon it at the first sign of its weakness. When the tide of military battles turns against this state, its coalition can quickly disintegrate as in the wake of Napoleon's and Hitler's offensives running into difficulties in their respective campaigns against Russia/the USSR. Their and other would-be hegemons' allies are often unreliable and can quickly abandon and even turn on them, switching sides and fighting back. Italy's role reversals in both world wars offer just one prominent example. The would-be hegemons' coalitions are thus fragile as countries join them in the first place primarily due to greed or fear rather than loyalty or identity.

Therefore, when the would-be hegemons' overweening ambitions cause them to overreach, they weaken and expose themselves to the danger of backlash by their victims and even allies. When their coalitions begin to unravel, it can happen abruptly and cascade widely. This process can create an accelerating momentum so that there is a collective rush to "pile on" the aggressor states now that they have shown themselves to be vulnerable. These states also sometimes experience challenges or wars simultaneously on multiple fronts such as for Philip IV of Spain. The change in their former allies' behavior can be both quick and sharp—as shown most recently by the conduct of the former member states of the Warsaw Pact in becoming the most vociferous critics of the Kremlin, albeit in this case the collapse of the USSR was due to internal decay rather than external war. Anger and resentment accumulated over time can be released suddenly to cause this massive backlash brought about by the hegemon or would-be hegemons' own prior behavior.

Of course, this self-encirclement can manifest itself in a less dramatic fashion. In his interview with Iran's President Ebrahim Raisi broadcast on September 23, 2023, on CNN's GPS (Global Public Square) Program, Fareed Zakaria (2023) asked whether Tehran's assertive policies have brought about something quite unexpected, namely, the rapprochement between Israel and several Arab countries, including Saudi Arabia. Others had made the same general point, arguing that the USSR's aggressive policies had brought together China and the United States to oppose it in the 1980s. More recently, in her book *Overreach* Susan Shirk (2023) has argued China's conduct has alienated other countries, causing a backlash against Beijing, including the opposition of Southeast Asian countries against its extensive sovereignty claims over the South China Sea.

This phenomenon, however, does not necessarily suggest that China's neighbors have begun to balance against it (Chan 2010b; Kang 2007; 2010; 2012; 2020a; 2020b; 2023), that a countervailing coalition is forming against Beijing, or that East Asian countries are flocking to the US side to oppose China, as I will explain in Chapter 5. Moreover, not all Southeast Asian countries have sovereignty disputes with China over the South China Sea, and those that do face the classic challenge of collective action. The first one that breaks ranks and negotiates a deal with Beijing is likely to receive the most favorable settlement terms, whereas the last one can end up with little or nothing (Chan 2016). Some of these countries also have competing sovereignty claims among themselves over some parts of the South China Sea. Although inexact, these aspects of the situation invoke some parallels with the story of hunting stag versus hare told by Jean-Jacques Rousseau.

For now, let us recall that Paul Schroeder (1994b) mentioned hiding and transcending in addition to balancing as states' responses to a strong, aggressive power among them. Moreover, Thomas Christensen and Jack Snyder (1990) have pointed to buck-passing as another possibility in states' behavior when confronted with the rise of a strong, aggressor state, such as prior to World War II. When referring to hiding, Schroeder was pointing to the smaller states' efforts to avoid becoming the target of a strong, aggressive power, such as by staying neutral and even trying to deflect the latter's antagonism to another possible prey. *Transcending* refers to their efforts to rise above the fray such as by offering to serve as bridges or mediators among contending states, a role that was sometimes performed by the Vatican in the past and more recently by countries such as Switzerland, Sweden, Austria, and Finland. In Schroeder's words (1994b, 110), it means efforts to "surmount international anarchy and go beyond the normal limits of conflictual politics; to solve the problem, end the threat, and prevent its recurrence through some institutional arrangement involving an international consensus or formal agreement on norms, rules, and procedures for these purposes." Finally, as discussed previously, buck-passing behavior seeks to free-ride on the efforts of other states to oppose a strong, aggressive state.

The interstate system's structure is important in influencing these different patterns of behavior. When a system verges on unipolarity, there is no other state strong enough to pass the buck to, and it offers few places to hide. Since balancing means coming into the preponderant state's crosshairs, it is dangerous. The remaining options for the smaller states appear to be limited to sullen submission and even bandwagoning. But they need not be. As T. V. Paul (2005; 2018) and other scholars have written, small and middle powers have engaged in "soft balancing" in the shadow of preponderant power (Bobrow 2008; Brooks and Wohlforth 2005; Friedman and Long 2015; He and Feng 2008; Khong 2004; Lieber and Alexander 2005; Pape 2005; Pempel 2016; Saltzman 2012). I will return to this topic in Chapter 5.

It is important to recognize that the regional structure and the global structure do not have to be the same. The United States towered over other countries in the Western Hemisphere, even though over many years when it was rising, the interstate system was still Europe-centric and even though Britain continued to be an important extra-regional power in the Americas. Anglo–French rivalry, however, distracted these countries' attention to block this rising colossus and, indeed, even inclined them to occasionally solicit US assistance to check each other (Elman 2004). As mentioned earlier, after the conclusion of the American Civil War, London came increasingly to the conclusion that the US rise was unstoppable and that it was better to befriend rather than resist it to focus its energy and resources to check threats closer to home (P. Thompson 2007). Britain's decision to accommodate the rising United States denied the rest of the region a core around which a countervailing coalition could be formed to contain or balance against the United States. No other country in the region was strong enough to check US power—in contrast to Europe, which in the past had usually been characterized by multipolarity, and in contrast to Asia today, with China being surrounded by Russia, Japan, India, and the incomparable United States, which is practically a resident country in the region. As Elman (2004) argued, the unique set of historical circumstances that enabled the United States to become a regional hegemon is unlikely to be repeatable.

As suggested in the last two chapters, small countries have more space to operate in a bipolar world, which even sometimes gives them the opportunity to entice and exploit competition between the two strongest countries to advance their own cause. Hiding and transcending are also more viable under this circumstance. Indeed, these last two categories of behavior do not perhaps give enough credit to the smaller countries' diplomacy. Not only does bipolar rivalry enable them sometimes to extract resources and support from the two competing superpowers, but it also allows them to practice the diplomacy of hedging and enmeshment. Even though Shirk (2023) may be correct that Beijing's more assertive policies have created a backlash effect among its neighbors, this does not mean that they will necessarily rush to the embrace of the United States. While China's neighbors would surely welcome a US presence to provide a counterweight to China, they are also reluctant to choose sides between these countries. They would rather not be forced into either camp, and they prefer to enmesh both countries in a web of multilateral institutions and norms to tame their power and have Beijing and Washington restrain each other from excessive and wanton use of military force—and limiting the danger of any confrontation between them from escalating into a conflagration (Goh 2013; 2019). Evelyn Goh (2007/2008) has used "omni-enmeshment" and "complex balancing" to describe Southeast Asian countries' multilateral diplomacy to engage, influence, and socialize China. In short, their behavior is more nuanced than the categorical distinctions as suggested by the ideas of balancing, buck-passing, and bandwagoning. Their behavior is instead characterized by all these elements as well as hedging and enmeshment. Moreover, the meaning of balancing is extended beyond binary choices of funding armament and joining alliances.

Conclusion

History is replete with examples of self-defeating policies that have brought ruin to many leaders and their countries. Napoleon's repeated assaults on his neighbors brought about a countervailing coalition that British diplomacy had failed to forge, one that eventually led to his defeat. Hitler and Tojo committed the same error. Their serial aggression subjected their country to fighting a much stronger coalition of their victims in a war that they could not have won. Similarly, Philip IV's determination to confront and fight all challengers caused Spain's overextension and its eventual exhaustion. Arguably, Moscow's competition with the United States during the Cold War took a heavy toll on its economy, contributing to the demise of communist rule and the disintegration of the Soviet Union (e.g., Wohlforth 2003).

Admonitions to guard against self-defeating policies certainly warrant close attention, and those examples just mentioned surely have much popular resonance and policy relevance. Chinese folklore claims that "while disasters of nature can be overcome, self-inflicted errors are much more difficult to rectify." In international relations, it often seems that some states prevail not only because of their own clever strategies but also and sometimes almost by default due to their adversaries' follies. Just to cite one quick example from China's Warring States period which culminated in Qin's defeat of its rivals and its unification of China, Victoria Hui (2005) attributed these outcomes to not only Qin's own institutional reforms but also its counterparts' dysfunctional practices such as their reliance on mercenaries, tax farming, and the venality of office. Studying the fall of past empires, Paul Kennedy (1987) has focused on imperial overstretch as a common cause.

Recently, China's claim of sovereignty over the South China Sea has had the objective effect of putting itself in opposition to several other claimant states and motivating them to form, even if only tacitly, a united front against it. By changing the perceptions of even bystanders that were not initially committed to oppose it, a country's own actions can contribute to bringing about a countervailing coalition against it. This country can accelerate the formation of such an incipient bloc consisting of countries that are already deeply suspicious of its motivations. The emergence of the Quad illustrates this dynamic. It shows that China's assertive behavior can cause its self-encirclement.

One also encounters evidence of US overreach such as its insistence on invading Iraq without United Nations authorization. Its claims that Saddam Hussein had weapons of mass destruction and that he had connections with Al Qaeda were received skeptically even before the war (Kaufman 2004; Mearsheimer and Walt 2003) and further damaged its credibility when they were disproved after the war. This war undermined even the trust of US allies France and Germany, not to mention Russia and China—who became even more mistrustful of Washington's intentions after NATO's bombing campaigns against Libya and Serbia in the name of humanitarian intervention when they suspected that the West's agenda was in fact regime change.

A similar process of backlash may be unfolding regarding the US dollar, which has been the world's dominant currency for some considerable time now. Washington has used this dominance to its advantage. For instance, its exclusive access to issuing the dollar, a currency that other countries cannot refuse to accept except under the direst circumstances, has enabled the United States to spend extravagantly and export the inflation caused by this extravagance. By declining to exercise fiscal responsibility, it devalues the dollar and thus depreciates dollar-denominated assets held by foreigners, at the same time making

American exports more competitive in the international market. This practice eventually reduces the dollar's attractiveness as a store of value.

Washington's control of international banking and the dollar's dominant status give the United States a powerful financial weapon to punish those governments that it dislikes. It uses the SWIFT (the Society for Worldwide Interbank Financial Telecommunications System) routinely to impose financial blockades against countries such as Iran, North Korea, and Russia, hampering their ability to engage in international trade. It also often freezes foreign countries' assets held in US bank accounts, thus preventing their access to these funds. Its economic sanctions and financial embargoes have been largely ineffective (Hufbauer, Schott, and Elliott 1990; Pape 1997), producing diminishing return over time as more and more countries make anticipatory adjustments to protect themselves against being potentially subjected to such coercion in the future.

Therefore, more and more countries are taking steps to lessen their dependency on the dollar and to look for alternative ways to settle their trade accounts. Media reports indicate that an increasing number of countries are settling their foreign trade in local currency, such as India's purchase of oil from the United Arab Emirates in summer 2023. The BRICS group has reportedly offloaded $123 billion in US treasuries in the first nine months of 2023 (and $18.9 billion in September 2023 alone), with China reducing its ownership of US government debt by $117.4 billion (Dsouza 2023). It trimmed its dollar holdings by $13.6 billion in July 2023 alone, followed by Brazil ($2.7 billion) and India ($2.3 billion).

In the meantime, the US Congress continues to be mired in a gridlock, presenting a recurrent danger that government operations have to shut down because it is unable to pass the necessary legislation to fund them. The United States is a rare country where congressional appropriation of expenditures is not directly coupled with legislation to raise the necessary funds to pay for these expenditures. Chronic deficit spending leads to ballooning national debt, which in turn undermines confidence in the US dollar. These phenomena are again examples of self-inflicted injury and unforced errors with consequential ramifications abroad.

The US federal government's deficit reached almost $33.7 trillion in October 2023. The budgetary impasse facing Washington had its fundamental cause in Democrats' reluctance to lower spending and Republicans' aversion to raise taxes. With discretionary spending constituting less than one-third of the federal budget and intense partisan disagreement over which of a small number of the remaining programs to subject to funding cuts, there is little wriggle room to reach an agreement to overcome the deadlock. The deficit is projected to rise to about 10% of the US gross domestic product due to further government borrowing to cover the increasing gap between expenditures and revenues. As the 10-year treasury bill has already reached a 5.0% annual interest rate, the country's debt burden will become heavier in the coming years. This development will in turn increase US dependence on foreigners' willingness to loan money to Washington, and of course this deficit financing will further weaken the value of the dollar. It is true that Congress has thus far always managed to act before going over the fiscal cliff, but its chaotic process and brinksmanship are not reassuring to observers, including federal workers whose paychecks depend on its timely action.

Multiple ongoing processes portend potentially profound transformation of international relations, which may start with seemingly small, even barely visible, changes. But they can cumulate and pick up momentum suddenly. This phenomenon may resemble punctuated equilibrium, a concept used by paleontologists to describe biological evolution (Gould and Eldredge 1977). There tends to be a long period of gestation with few overt signs of change. It is followed by an abrupt and sharp transformation of the organism in question. We are perhaps in a period for such dramatic change to occur in international relations.

Many countries are wary of openly challenging the peerless United States lest they call attention to themselves and become the target of Washington's retaliation. Thus, I have mentioned that an anti-hegemonic coalition has difficulty forming, but if it forms, it will do so quickly and even appear suddenly—thus resembling the process of punctuated equilibrium. This phenomenon can reflect a backlash effect due to the accumulation of resentment against overbearing US conduct. Signs of such a movement afoot may not be discernible initially and for a long time, but it can accelerate unexpectedly. As discussed earlier, states often do not balance against the strongest—even the most aggressive—one in their midst in part because it is hazardous to confront a hegemon or would-be hegemon. However, hegemonic coalitions can disintegrate rapidly when their leaders encounter a serious setback. As Thucydides had warned, such setbacks are often due to these states' own mistakes.

Chapter 5
The Dynamics of Sino–American Tension

Overview

How do fuses, chains, and backlashes interact? It should be evident from the previous discussion that the short answer is "it depends." A fuse requires a conducive environment to start a fire. Even though Taiwan has always been a contentious issue for China and the United States, when these countries' relations are friendly the danger of this island's status causing a war is contained. In other words, in the absence of a conducive environment, a fuse cannot by itself produce a blaze. Conversely, even when macro conditions are volatile, in the absence of a catalyst such as the assassination of Archduke Ferdinand, war may still not occur. Accumulated debris, a prolonged period of drought, and strong winds create conditions to start a large blaze.

When in the following discussion I bring up factors such as incipient signs of competing alliances (e.g., with respect to the Quadrilateral Security Dialogue [Quad] and Shanghai Cooperation Organization [SCO]), recent increases of military expenditures by China's neighbors, and the intensification of commercial and technological competition between China and the United States, it is to show that a more ominous environment is developing in East Asia. Similarly, when I refer to "economic decoupling" between China and the United States and their leaders losing trust in their counterpart, it is intended to point to the removal of a source of stability that has heretofore acted to contain disputes and defuse crises. In short, these developments show what is new and concerning about an emergent situation.

A fuse such as a lightning strike, a downed power line, or a carelessly discarded cigarette butt is required to ignite fire. The danger of a contingency involving Taiwan to trigger a Sino–American confrontation has increased in recent days because, among other things, these countries' relations have deteriorated seriously. When this development is combined with other conditions conducive to war, it is easier for any number of things to provide the fuse to cause a confrontation, and it is also easier for any of them to start one. Domestic politics on all three sides—Beijing, Taipei, and Washington—have taken a turn such that Taiwan's status is now more likely to become a trigger for war than at any other time in recent memory, Naturally, we can imagine other places such as

Fuses, Chains, and Backlashes. Steve Chan, Oxford University Press. © Oxford University Press (2025).
DOI: 10.1093/9780197812907.003.0005

the South China Sea and the Korean peninsula that might also ignite a conflict. As remarked earlier, weaker disputants—such as Taiwan, the Philippines, and North Korea—may be motivated by loss aversion or the desire for gain to internationalize their local feuds to offset their lopsided disadvantages in these conflicts.

Once a conflict starts, the actions of third parties can cause it to spread or to be contained. Alliances have been usually seen as a transmission mechanism for a war to spread and escalate. However, as with the role of fuses, the effects of alliances on conflict contagion and escalation are conditional on other factors. Alliances can restrain the partners in these arrangements from undertaking reckless policies and, conversely, encourage them to get into a war in lockstep. Alliances can therefore have the effects of "balls" in immobilizing belligerent states or at least slowing down their rush to war or, alternatively, increasing this danger of conflict enlargement due to the dynamics of chain-ganging. Which of these tendencies prevails depends on considerations such as whether the allies have similar or different preferences, their respective policy inclinations (dovish vs. hawkish), their relative power, and their perception of whether the offense or defense has the edge.

Therefore, the effect that alliances can have on the outbreak and spread of war is contingent. Ceteris paribus, contagion is more likely when components of a system are closely coupled, such as when partners in an alliance or leaders of opposing alliances in a tight bipolar system believe that their security is highly interdependent. Recent developments are concerning because, in contrast to the past, Washington seems to be less interested in restraining Taipei and more inclined to support it even if it chooses to declare formal independence. Beijing may also have become less disposed to restraining its ally in Pyongyang. In my view, Washington's and Beijing's postures toward Taiwan and Pyongyang, respectively, are derivative and indicative of their bilateral relations. As suggested earlier, the hawkish or dovish predisposition of the dominant party in an alliance is pertinent as to whether these security relationships will raise or reduce the danger of war. Moreover, the very existence of such a relationship may incline the weaker partner to drive a harder bargain with its adversary, rejecting an offer that it would otherwise have accepted in the absence of support from its stronger partner. Being thus more intransigent and less willing to compromise, this behavior can make a dispute last longer and a war more likely.

Domestic politics in the United States appear to be in flux so that it is difficult to predict whether, where, and how Washington would intervene abroad. The debate on funding Ukraine's fight against Russia shows discord. With respect to Taiwan, however, US public and elite opinion has changed significantly compared to just a few years ago. Washington now appears to be less willing to "let Taiwan go." There is, of course, an ongoing debate about whether the United

States should abandon its policy of strategic ambiguity and replace it with a definite commitment to defend Taiwan. We do not know whether this debate is just "atmospherics" or "hot air," but the very fact that it is occurring should be concerning to Beijing.

Backlash happens when aggressive states lash out repeatedly against their victims, forcing them to fight back. These actions and reactions enlarge a conflict. By attacking their neighbors repeatedly, aggressive states cause a backlash. Their actions are self-defeating because they cause a countervailing coalition to form and eventually defeat them. Thus, aggressor states' reckless behavior is often a reason for wars to spread and escalate. Less obviously, foreign intervention motivated by good intentions can also have a backlash effect due to the moral hazard created by this intervention. When foreign powers intervene to stop fighting before war ends in the decisive defeat of the weaker belligerent, or when they provide humanitarian aid, their actions have the effect of limiting the costs of fighting and abetting incentives to start a conflict or repeat it—when prospective belligerents sense that they are extended a safety net by the prospect of foreign intervention.

Even worse, some states or insurgency groups may deliberately provoke their adversary to overreact in the hope that civilian sufferings and war atrocities would galvanize foreigners to provide humanitarian assistance and prevent the stronger belligerent from utterly crushing the weaker opponent. By sparing the latter belligerent from utter destruction, this intervention enables it to live and fight another day. Thus, even foreign intervention with good intentions can backfire by encouraging states or groups to start new rounds of conflict and even to deliberately escalate them in an effort to internationalize their feuds. This intervention causes these feuds to persist and conflicts to recur. I have called attention to moral hazard. Being reassured that Washington "has its back," Taipei may be emboldened to take actions that provoke Beijing to react, which in turn can ensnare Washington in an unwanted conflict.

My brief discussion earlier about Washington's fiscal and monetary extravagance and its frequent resort to commercial and financial sanctions points to the possibility of backlash in the long term. They cause other states to lessen their dependency on the dollar and divert their trade from the United States. Tariffs imposed on imports from China can also have an effect such as by abetting domestic inflation (Zakaria 2024).

A Gathering Storm?

A match cannot easily ignite a pile of wet wood, but it will quickly set on fire one that has been previously doused with gasoline. Thus, preexisting conditions are relevant to how easily a fuse can cause a conflagration. I therefore start with a discussion of the macro conditions characterizing the world today and especially recent and ongoing developments that have made East Asia's environment more combustible. Following my conjunctive logic explained earlier, I focus on the confluence of factors that has made this region more susceptible to the danger of war than before. In combination, these factors tend to augur a more tumultuous East Asia, a region that has actually been more stable and peaceful than other parts of the world in recent decades, contrary to some prior expectations (e.g., Friedberg 1993/1994).

This book's perspective argues for considering multiple factors whose interactions can produce nonlinear effects. We know, for example, obesity, unhealthy diets, tobacco use, high cholesterol, high blood pressure, diabetes, and genetics all contribute to the risk of suffering a heart attack. Similarly, the danger of war becomes elevated in the presence of several variables. Paul Senese and John Vasquez (2008, 197) offer generic benchmark figures to gauge the level of this danger. When two states have a militarized dispute over contested territory, they have a 0.165 chance of going to war in the next five years. When these disputants are allied with other countries, the odds of war increase almost threefold to 0.486. If these countries have a history of recurrent confrontations, the danger rises even further to 0.692. Finally, when we add the presence of an arms race to the combination, the probability of war reaches 0.921. We do not have to accept these figures as exact estimates of war occurrence, but they illustrate nicely the compounding effects of actions and policies that can send two countries on a collision course. The United States and China do not have a direct territorial dispute, but Washington is indirectly involved because its allies Japan and the Philippines have contested China's sovereignty claims in the East China Sea and South China Sea, respectively. To varying degrees the other three ingredients conducive to conflict escalation—recurrent confrontations, arms racing, and alliance ties—are present. Moreover, another ingredient—the turbulence and uncertainty stemming from power shifts, not included in Senese and Vasquez's statistical equations—is also a factor in Sino-American relations endangering war.

There are unmistakable signs suggesting that the euphoria celebrating the end of the Cold War was at least overblown and premature (e.g., Fukuyama 1989; 1992) and that we have returned to a more uncertain, tumultuous, and even dangerous time for international relations. As discussed earlier, Europe in 1914 was a powder keg poised to explode. Sarajevo came along to set off this explosion because preexisting conditions had already primed the continent for war. In the views of some historians, if the assassination of the archduke had not happened, some other event would or could also have precipitated war.

In William Thompson's (2003) study referenced earlier, Europe in 1914 was experiencing a convergence of several trends: the alignment of major states in two opposing camps, the intensification of armament races, and the recurrence of militarized disputes. There were also ongoing processes of power shifts that augur a reshuffling of the existing interstate hierarchy, intense commercial competition, and scramble for extra-regional conquests in Asia and Africa. Each of these developments contributed to tension, mistrust, and a pervasive feeling of insecurity. It was, however, their compounding or multiplicative effect that created a combustible environment.

I review below these different ingredients contributing to a more dangerous environment, starting with recent and ongoing power shifts and followed by other sections addressing other contributing factors to a combustible environment such as tightening alignment patterns, military expenditures, and domestic partisan politics. To recapitulate, this discussion of the regional environment is relevant because a fuse is only likely to start a blaze when a conducive environment, produced by a confluence of enabling factors, exists. Because this discussion of the security environment reflects that of 1914 Europe as an analog, there is also a later section discussing the differences between then and now. After discussing the macro conditions characterizing East Asia's security environment that incorporates both old conditions and new developments, I finally turn to how fuses, chains, and backlashes pertain to this environment.

Power Shifts and Their Consequences

We are today revisiting an environment that shows several worrisome parallels with the one prior to the Great War. The relationship between Beijing and Washington has deteriorated significantly, with US president Joe Biden describing it as one of "extreme competition" across an array of diplomatic, military, commercial, and technological spectra (Biden 2021, n.p.). The intensification of this competition is unfolding in the context of a power shift between these two countries, an ongoing process that has alarmed many Americans and has led some of them to warn about the so-called Thucydides' Trap (Allison 2015; 2017). This warning refers to the aphorism attributed to this Athenian historian, claiming that Sparta's fear of Athens' rise was the basic cause of the Peloponnesian War, a devastating conflict that had laid waste to the ancient Greek world some 2,500 years ago. This warning resonated with many scholars, pundits, and the informed public, and it has even reached the highest levels of government. China's President Xi Jinping was quoted as saying that "we must all strive to avoid falling into Thucydides Trap" (Yicai Global 2017, n.p.) and that this trap "can be avoided . . . as long as we maintain communication and treat each other with sincerity" (quoted in Shi 2020, n.p.).

Although, as mentioned earlier, formulations such as power-transition theory and Thucydides' Trap have not specified or tested those intermediate steps that lead from power shifts at the international level to officials' decisions to go to war, such as various cognitive and psychological effects that can be induced by large and rapid power shifts, they have staked out bold claims that changing international power balance is *the* leading cause of war. Although the United States continues to be the world's undisputed dominant power, China's rise represents a seismic transformation of the post-1945 international system, and the importance of this development is matched only by the USSR's collapse and the invention of nuclear weapons. Parenthetically, although power-transition theory argues that systemic wars are started by a cocky, impatient latecomer, some researchers on the origin of World War I have argued that it was due to a preventive motivation on the part of a dominant power poised to decline—namely, Germany deliberately choosing war to forestall a rising Russia that could present a future threat to it. Regardless, the key point of this discussion is, of course, that power shifts present an important ingredient to an environment conducive to war, one that is more easily ignited by a fuse—any fuse.

Power-transition theory points to the changing power balance between Britain and Germany as the main reason for the outbreak of the Great War. Other scholars have preferred to study power shifts among multiple great powers rather than just the top two (e.g., Doran 1991; Doran and Parsons 1980). This broader perspective suggests that even a relatively small change involving the power of a lesser great power can create a large perturbation in the relative standing of other members of this select club. This situation therefore points to the arrival of an environment of greater uncertainty and concomitantly greater anxiety for the relevant countries' officials. Even a relatively small increase in Russia's power was a source of serious concern for Germany's leaders before World War I. Today, we are seeing economic forces affecting multiple countries simultaneously. There is an ongoing process pointing to the relative decline of established Western economies and relative gain on the part of large, emergent non-Western economies. There is therefore concurrent upward and downward mobility for major states. China's rise cannot but affect the relative positions of other countries such as Japan, Germany, and Russia, and thus has multilateral ramifications. Power shifts are likely to arouse feelings of anxiety, alarm, arrogance, fear, pride, overconfidence, and other emotions. These feelings as well as increased uncertainties can impair judgment and cause policy mistakes during periods when the distribution of interstate power is undergoing rapid change.

Although Europe had been the central arena of international relations during a very long period of the modern era of international relations, its influence had already been eclipsed by the United States after World War I and even more so after World War II. In the next several decades, the center of gravity for international relations will move further to the west across the Pacific. According to Marcus Lu (2023), by 2050 four of the world's top six economies would be from Asia (China, India, Indonesia, and Japan). This change augurs a major reshuffling of the interstate hierarchy, a profound transformation of the traditional international system from one dominated by European countries to one that is Asia-Pacific-centric.

The interstate hierarchy has become more fluid, unstable, and vulnerable to challenge due to the uneven economic growth among major powers (Gilpin 1981; 1987; Organski and Kugler 1980; W. Thompson 1983). We are clearly entering a period of global power deconcentration, that is, a period when there is a more diffuse distribution of power among states, a development that in the past has presaged more intense conflict and even systemic war before introducing a new global hegemon (Modelski 1987a; 1987b; Rasler and Thompson 1991; 1994; W. Thompson 1983; 1990; 2020).

International relations scholars have been mostly concerned about the conduct of rising powers, seeing them as the main source of challenge to international stability and order. They are the ones usually seen as predisposed to start war. Yet Germany's policies prior to both world wars indicate that an established power but one that is poised to decline can also initiate conflict, specifically in Germany's case to wage a preventive war against a rising power to its east. Thus, declining powers can also be a source of international instability. Thomas Christensen (2001) has written that China can pose problems for the United States without catching up. A China whose growth has stalled or even reversed can be perhaps even more worrisome for those concerned about international stability.

During times of large and rapid power shifts, the old pecking order fails increasingly to reflect the new reality. For example, although Britain and France continue to hold on to their permanent seats on the United Nations Security Council, their power has slipped considerably compared to other countries such as Japan, Germany, and India. Naturally, established states do not readily yield their privileged positions to newcomers. There can then be an increasing mismatch between a rising state's objective power and the status accoutrements accorded to it by other countries. The faster and greater that power shifts are occurring among countries in the top tier of the international hierarchy and the slower and less adequate the process to accommodate new arrivals knocking on the door of this select club, the greater is this disparity that has been a significant source of instability and war in the past (e.g., East 1972; Gochman 1980; Ray 1974; Renshon 2016; 2017; Wallace 1973; Ward 2017).

How does this phenomenon relate to this book's central concern? To state the obvious, power shifts cause status frictions, which are in turn a major source of international instability according to status-inconsistency theory (which argues that wars are more likely to happen when states feel frustrated because they do not feel that they are accorded the international status that their capabilities should entitle them to). Status pursuit and its flip side, status denial, have been recurrent reasons for international tension (e.g., Renshon 2017; Ward 2017). Ned Lebow (2010) has argued that the desire for status recognition, prestige, or *gloire* has been an important cause of warfare—even more so than states' pursuit of their security concerns. He reports that the quest for status was present as a primary or secondary motivation in 62 of 94 wars involving great powers since 1648 (Lebow 2010, 18). The converse of status quest is perceived attempts to deny or block the legitimate aspirations of newcomers by the established powers. The "chip on the shoulder" phenomenon tends to be a common characteristic of rising or re-emergent powers. It has been attributed to Wilhelmine Germany and, more recently, China and Russia (Krickovic 2017; Krickovic and Zhang 2020; Larson and Shevchenko 2010; 2019; Murray 2019; Wolf 2014). Perceptions of gratuitous insult and deliberate obstruction can arouse strong resentments, as these studies show. One often hears, for example, the complaint that a foreign country's action "has seriously hurt the feelings of the Chinese people."

Mismatch of Economic and Military Power

The speed and size of power shifts matter, as does the extent of power deconcentration in international relations that has in the past portended a more tumultuous time ahead. A mismatch in a country's economic and military power can also be a source of concern. Although the United States has suffered relative economic decline since the 1970s, it continues to be a preponderant military power that no other country comes close to matching (W. Thompson 2022). This situation naturally reminds one of Paul Kennedy's (1987) warning about imperial overstretch, a self-inflicted error, so that excessive foreign policy commitments have a backlash effect hurting domestic economic well-being and social cohesion. There are, of course, also other states whose military capabilities exceed their economic capabilities (e.g., Russia) and vice versa (e.g., Japan, Germany). These status inconsistencies can introduce another source of international instability.

To conserve space, I will limit my discussion below to only the United States and China with respect to their evolving economic and military positions. Scholars have used different indicators to define or measure national power and the changing power relationships among countries (e.g., Baldwin 1979; Beckley 2018; Cline 2002; Hart 1976; Kugler and Arbetman 1989; Merritt and Zinnes 1988; 1989; Moyer et al. 2021; Nye 1990; 2002; 2004; Rauch 2017; Snider 1987; Taber 1989; Tellis 2015). According to Organski and Kugler (1980) who formulated the power-transition theory, when a rising state reaches 80% of the leading state's power, it has entered a period of rough parity, a period during which a systemic war is most likely to happen. A systemic war is an intense armed conflict involving most or all of the world's great powers, one that augurs a major transformation of international order and interstate hierarchy. Organski and Kugler (1980) have argued that the simplest and most appropriate measure of national power is a country's gross national product or its gross domestic product (GDP).

In 1960, China's GDP was US$59.7 billion compared to US$543.3 billion for the United States (https://www.macrotrends.net/countries/CHN/china/gdp-gross-domestic-product; https://www.macrotrends.net/countries/USA/united-states/gdp-gross-domestic-product). China's economy was thus about 11% of the US economy at that time. In terms of China's GDP per capita (US$90), it was even further behind the United States (US$3,007). In 1978, the year when China started its economic reform, its GDP was US$149.54 billion compared to US$2,351.6 billion for the United States. Representing less than 6.4% of the US economy, China was further behind the United States in 1978 than 1960. The disparity between these two countries was even greater when assessed in terms of GDP per capita: US$156 for China compared to US$10,565 for the United States. By 2021, however, this relationship had changed significantly. China's GDP (US$17,734.06 billion) had grown to be 76% of the US GDP (US$23,315.08 billion). Although not yet meeting the 80% threshold suggested by Organski and Kugler, China had made great strides in narrowing the gap separating it from the United States. By 2021, China's GDP per capita (US$12,556) had also shown significant relative gain (the US GDP per capita was US$70,249 in 2021), even though it was still significantly behind the US level.

Another way of looking at China's economic advance is to examine its performance over time. China's economy was almost 300 times larger in 2021 than in 1960 and almost 120 times larger when compared to 1978. In contrast, the US economy had grown more slowly; it was only about 43 times larger in 2021 than 1960 and not quite 10 times larger than 1978. For more than three decades following its economic reform in 1978, China's economy grew at about a double-digit rate. In the first half of 2023, after the COVID lockdowns and disruptions of supply chains, this rate slowed to 5.5%; and it was expected to be lower still at 5.2% for the entire year 2023, 4.5% in 2024, and 4.8% in 2025 (https://www.theguardian.com/business/2023/jul/17/china-gdp-growth-down-economy-june-quarter-gross-domestic-profit). The Conference Board's forecast for the US economy's growth was 1.3% for 2023 and 0.1% for 2024 (https://www.conference-board.org/research/us-forecast). Officials make policies based on their anticipation of future conditions. They pay attention to the direction, pace, and trajectory of changes in their national power compared to that of their foreign counterparts. Although they are not infallible, the estimates reported above suggest that China's economy would soon exceed 80% of the US economy (if it has not already done so, especially if one uses purchasing power parity to measure an economy's size), and many people expect it to overtake the US economy in the next 25 years.

In the meantime, defense expenditures have been rising and are poised to increase further for many countries. NATO members have pledged to increase these expenditures to 2% of their respective GDP in the wake of Russia's invasion of Ukraine (Drozdiak 2023), and Japan has breached its longstanding practice of limiting this spending to 1% of its GDP. The United States has always been by far the world's biggest spender on defense. In 2019, it outspent the *combined* military expenditures of the next 11 highest countries (Stockholm International Peace Research Institute 2020). The US defense budget for 2023 is about as large as the *combined* total for the next 12 countries with the largest defense budgets (https://www.globalfirepower.com/defense-spending-budget.php).

The amount of Chinese military expenditures has been the second highest in the world, albeit still much lower than that of the United States both absolutely and relatively (as a proportion of their respective GDP). According to the Stockholm International Peace Research Institute, the United States had spent 2.73 times more than China on its military in 2021, or about 3.5% of its GDP compared to 1.7% for China (https://www.sipri.org/research/armament-and-disarmament/arms-and-military-expenditure/military-expenditure). These countries and others have been raising their defense spending. The expected "peace dividend" after the Cold War's end has long since disappeared.

Tighter Alignment Patterns

As mentioned earlier, when components of a system are closely coupled, one component's failure can more easily cause others to fail as well. Tight alliances are one condition that can cause an original bilateral conflict to become a larger, multilateral struggle. Therefore, tighter alignment patterns are a worrisome development contributing to a more combustible international environment. The danger of an armed confrontation is greater today than during the Cold War, when Washington refrained from interfering in the USSR's sphere of influence in Central and Eastern Europe (e.g., the Hungarian uprising in 1956, the crushing of the "Prague Spring" in 1968). The zone of contest in Ukraine has been moved right up to Russia's border, and the buffer zone provided by Russia's former allies in Eastern and Central Europe has been removed. Moreover, this buffer and the intermediary role played by Finland and Sweden have also disappeared with these latter countries' recent membership in NATO. Of course, Taiwan is also within close physical proximity of China.

There has recently been an increasing trend for countries to select themselves into opposing camps. Although NATO was described by France's president Emmanuel Macron as "brain dead" not so long ago ("Emmanuel Macron Warns Europe" 2019, n.p.), this alliance has been reinvigorated by Russia's invasion of Ukraine. It has presented a united front to oppose this aggression and has even added Finland and Sweden as its newest members. For a second year, leaders from four Asia-Pacific countries—Australia, Japan, South Korea, and New Zealand—attended the NATO summit meeting, held in Vilnius, Lithuania, in July 2023. This development was seen by Beijing as a continuation of this Western alliance extending its reach eastward. In addition, in the Indo-Pacific region the United States has taken the lead to organize the Quad, an incipient alliance clearly with China as its target.

At the same time, even though they had at one time perceived each other as the principal enemy, there has been a rapprochement between Beijing and Moscow. China and Russia have proclaimed a partnership "without limits." This combination presents a nightmare scenario to those who subscribe to traditional geopolitical and geostrategic thinking. Halford Mackinder (1904; 1919; 1943), who pioneered this tradition, had written that control of Eurasia, the world's heartland, holds the key to commanding the rest of the world. Other leading geostrategic writers, such as Alfred Mahan ([1890] 1980) and Nicholas Spykman (1942; 1944), would also be alarmed by the security implications of a Sino-Russian alliance. They had urged the US and British governments to contain the influence of a rising Germany and an emergent Russia/USSR, or a union of the two, prior to the two world wars and in the post-1945 Cold War. An alignment drawing China and Russia closer today would be equally alarming to these geostrategic thinkers as these two countries together can potentially dominate the world's heartland.

There are other signs of ongoing realignment of international relations with more and more countries—many of whom were non-aligned during the Cold War and even some traditional US allies—expressing an interest in joining the BRICS group, which had its first summit meeting in 2009 (South Africa joined the following year). The United Arab Emirates, Iran, Egypt, and Ethiopia are scheduled to join this association as its newest members (Argentina has declined its invitation to join, and Saudi Arabia has reportedly decided to postpone its membership; https://www.cnn.com/2023/08/24/business/saudi-arabia-brics-invitation-intl/index.html). Other countries, such as Indonesia, Algeria, and Belarus, are rumored to be waiting in the wings. Media reports suggest this group's expansion as a possible sign of an emergent anti-Western coalition, portending and accelerating perhaps a process of "de-dollarization" (that is, abandoning the US dollar, currently the dominant international currency, to conduct trade and financial transactions).

As mentioned earlier, the Quad has also been revived under Washington's leadership after having been dormant for an interval after 2008. At the same time, the SCO has developed into an incipient Eurasian bloc led by China and Russia, and includes member states such as India, Iran, Pakistan, Kazakhstan, Kyrgyzstan, Tajikistan, and Uzbekistan. Iran joined as its newest member in July 2023. As with the BRICS group, its expansion and institutionalization may augur the potential formation of an anti-Western coalition.

Recurrent Encounters and Multiple Webs That Can Ensnare

Compared to China, the United States has far more interests and allies spanning the globe. Ipso facto, it runs the greater danger of becoming engulfed in conflicts abroad, in contrast to China whose focus is more on its immediate neighborhood and who has only one formal ally (North Korea). The incidence of Washington's military intervention abroad has more than tripled from 46 during 1948–91 to 188 during 1992–2017 (Toft 2017). To my knowledge, China has not taken any such military intervention abroad—which is not to deny that it has militarized disputes with its neighbors over contested sovereignty claims, whether over Taiwan, with India, or concerning portions of the East China Sea and the South China Sea. Because of its more active and prominent global profile, Washington is more likely to be ensnared in a foreign crisis than Beijing. Singapore's former ambassador to the United Nations, Kishore Mahbubani, was quoted as saying that even during the relatively peaceful administration of Barack Obama, the United States had dropped 26,000 bombs on seven countries in 2016 alone, whereas China has not fired a single shot across its border since 1979 when it fought its last war with Vietnam (Kang 2020a, 140).

Naturally, the frequency of "close encounters" matters if for no other reason than statistical probability. The more points of contact two rival countries' militaries have, the greater is the probability for a mishap or accident to happen. From this perspective, the rising incidence of "freedom of navigation" show of flag in contested waters, more frequent overflights over another country's declared air defense identification zone, more intrusive patrols or fishing expeditions in another country's economic zone, and more deliberate challenges by Chinese fighter jets in crossing the median line in the Taiwan Strait or US long-range bombers such as the B-52 in approaching China's air space, the more likely that they can produce some unintended consequences. Naturally, displays of military force such as joint naval exercises and diplomatic brinksmanship can also have these consequences. This is one reason why research on enduring rivalries shows the tendency for militarized disputes to increase the probability of further such disputes, causing the phenomenon of conflict recidivism.

As mentioned in Chapter 2, one definition of an enduring rivalry is simply the frequency of militarized disputes between two countries. The United States and China have had many such encounters in the past. However, lopsided Chinese weakness had limited the escalatory potential of these incidents. This situation has changed in recent days. Chinese vessels and aircraft have increasingly ventured beyond their traditional areas of operation. Chinese coastguard vessels have also participated in increasing incidents of harassment against foreign encroachments in contested areas being claimed by Beijing in the South China Sea and the East China Sea. China's navy has also undertaken longer voyages farther from its shores to show the flag. At the same time, the US Navy has increased its excursions to contest Chinese claims of sovereignty over disputed waters in the name of freedom of navigation. Therefore, we can expect more frequent encounters between the two sides, thus raising the danger that they can produce unexpected and unwanted clashes, which in the context of a more combustible environment present a higher risk of conflict escalation—especially because leaders in both countries have become highly suspicious of their counterparts' intentions and are under domestic pressure to demonstrate their patriotic credentials.

Contesting Regionalisms: Asia-Pacific versus Indo-Pacific

Washington has introduced a new concept—the idea of Indo-Pacific—to replace its predecessor, Asia-Pacific. In March 2021, US president Joe Biden pledged commitment to a "free, open, secure" Indo-Pacific (Wright 2021). As I have argued elsewhere (Chan 2023a, 117),

> the U.S. has interjected itself as an extra-regional actor by successfully constructing and institutionalizing imagined communities of super-regions such as "Atlanticism," "Asia Pacific," "Pan Americanism," and most recently, "Indo-Pacific" (or the "Quad" consisting of Japan, India, Australia, and the U.S.). These moves enable Washington to play a "swing strategy" whereby it gains leverage in all regions. . . . Naturally, the U.S. construction of and embeddedness in these super-regions help Washington to forestall any attempt by a regional actor to shut it out and obviously, also to prevent the rise of a potential competitor to its superpower status. No other country, including China, enjoys this positional advantage.

"Because it has the option to delink from, or reduce the priority of its engagement in, in any region, the US can use threats and inducements of increasing or decreasing its levels of engagement as a means of playing one region against another" (Buzan 2004, 105).

The switch from the verbiage of *Asia-Pacific* to *Indo-Pacific* is significant and concerning for two reasons. First, whereas *Asia-Pacific* is associated specifically with the idea of open regionalism that welcomes dialogue with and participation by countries with different political and economic orientations, *Indo-Pacific* is the opposite of an inclusive group. It is exclusionary, led by four large countries with China evidently as their target. Second, whereas the United States has previously pushed to foster both democracy and capitalism abroad—even sometimes compromising its democratic ideals in favor of economic interests—the Indo-Pacific arrangement reverses this priority, promoting the idea that there is now an existential struggle between democracy and autocracy (Beckley 2022). The policy implications are equally clear. Whereas authoritarian states, such as China and Burma, can be accommodated within the rubric of Asia-Pacific regionalism and enjoined to set aside political differences in favor of pursuing economic cooperation and development, the idea of Indo-Pacific has the opposite connotation and even the intended purpose of dividing countries politically.

Paul Evans and Cheng-Chwee Kuik (2023, n.p.) describe the concepts of Asia-Pacific and Indo-Pacific more fully and elegantly than I can, in the following words:

> In its starkest form, the Asia-Pacific emerged as an aspiration in the late 1980s for a new regional framework built on the principles of market economics and free trade, open regionalism, inclusive multilateralism, co-operative and comprehensive security, and the engagement of China. It eschewed drawing lines on the basis of political regimes and, at its boldest, envisioned an Asia-Pacific community that would transcend or at least mitigate national rivalries.
>
> The Indo-Pacific, in contrast, is a construction promoted most strongly by Japan and the US, and a range of other countries in what they see as a new strategic setting defined by a deepening competition between the US and China, increasing anxiety about Chinese intentions and rising influence, a skepticism about open markets and free trade in a fragmenting global economy, and a belief that regional economic integration is as much a source of vulnerability and risk as it is opportunity.

As these authors point out, although the tenets of the Indo-Pacific concept may play well in North America and some parts of Europe, they are received skeptically in some countries in the geographic region covered by it and hotly contested and even resisted in many other countries. Elite associations of big countries based on exclusionary criteria and transparently targeting a specific country—such as the Indo-Pacific concept—cause skepticism, discomfiture, and even alarm among some countries (e.g., Goh 2023; Moon 2023). "A shifting regional discourse reflects a changing reality but is also shaping it. If the Asia-Pacific was an institution and identity-building instrument put in place at the end of one cold war, the Indo-Pacific has more than a whiff of being constructed on the verge of a second" (Evans and Kuik 2023, n.p.). A final concern about and therefore objection to the nomenclature of the Indo-Pacific era is that by pitching it as an existential struggle between democracy and autocracy, this presentation boxes the United States and its allies in—creating a self-imposed strategic cul de sac from which neither Washington nor its supposed adversary Beijing can easily reverse course and extricate itself from the security dilemma.

Arms Spending in East Asia

Still another ingredient creating the dangerous brew in Europe prior to 1914 was rising armament by the then future belligerent states. The Anglo-German naval race played an especially prominent role in traditional accounts of the sources of World War I, although more recently there has been a reappraisal of its importance. Naturally, a pertinent question for this discussion of East Asia's security environment is whether countries in this region are arming themselves to balance against a rising China (Beckley 2022; Brzezinski and Mearsheimer 2005; Kang 2003; 2007; 2023; Liff and Ikenberry 2014; Ross 1999; 2004; 2006; Shambaugh 2004/2005). Rising armament spending could be an indicator that the danger of regional war is increasing because obviously countries commit to more military expenditures when they see a higher probability of getting into a conflict.

It is important to recognize that rising defense spending on the part of China's neighbors does not necessarily indicate that they are balancing against China. After all, South Korea's and Japan's military expenditures could also be directed against North Korea. Similarly, military spending by Laos, Cambodia, and Thailand may have Vietnam more than China as the intended target; and Singapore, Malaysia, and Indonesia may be more wary of each other than a more distant China. There are also other reasons for a country to spend money on its military, such as to stimulate its domestic economy. A large part of defense spending may also reflect bureaucratic interests, political logrolling, and budgetary inertia. There were years after the Cold War's end that the United States kept a high level of defense spending even without any enemy in sight.

These remarks thus suggest that rising defense expenditures by China's neighbors are a necessary condition for substantiating the claim that they are balancing against China, but this phenomenon is not a sufficient condition for proving this claim. This logic, of course, also means that in the absence of these countries spending more money on their military, it would be hard to argue that they are balancing against China. The one place to look for evidence of such balancing behavior is, of course, Taiwan, which faces an exclusive and existential threat from China and therefore whose military expenditures can arguably be said to be directed solely against China. This is the "most likely case" to confirm realist expectation. If supportive evidence is not forthcoming from this case, it is difficult to imagine where else one should expect realism to be supported.

Parenthetically, if some countries are not increasing their defense spending—and hence cannot be said to be balancing against China—this phenomenon may not be construed by some people as evidence against realism. For example, some realists may argue that Indonesia, Malaysia, or Brunei may simply be passing the buck to other countries closer to China, especially presumably those sharing a land border with China such as India and Vietnam, to balance against Beijing.

Taiwan has announced a record defense budget for 2023. It will spend $19.1 billion, but this amount constitutes only 2.6% of its GDP (Sacks 2023). This budgeted increase will represent a nominal increase of 3.5% from the previous year, but it must be seen in the context of inflation running at about 2%, and thus represents, in fact, the smallest real increase in the past half-decade. From 2001 to 2019, defense spending has remained remarkably stable at about 11% of the government's budget (Sacks 2023, n.p.). Compared to possible counterparts that also face external threat, such as South Korea and Israel, Taiwan has spent less proportionately on its defense as a share of its economy.

Using data from the Stockholm International Peace Research Institute, David Kang (2023, 16) shows that Taiwan's defense burden (defense spending as a percentage of GDP) was 2.04% in 2010, 1.87% in 2015, and 1.74% in 2021. This defense burden *declined* 0.29% between 2010 and 2021 and 0.12% between 2015 and 2021. Thus, when it announced its record defense budget for 2023, Taiwan was catching up from years of stagnant and even decreasing defense burden. At 1.74%, Taiwan's defense burden in 2021 was low, but some of China's other neighbors had even lower defense burdens in 2021, such as Japan at 1.07%, the Philippines at 1.04%, Indonesia at 0.7%, Malaysia at 1.06%, and Thailand at 1.32%. Even South Korea and Singapore, which led the group, featured a defense burden of only 2.78% and 2.98%, respectively. By comparison, the United States spent more than 3.45% of its GDP on defense in 2022.

The comparatively low levels of defense burden for China's neighbors and especially for Taiwan are instructive. Equally important, however, are their trend lines. One would expect that their defense burdens will rise over time, especially during recent years when China was accused of engaging in assertive or aggressive behavior. Yet significantly, Kang (2023, 16) shows that these changes are often negative or only slightly positive. This change in defense burden between 2015 and 2021 was −0.05% for the Philippines, −0.07% for Singapore, −0.11% for Thailand, −0.12% for Taiwan, −0.19% for Indonesia, and −0.45% for Malaysia. Even for the three countries showing positive changes, the increase was quite small: 0.03% for Australia, 0.11% for Japan, and 0.28% for South Korea. Overall, these figures do not provide strong support for the proposition that China's neighbors have been balancing against it. In a more recent publication, Xinru Ma and David Kang (2024) again emphasized that international politics in East Asia should not be seen through a European or American prism. Moreover, in contrast to Europe, characterized by frequent warfare and balance-of-power considerations, East Asia has enjoyed long periods of peace; and countries in this region accept a shared understanding of regional hierarchy with scant attention to those concerns highlighted by the European tradition of realpolitik.

When compared to 1990, the relevant trends, in fact, point in the opposite direction of the expectation of increasing balancing behavior by China's neighbors. Kang (2023, 14) remarks,

> The proportion of the economy devoted to defense spending is now almost half of what it was in 1990 and shows no sign of increasing. . . . Specifically, the defense spending of nine main East Asian countries declined from an average of 2.88% of GDP in 1990 to an average of 1.6% in 2021. That is, the overall reduction in defense effort in East Asia is a generations-long and region-wide phenomenon. It is not a spurious result driven by a few outlier countries or outlier years.

These remarks confirm and reinforce earlier results, and they also support congruent trade patterns pointing to China's rise to become its neighbors' most important commercial partner (Chan 2010b). Here again, Taiwan provides the most decisive evidence. In 2021, 42% of its exports went to China, and 22% of its imports came from China (Cheng 2022). This extraordinary extent of trade dependency on China belies any claim of balancing behavior—and for the one entity that should have the most to fear from China's increasing power (for studies on trade as a costly signal, see Chan 2009; Morrow 2003).

Naturally, these comments do not rule out future changes in the opposite direction, and indeed there have been some adverse reactions to Beijing's recent conduct, as Susan Shirk (2023) has indicated in her observations about China's overreach. Yet, at least until very recently, the overall picture does not suggest balancing behavior against China by its neighbors—which in turn implies that they do not see an imminent danger of war. Naturally, this remark does not rule out the possibility of change. Indeed, there are some signs indicating that Japan, Taiwan, and the Philippines may be ramping up their military spending.

David Kang (2023, 7) observes,

> the evidence leads to the conclusion that China's dramatic growth has provoked very little response from its neighbors. As of 2022, there is still no nascent East Asian containment coalition against China. There is little evidence of an East Asian balancing against China through either build ups of their own military forces, or pursuit of military alliances. Furthermore, rather than East Asian efforts to limit economic interactions with China, most East Asian countries are steadily deepening their economic and diplomatic relations with China, not moving farther away. China has already completed a regional power transition in East Asia. China has done so quickly, and it has done so peacefully.

His observation naturally contradicts my view that East Asia has become a more dangerous place. More recent evidence on defense spending by countries in this region can indicate a changing picture. Nevertheless, Kang makes an important point about the dense and extensive economic relations that exist between China and its neighbors. These commercial and financial ties are important to stabilize their relationships during times of turbulence. These ties are also indicative of the expectations of China's economic partners because obviously states that anticipate getting into a conflict do not trade or invest heavily in each other.

Domestic Politics and Rhetoric

I would be remiss if I overlooked the role of domestic politics in encouraging states to adopt belligerent and expansionist policies abroad. The iron–rye coalition in pre-1914 Germany and this country's Navy League (*Deutscher Flottenverein*) pushing for naval buildup and *Weltpolitik* were important parts of its political landscape. Conversative German politicians were also preoccupied with the influence of Social Democrats, fearful that they could threaten the monarchical order. Imperial expansion was the formula that they settled on to appease and appeal to the working class. These domestic factors combined with international ones contributed to the occurrence of war (Albertini 1980; Berghahn 1973; Fischer 1967; Herrmann 1997; Hilgruber 1981; Schroeder 2004). We saw similar dynamics operating in Japan's domestic politics in the 1930s. Industrialists, militarists, and ultra-nationalists engaged in logrolling and promoted the "myth of empire" in the leadup to World War II (J. Snyder 1991).

Rising Serbian (Slavic) nationalism and increasing ethnic discord in Austria–Hungary also contributed to the tension between these countries. Officials in Vienna were especially gripped by a sense of fear and anxiety about the deterioration of their country's domestic and foreign environment, a combination that encouraged their bellicosity in July 1914.

We do not have the same exact dangerous brew fomenting today. Nevertheless, Beijing has been busy dealing with restless ethnic minorities in Xinjiang and Tibet, political dissidents in Hong Kong, and a recalcitrant Taiwan. At the same time, the United States has faced its own minority issues, such as that articulated by the Black Lives Matter movement. Moreover, political discord and cultural clashes have clearly been on the rise. Democrats and Republicans rarely agree on any issue—except both now favor "getting tough" on China. Chinese nationalism has also been on the rise, with netizens increasingly criticizing their government for being too soft on Taiwan and the United States. In times of domestic hardship or turmoil, politicians often engage in demonizing and scapegoating real or imagined foreign enemies (Colaresi 2005). There is a large body of literature on the so-called diversionary theory of war, hypothesizing that leaders often escalate foreign tension and manipulate international crises to deflect their citizens' dissatisfaction with the government's job performance (e.g., Chiozza and Goemans 2003; DeRouen 2000; Haynes 2017; Meernik and Waterman 1996; Morgan 1999; Richards et al. 1993; Smith 1996a; Sobek 2007).

Elite and mass opinion in both China and the United States has become more hawkish so that those who favor conflict de-escalation and reconciliation face strong political headwinds. As already noted, Democrats and Republicans rarely agree on important issues, but they both favor a more hardline policy on China. Popular opinion and elite pronouncements have also hardened in China. Surveys of public opinion in different Asian countries also show a sharp decline in their peoples' favorable views of China, with a large percentage in practically all countries expressing negative sentiments and a lack of trust in China. In short, the domestic climate does not favor the prospect of politicians reaching out to their counterparts to settle disputes or defuse tension. If anything, the prevailing incentive is for politicians to demonstrate their patriotic credentials by "standing up" to their foreign adversaries. Wars can occur due to the pull of alliances or the push of domestic politics (Welch 2015). If foreign conditions tend to raise the danger of conflict, countervailing influence from domestic politics can help to limit this danger—and vice versa. However, if both foreign and domestic conditions are working in the same direction to increase international tension, they create a more acute danger. My discussion in this chapter on competitive armament, tightening alignments, and shifting power balance shows that these developments, when combined with more jingoistic domestic politics, are converging to present a more combustible foreign environment.

International Norms and Rules

Whether countries agree on the norms and rules of international conduct is another factor that determines the probability of war and peace. Charles Kegley and Gregory Raymond (1994) have studied the incidence of interstate conflict during periods of permissive international order and during periods of restrictive international order. A restrictive international order is characterized by states that respect one another's sphere of influence and that recognize principles such as upholding another country's sovereignty, noninterference in its domestic affairs, the sanctity of treaties, and limits on the use of force. Conversely, when states disregard these norms and principles, a permissive international order prevails. Not surprisingly, these researchers found that during times of restrictive order peace and stability are likely to prevail. In contrast, during times of permissive order, there tend to be more wars and disputes.

At a meeting held in March 2021 in Alaska, US secretary of state Antony Blinken criticized China, saying that "Beijing's actions threaten the rules-based order that maintains global stability" (Rising Power Initiative 2021, n.p.). His Chinese counterpart, Yang Jiechi, China's director of the Office of Central Commission for Foreign Affairs, pushed back, stating that the United States should "rectify its mistakes made over a period of time and work with China to uphold the spirit of no conflict, no confrontation, mutual respect and win–win cooperation, focus on cooperation and manage differences," while also stressing that "the two sides should respect each other's core interests and choices of political system and development path, and manage their domestic affairs well." Yang Jiechi reminded Blinken that "it is not for the U.S. alone to evaluate its democracy" ("It Is Not Up to the U.S. Alone" 2021, n.p.), suggesting that even many Americans have questioned the state of democracy in the United States.

Yang challenged Blinken to specify which and whose rules of world order that Blinken had in mind when criticizing China, stating that China would only follow "the United Nations–centered international system and the international order underpinned by international law, not what is advocated by a small number of countries of the so-called 'rules-based' international order" (Rising Power Initiative 2021, n.p.). Beijing argues that the rules being propagated by Washington are "house rules" determined by the United States and a small handful of its allies to dominate the world. Chinese Foreign Ministry spokesperson Zhao Lijian characterizes the "rules-based international order" as actually a "US rules-based international order," a hegemonic order to dominate the world with Washington's "house rules" (Zhao 2022).

Xi Jinping, China's president, has stated pointedly that "China welcomes helpful suggestions, but will not accept sanctimonious preaching" (quoted in Xi

2021, n.p.). Naturally, it would be a gross simplification to characterize this debate as one between a US preference for a "rules-based order" and a China determined to overthrow it. Rather, "the question is who gets to write the codes—and whether the United States will live up to its own" (Walt 2021, n.p.).

Relative US international decline and the rise of protectionist and anti-immigrant sentiments have undermined the so-called liberal international order led by the United States—which, according to G. John Ikenberry (2008, 28),

> is distinctive in that it has been more liberal than imperial—and so unusually accessible, legitimate, and durable. Its rules and institutions are rooted in, and thus reinforced by, the evolving global forces of democracy and capitalism. It is expansive, with a wide and widening array of participants and stakeholders. It is capable of generating tremendous economic growth and power while also signaling restraint—all of which make it hard to overturn and easy to join.

Other scholars have questioned the extent to which the relevant institutions, rules, and outcomes have been truly liberal, international, or even orderly (e.g., Mearsheimer 2019; Nye 2019; Schweller 2001; Zakaria 2020). The agriculture and service sectors, for example, were largely excluded from this order, which also included countries that could hardly be considered liberal. Moreover, various forms of state-sponsored industrial policy and government subsidies for strategic sectors (e.g., semiconductors, electric vehicles) continue to this day. This order excluded the communist countries and developing countries. Michael Beckley (2022) points out that order building has always been motivated by considerations of security competition and intended to be exclusionary rather than inclusive. As John Mearsheimer (2019) also notes, Washington's efforts to expand this order after the Cold War by promoting regime change have encountered fierce resistance abroad and pervasive disaffection at home. Finally, this liberal international order was not that orderly. Just recall various shocks initiated by Washington, including Richard Nixon's abandonment of the US commitment to exchange the dollar for gold and his visit to Beijing in 1972. Randall Schweller (2001) argues that when multilateralism and liberalism clash with realpolitik interests, the latter always prevails in US foreign policy. The thrust of this discussion is that the liberal international order is now in serious jeopardy if it ever operated in the way its proponents have claimed. It is being undermined by the very country that had supported and sponsored it previously, namely, the United States, due to the rise of nativism, backlash against globalization, and Donald Trump's brand of Make America Great Again.

Some Important Differences to Keep in Mind

Today's relationship between China and the United States is different from that between the USSR and the United States during the Cold War for two main reasons. First, the Soviet Union was never as embedded in the international economy as China is today. Second, unlike the Soviet Union, China is not trying to propagate its ideology or export its model of governance in competition with the United States. Both observations have much merit. At the same time, globalization is now encountering more intense political opposition in Western developed economies, and the United States has openly declared that it is seeking economic decoupling from China. Washington has imposed a technological embargo and investment blockade against China, and it has lobbied other countries to boycott Chinese products and technology such as banning the Chinese telecommunication company Huawei from installing its 5G internet infrastructure. Economic interdependence between China and the United States has provided a ballast to steady their stormy relationship in the past. It has become less certain whether their commercial and financial relations will continue to play this role in the future.

Of course, we are also reminded that the dense commercial and financial ties between Britain and Germany did not prevent them from going to war in 1914. Moreover, these countries were not engaged in an ideological contest at that time. Thus, the absence of ideological rivalry does not appear to have made a difference in preventing World War I. Indeed, the royal families of Russia, Germany, and Britain were literally blood relatives. Furthermore, even if one accepts the proposition that Beijing is not competing with the United States for ideological converts abroad, Western leaders have increasingly depicted current international relations as a struggle between democracies and autocracies. They have therefore been adopting rhetoric that is reminiscent of the Cold War years.

Regarding parallels between 1914 Europe and today's East Asia, Etel Solingen (2014, 45) argues that China is far more embedded in the global economy today than Germany and the other belligerent states such as Austria–Hungary, Russia, and Serbia on the eve of World War I. Others like Chong and Hall (2014, 15) also have a relatively optimistic view, arguing that "much less hangs in the balance for either [China or the United States]" today, in contrast to the Anglo–German rivalry. Most important, today's world is different from that of Europe in 1914 because of the advent of nuclear weapons. That both China and the United States have these awesome weapons of mass destruction provides a compelling reason for these countries to be ever more cautious about getting into a direct confrontation. One can, of course, point to the fact that two states with nuclear arms, namely, India and Pakistan, had fought the Kargil War in 1998–99. Still, it is sobering to ponder the possible consequences of such states going to war. Their mutual restraint provides a reason to hope that a Sino–American conflict will not occur.

Naturally, this discussion of ingredients forming a dangerous mixture abetting conflict diffusion and escalation reminiscent of World War I and the brief remarks about the Cold War era are not meant to suggest that history is destined to repeat itself. While there may be some structural similarities between then and now, there is still the important role of human agency. Chinese and American leaders remain coauthors of their future. Even though their policy choices may be constrained by their domestic and international environment, the choices are still theirs to make. This said, one is also reminded of Karl Marx's remark that "Men make their own history, but they do not make it as they please; they do not make it under self-selected circumstances, but under circumstances existing already, given and transmitted from the past" (https://www.goodreads.com/quotes/114782-men-make-their-own-history-but-they-do-not-make).

Europe in 1914 may be deficient or inappropriate for viewing and comparing with East Asia today for another reason. East Asian countries' conduct is often more subtle, nuanced, and variegated than Western analytic categories and labels suggest. Concepts such as balancing, bandwagoning, and buck-passing do not fit neatly with Asian conduct; and they may even not apply well to Western countries' own past conduct. Perhaps East Asians' behavior can be best described as "soft balancing" (e.g., Bobrow 2008; He and Feng 2008; Pape 2005; Paul 2005; 2018).

Whereas hard balancing involves direct confrontation, soft balancing entails indirect restraint; whereas hard balancing suggests active opposition, soft balancing often points to passive resistance; and whereas hard balancing relies on armament and alliance, soft balancing typically resorts to institutional integration, normative socialization, and economic statecraft. Soft balancing includes attempts to engage with and enmesh a potentially threatening state in multilateral diplomacy and international institutions and binding it to consensual norms and dense, interwoven networks of ties, including and especially economic ties. Soft balancing can simply involve denial of legitimacy to the target state by withholding support in the form of inaction, noncompliance, boycott, and other subtle forms of absenteeism, such as going through the motions without actually trying. Foot dragging, obstructionism, failure to deliver on promises, and a refusal to extend tangible support beyond verbal endorsement are other means available to the weak to impede, hinder, hamstring, complicate, and frustrate by other means (such as increasing the target's costs of implementing its policies) the strong without having to confront or challenge it directly (Bobrow 2008).

That countries must pick sides between China and the United States is alien to Asian thinking, and this view of international relations is not reflected in their actual conduct. They would rather not be forced to make such binary choices that would limit their options and constrain their behavior. As just discussed, although there are certainly signs of some countries shifting their alignment closer to the United States, there have been scant indications that they are forming formal alliances in opposition to China. Moreover, expectations that China's neighbors are or should be ramping up their armament spending to balance against Beijing have thus far received only limited support, if not being entirely contradicted. The ideas of omnidirectional balancing (Ciorciari 2009; 2010), enmeshment (Goh 2013; 2019), and engagement (Shambaugh 2004/2005) provide more accurate descriptions of their strategic conduct.

Leaders of East Asian countries do not see why they will have to sacrifice their economic relations with China, which is their biggest trade partner and, for some of them, the largest foreign investor in return for US military protection— or vice versa. They see no reason to be boxed in, having to join exclusionary blocks in opposition to either China or the United States. They understand that in some situations both Beijing and Washington can be useful or beneficial for them, while in other circumstances neither may be relevant. Binary visions such as either accommodating China or balancing against it appear to them as false binary choices. Their preferred menu includes "all of the above," "some of the above," and the choice of not having to choose. Instead of categorical choices such as appeasement versus bandwagoning or accommodation versus balancing, statecraft to these leaders appears more as a matter of gradations such as moving closer to or distancing further away from Beijing or Washington, always keeping the speed, amount, and even the possibility of reversing course as options. Even when attempting to balance against another country, their policy repertoire contains more than just the alternatives of armament and alliances offered by neorealism. Their actual conduct can reflect a rich mixture of shirking, delaying, evading, equivocating, hedging, dodging, hiding, and even binding.

Taiwan and Other Fuses

Having surveyed the macro conditions characterizing East Asia today, I now turn to a discussion of fuses that can ignite a Sino–American conflict. We learn from a large body of international relations research that territorial contests or border disputes are the most common reasons for countries to quarrel and go to war (Senese and Vasquez 2008; Vasquez 1993; 2009b; Vasquez and Henehan

2011). The good news is that being separated by the Pacific Ocean, China and the United States do not have any conflict over disputed land. In other words, contested territory will not be a fuse for a Sino-American conflict.

This said, the bad news is that the United States has allies that have territorial disputes with China—such as Japan and China in their dispute over the Senkaku/Diaoyutai islands, the Philippines and China in their dispute over the Spratly islands, and, of course, Taiwan and China in their dispute over the former's political status. Being a formal or informal ally of one of these contestants can engulf the United States in a conflict with China. Washington has shifted its official policy on whether it has an obligation to intervene on behalf of its protégés in these cases, and in recent years it has committed itself more firmly to coming to their defense should there be a military contingency involving them. At the same time, Beijing has also hardened its positions. It has always indicated that Taiwan's status is at the top of its core interests but has more recently widened the definition of its core interests to include its sovereignty claims in the South China Sea. Thus, to borrow an analogy from Nikita Khrushchev's metaphor in his communication to John F. Kennedy during the Cuban Missile Crisis, the two contending sides have been pulling at the opposite ends of a rope, making a knot tighter and thus more difficult to untie.

Of all possible fuses that may spark a Sino-American confrontation, Taiwan is the most likely one. Washington's recent conduct is inching closer to Beijing's red line. It also belies earlier formal and informal commitments that Washington has made to Beijing. Yet domestic politics seems to be incentivizing politicians from both political parties in the United States to outbid each other in expressing their support for Taiwan even at the risk of war with China. This remark suggests that Taiwan has become a more dangerous point of contention *compared* to any time since Sino-American rapprochement in 1972 when Nixon visited Beijing. It is certainly the most likely fuse to set off a Sino-American confrontation.

Taiwan has always been a source of friction in Sino-American relations. Several recent developments, however, have made this island a more likely fuse for a conflict between these countries (Chan 2021c; 2024b). The most important of these developments is that the relationship between Beijing and Washington has deteriorated seriously. When their relations were friendlier, both sides were willing to subordinate the Taiwan issue to other higher priorities or at least to set it aside for the time being. As already remarked, Washington indicated publicly its intention to economically "decouple" from China, thereby removing an important factor that has heretofore stabilized its relations with Beijing. When Sino-American relations turned negative, both began often to use the Taiwan issue to challenge or irritate the other party. This remark suggests that to some extent Taiwan's importance tends to be derivative of the state of the relationship between China and the United States and that they can ratchet up or down tension over their disagreement concerning this island's status depending on their overall relationship. This tendency is certainly more evident in Washington's policies toward China than Beijing's policies toward the United States.

As already remarked on several occasions, Sino–American competition has intensified recently. The United States has asserted its freedom of passage in the South China Sea, claimed by Beijing to be under its sovereignty; it has placed individual Chinese officials on its sanction list for violating human rights in China; and it has banned the transfer of sensitive technology to China and prohibited investments by American companies in China in areas such as artificial intelligence, semiconductors, and quantum computing. Beijing has retaliated by restricting its export of certain strategic material such as gallium and germanium, which are critical to the manufacturing of semiconductors. It has also raised tariffs on US goods after Washington imposed tariffs on Chinese goods during the Trump administration. Both sides have openly identified the other party as a competitor and a security threat—indeed, as the only other country in the world that is in its view capable of seriously challenging its international position. Although on prior occasions China had backed down or sought compromises when caught in a standoff with the United States—such as in episodes involving the US EP-3 spy plane forced to land on China's Hainan Island, US bombing of China's embassy in Belgrade, and Washington's issuance of a visa for Taiwan's president Lee Tenghui to visit his alma mater, Cornell University—it is becoming more assertive and less inclined to yield to US pressure.

Other developments that have made Taiwan a more dangerous fuse pertain to developments on the two sides of the Taiwan Strait. Public opinion in Taiwan has increasingly moved further away from a Chinese identity to a Taiwanese identity, and the pro-independence Democratic Progressive Party has established a larger electoral base compared to the Kuomintang or the Nationalist Party, which has traditionally been more inclined to accept the principle of One China—albeit in its eyes this term refers to the Republic of China. Beijing's efforts to persuade the people of Taiwan to accept reunification by "soft" means have largely failed. Even though Taiwan is highly dependent on trade with and investment in mainland China, this intense and asymmetric economic relationship has not produced a greater acceptance or receptivity on the part of Taiwan's populace with respect to Beijing's political goal of national reunification.

Another concomitant development concerns the military balance across the Taiwan Strait, which has increasingly shifted in Beijing's favor. Even though as recently as 30 years ago Beijing could not do anything about Bill Clinton's order for two US carrier groups to transit the Taiwan Strait in 1995, China has now acquired long-range missiles that can deny US access right up to the Chinese coast. Although it is still debatable whether China can launch a successful amphibious invasion of Taiwan, Beijing is acquiring more capabilities over time, such as to impose a blockade of the island. Chinese leaders have also professed an impatience to settle Taiwan's status, suggesting that this issue cannot be left unresolved and passed from generation to generation. Having failed in its "softer" approach, Beijing may be considering a "harder" one. Thus, in addition to deteriorating relations with Washington and the adverse trend in Taiwan's public opinion from Beijing's perspective, changes in the military balance across the Taiwan Strait have also made a military clash more likely than before.

This said, I have also argued elsewhere that prevailing discourse may have overstated the prospect of US military intervention on Taiwan's behalf. To be sure, the danger of conflict is real, but it should also not be exaggerated (Kastner 2022). Space does not permit an extended discussion of this topic here; suffice it to say that several considerations, including past US actions and inaction (since the Korean War) in situations that might put it in a direct conflict with Russia/the USSR or China, indicate that Washington has acted prudently, with the Russo–Ukrainian War offering one powerful example. In his careful analysis of the Johnson administration's policymaking on the Vietnam War in 1965, Yuen Foong Khong (1992) offers a compelling argument that top US officials consistently chose policy options that they knew would be less effective in coercing Hanoi in favor of other less escalatory alternatives because they wanted to avoid the danger of Chinese military intervention—even though they were told by their intelligence agencies that, short of a US invasion of North Vietnam, this intervention would be unlikely. He writes that of all the historical lessons learned by the top officials in the Johnson administration, "the need to avoid drawing China into the [Vietnam] war, seems to have been most influential" (Khong 1992, 146).

When these words were being written, news media were reporting that Joe Biden had told Benjamin Netanyahu that the United States would not participate in any Israeli retaliation against Iran in the wake of Tehran's drone and missile attack on Israel on April 13, 2024. China is not Iran, and it will be a more formidable adversary than even Russia, thus suggesting that Washington would act even more cautiously in a situation involving Taiwan that can put it on a direct collision course with Beijing. Naturally, I cannot assert categorically that the possibility of US intervention in this case does not exist.

China has been traditionally a land power, featuring a large infantry. The United States has been primarily a maritime power that has relied on its navy to project influence abroad. Some observers (e.g., Ross 1999) see this situation as reassuring because they expect it to facilitate mutual accommodation. However, Beijing has invested heavily in its navy in recent years, and it is thus developing into a hybrid power—another concerning sign for traditional geopolitical and geostrategic writers because China straddles the world's so-called heartland and rimland. For those who recall the history of the Anglo–German naval race before World War I (Kennedy 1980; Murray 2010), Beijing's effort to develop a blue-water navy would also be concerning. In the meantime, the Obama administration declared its "pivot to Asia," reallocating US military assets to that region and increasing its defense cooperation with allies such as Australia, Japan, South Korea, and the Philippines. The Biden administration also announced in July 2023 the largest arms sales to Taiwan, with a potential value of US$440 million (Callahan 2023).

Parenthetically, the most devastating conflicts in the past, including the two world wars, were titanic struggles between a maritime power and a continental power. These were intense fights pitting a global naval power (a whale) against a regional powerhouse with a large army (an elephant) (Levy and Thompson 2006; 2010).

I have remarked earlier about the strategic and symbolic relevance of Belgium and the Balkans for leaders of major European states on the eve of World War I. Ukraine and Taiwan have recently acquired the same importance (Chan and Hu 2025). Ukraine is located right on the traditional path to invade Russia from its west. It provides a defense buffer for Russia, which also sees this country as being within its traditional sphere of influence. NATO's eastward expansion had become intolerable to Moscow. Conversely, Halford Mackinder (1904; 1919; 1943) had claimed that whoever controls eastern Europe would command Eurasia's heartland and that whoever controls Eurasia's heartland would command the "World Island" (meaning the Eurasian landmass plus Africa) and, ipso facto, the entire world. From the West's perspective, Russia's control of Ukraine would also be dangerous because it would enable Moscow to project its influence and expand its ambitions westward. Thus, the perceived stakes of this conflict are high for both sides.

Taiwan is also of great importance to China. Besides its symbol as the last holdout against China's goal of national reunification, it is of vital strategic importance to Beijing. Under Chinese control, this island provides a barrier or shield against foreign attack. But in hostile hands, it can be a staging area for launching an attack on China (Wachman 2007). In General Douglas MacArthur's words, Taiwan is an "unsinkable aircraft carrier." Its importance to China is no less than that of Cuba for the United States. In fact, strategically Taiwan is far more important to China than Cuba is to the United States because Cuba cannot present a threat to block US access to the Pacific and Atlantic Oceans. In contrast, Taiwan is the linchpin in the so-called first island chain erected by the United States to contain China's maritime access. This first island chain runs from Japan, through the Ryukyus, then Taiwan, to the South

China Sea and the Philippines. China's navy and merchant fleet—including its submarines—must pass narrow transit straits and shallow channels before they can reach the open sea. They are therefore vulnerable to interdiction by hostile forces. The strategic importance of Taiwan is even greater (for Beijing) than that of Guam (for Washington), which serves as the pivot for the second island chain running from the Aleutian Islands to Papua New Guinea and Australia. In short, Taiwan represents the key to China's front door (just as Belgium in British, French, and German eyes in 1914), occupying a strategic location that can disrupt China's north–south communication and traffic. It can also serve as a launching pad for attacking China's economic and demographic center along its eastern coast, its soft underbelly. Why does the United States care about Taiwan? Largely for the same symbolic and strategic reasons for China—except, in this case, to deny the gains that Beijing seeks.

In the joint communiqué between the United States and China released on February 27, 1972, "The United States acknowledges that all Chinese on either side of the Taiwan Strait maintain there is but one China and that Taiwan is a part of China. The United States Government does not challenge that position. It reaffirms its interest in a peaceful settlement of the Taiwan question by the Chinese themselves. With this prospect in mind, it affirms the ultimate objective of the withdrawal of all US forces and military installations from Taiwan" (https://digitalarchive.wilsoncenter.org/document/joint-communique-between-united-states-and-china).

Prior to establishing diplomatic relations, the two countries issued another joint communiqué on December 15, 1978, in which the United States declares that "the United States of America recognizes the Government of the People's Republic of China as the sole legal Government of China. Within this context, the people of the United States will maintain cultural, commercial, and other unofficial relations with the people of Taiwan" (https://www.ait.org.tw/u-s-prc-joint-communique-1979/). It goes on to say that the "Government of the United States of America acknowledges the Chinese position that there is but one China and Taiwan is part of China."

Although these communiqués lack the binding force of a treaty, they nevertheless announce a country's intentions and pledges. The wording of these communiqués was deliberately constructed to leave some legal wriggle room (especially the word *acknowledges* as used here can have multiple meanings), but the basic ideas being expressed are quite clear. Washington's recent actions and statements contradict the spirit, if not the letter, of these declarations, thus compromising its reputation to abide by its words. They also contradict people's common-sense interpretation of these documents. As former US secretary of state Henry Kissinger put it, "[for] us to go to war with a recognized country where we have an ambassador over a part of what we would recognize as their country would be preposterous" (quoted in Tyler 1999, 225).

Several politicians have sounded the refrain, "Ukraine today, Taiwan tomorrow." In his recent (April 2024) visit to the White House, Japan's prime minister Fumio Kishida said something similar: "Ukraine today may be East Asia tomorrow" (White House 2024). Of course, there are differences between the two cases (Chan 2022). Ukraine has several friendly neighbors sharing a land border with it, facilitating the supply of assistance necessary for its war effort. In contrast, it is much more difficult to provide this supply to Taiwan, which is an island. At the first sign of danger, freight insurance for ships traveling to Taiwan will skyrocket, and many maritime companies will simply cease operations with Taiwan as their destination.

Most countries see the Taiwan issue as a matter of Chinese domestic affairs and would not therefore consider China's use of force in this case as international aggression. In other words, they would consider China's possible resort to force against Taiwan as a special case that is not generalizable to China's dealings with internationally recognized, sovereign countries (Kang 2007). Here is then another example pertaining to the question about states' reputation. Whereas the way in which the United States frames the Taiwan case suggests that Chinese conduct toward Taiwan discloses its general disposition to commit aggression and its inherent revisionist character, other countries are likely to disagree because they do not believe that Beijing's actions in this case can be used to infer how it will act in other situations.

To the extent that an overwhelming majority of countries in the world—including the United States itself—recognize the ruling authority in Beijing as the sole, legitimate government of China and Taiwan as part of China, it would be a hard sell for Washington to persuade others to join it in a military contingency involving Taiwan. Contrary to the US framing of the matter, most other countries would see US support for Taiwan as foreign intervention in favor of a secessionist movement, something that they would generally disapprove of and that the United States itself had opposed in its civil war, which was settled by bullets rather than ballots. Most recently, Washington has opposed the secession of Crimea and Donetsk and Luhansk in the Donbas region from Ukraine, condemning them as illegal acts even though it had previously recognized the independence of separatist movements in the former Yugoslavia.

In short, Washington's framing of the Taiwan matter would not attract much international traction. Most of the world would see it as a transparent cover for the United States to check China's rise—even though this pitch and the rhetoric of China presenting a threat to a rules-based international order may serve domestic political purposes and persuade the American people that vital national interests are at stake in confronting China. Yet, harsh US rhetoric and belligerent action can backfire around the world, thus compromising US credibility and undermining its moral leadership as suggested by the idea of the backlash effect.

The Risks of Chain-Ganging

Taiwan is not a formal ally of the United States, but as Joe Biden has stated publicly on four recent occasions, the United States will intervene on its behalf in a war. How seriously should one take his words is not something that can be decided easily, although clearly the prospect of US intervention has increased since his statements. Officials in Biden's own administration tried to "walk back" his statements each time, claiming that there has not been any change in US policy toward Taiwan. However, "Simply stating that U.S. policy has not shifted, as the White House has done following Biden's remarks [indicating that the United States would come to Taiwan's aid should it be attacked], rings hollow to Beijing and to any honest observer of U.S. policy over the past six years" (Blanchette and Hass 2023, 113). While it may suit Washington to maintain the current situation of Taiwan's de facto independence for as long as possible, why should Beijing accept the perpetuation of Taiwan's separation—especially if it perceives the chances of peaceful reunification to have greatly diminished?

Importantly, in this case, Washington as the preponderant partner in the security relationship with Taipei has control over the extent and circumstances of its possible involvement. As the much weaker junior partner, Taipei does not have nearly as much influence to shape this security relationship. This is another way of saying that the risk of Taipei trapping Washington in an unwanted conflict is low. If the United States gets involved and regrets this involvement subsequently, it would be due to self-entrapment.

If anything, it appears that Taipei may have more to worry about being trapped by the United States in an escalating crisis in which it would be the most direct and obvious casualty. The majority public opinion in Taiwan is to maintain the status quo for an indefinite future. Taiwan's economy is dependent on trading with China, and it clearly realizes that should there be a war, it would suffer the greatest damage. Taipei is also not so dense to overlook the fact that it has been abandoned by Washington once before when the United States switched its diplomatic recognition to Beijing and unilaterally and abruptly abrogated its defense treaty with Taipei. Stated bluntly, Taipei realizes that it is a pawn in the larger game of Sino–American competition. It is dispensable to the United States, which can always go home, whereas, like Ukraine, Taiwan would be stuck with its larger neighbor. Therefore, to repeat, the danger of entrapment is likely to operate in the opposite way than that which is typically thought of by Americans.

The same applies to other US allies in East Asia, specifically Japan and South Korea. The United States has significant military assets in these two countries, and in a contingency involving Taiwan it would want to use these assets. In other words, US personnel and bases on Japanese and South Korean soil could become involved in a contingency involving Taiwan, thereby getting Tokyo and Seoul into a possible unwanted conflict with China. Like Taiwan, these two East Asian countries are located closer to China and may be more vulnerable to Chinese retaliation. Indeed, it would appear that before China would attack the United States directly to cause a conflict to spiral out of control, an attack on Japanese and South Korean targets could be a more prudent intermediate step in the ladder of escalation. Here again, the dynamics of conflict contagion is likely to be one of US allies in East Asia becoming involved involuntarily in a conflict rather than the United States becoming so as a result of these allies' actions.

There is another even greater danger of conflict contagion. An abiding principle of Henry Kissinger's diplomacy is to keep Russia and China separate. In recent days, however, US policies have driven these countries closer together. Furthermore, having backed out of the Iran nuclear deal and having clearly singled out Tehran as its main nemesis in the Middle East, Washington has now become more reliant on Beijing and Moscow to exercise a restraining influence on Tehran such as in the ongoing (in April 2024) saga that threatens to widen Israel's war against Hamas to involve Iran and its proxies such as the Houthis in Yemen and Hezbollah in Lebanon.

To compound the problem, US policies have often alienated and even alarmed its allies, especially during the Trump administration. Donald Trump belittled and insulted US allies and pulled out of international accords and organizations such as the Iran nuclear deal, the Paris Climate Accord, the Trans-Pacific Partnership, and the World Health Organization. He also insisted on renegotiating the North American Free Trade Agreement to gain more favorable terms for the United States—only to raise tariffs against Mexico and Canada in the early days of his second presidential term by 25% on the grounds that these countries were not doing enough to interdict to the illegal inflow of immigrants and fentanyl into the United States. While on the campaign trail in February 2024, he was even quoted as saying that if a NATO ally did not pay enough for its own defense, his administration would not protect it and would instead "encourage [Russia] to do whatever the hell they want" (https://www.youtube.com/watch?v=HloWfFfXj7I). Although less bombastic than Trump and openly professing an interest to work with US allies, the Biden administration has also caused concerns in friendly countries. It ignored the Europeans' pleas for a more measured US withdrawal from Afghanistan, and it opposed Japanese ownership of U.S. Steel on national security grounds.

The preceding remarks suggest that ongoing US conflicts with Russia, China, and Iran are interrelated. There is accordingly an increasing risk that what is going on in Ukraine and Gaza can affect Taiwan and vice versa. The three chronic hot spots may become nested so that they can have a reciprocal influence on each other. Public media in the United States have indicated such a connection, reporting that Washington is pressuring Beijing to stop supplying war-related material to assist Russia in its war in Ukraine and urging it to restrain Iran from further escalating its armed conflict with Israel. This was happening at the same time that the US Senate was being asked to fund military assistance to Ukraine, Israel, and Taiwan. Yet there appears to be little recognition of the irony of this situation, asking Beijing to cease providing aid to Moscow while announcing Washington's largest sale of weapons to Taipei in recent history. Even so, Washington also wants Beijing to restrain Pyongyang when Seoul is becoming more closely tied to the trilateral defense arrangement involving Washington and Tokyo as well. In short, there is now a growing prospect that hot spots in different parts of the world are becoming connected, thus raising the danger of conflict contagion on a more global scale.

The logic of my perspective argues that conflicts in different parts of the world have become increasingly linked. If this logic is correct, it implies that China's response to increasing US support for Taiwan does not have to be limited to the Taiwan Strait. It can, for example, push back by increasing its support for Pyongyang or relaxing its restraint on North Korea's bellicosity in part to deter Seoul from becoming more actively involved in a contingency involving Taiwan and in part to remind Washington that it still needs Beijing's help to resolve inter-Korean issues. Similarly, Washington may prefer not to further inflame the situation across the Taiwan Strait but rather push other buttons to get under Beijing's skin, in a manner of speaking. It can, for example, choose to back the Philippines more strongly in Manila's dispute with Beijing in the South China Sea. Likewise, Beijing can push back against stronger US support for Taipei by increasing its own support for Moscow and Tehran. Such reciprocation, however, is a recipe for causing two opposing camps to become tighter and thus would create more conducive conditions for chain-ganging to occur. This contagion would now occur on a larger global scale, connecting conflicts in three different regions.

Thus, as remarked earlier, the number, density, and proximity of rivalry fields are important. How tightly are the pertinent rivalries coupled? As I have just suggested, conflict theaters in different parts of the world are now interrelated pieces on a global chessboard. There is nothing to prevent all the parties concerned from "jumping" from one arena to another to respond to one another's policy moves. At the same time, states appear increasingly disposed to resort to war by proxies in order to limit the risk of their direct involvement in a conflict. The war in Ukraine presents a classic case of Western efforts to tie down Russia's forces, deplete its resources, and exhaust its energy without getting directly into a fight with Moscow. Iran has also used its associates in the Middle East, such as the Houthis and Hezbollah, as its surrogates. There is, of course, nothing unusual or novel about these practices. After all, the United States had supported the mujahideen in Afghanistan to resist the Soviet invasion—although, to Washington's regret, these same fighters morphed later into the Taliban. The Vietnam War, of course, served the same purpose for Beijing and Moscow to distract, harass, and exhaust the United States without getting into a direct fight with Washington.

Backlash Effects of Imperial Overstretch

Remarks made in concluding the last section pertain directly to the risk of taking on more responsibilities and commitments abroad than one's resources—including time and attention—can afford. As already mentioned, Paul Kennedy (1987) has warned about this danger of imperial overstretch. Simply put, there are increasing signs that Washington's available resources cannot support all its foreign missions—the tendency for the United States to see its interests engaged everywhere in the world. The time has come for this "hyperactive" power to set priorities and nurse its resources. It cannot be everywhere all the time. A nightmare scenario for Washington is when it has to cope simultaneously with conflicts in East Asia, eastern Europe, and the Middle East.

This discussion also recalls David Treisman's (2004) analysis of the self-defeating policies of Spain's Philip III and Philip IV. By taking on multiple opponents, sometimes at the same time, these monarchs exhausted their country financially and militarily. This exhaustion in turn invited additional internal and external challengers to their rule, setting Spain on a course of inexorable decline. Their mistake was fundamentally one of not being able to set priorities, matching ends with means, and taking a long-term view. In their pursuit of a reputation for resolve and firmness, they actually brought about the opposite result from that which they had hoped for.

Interstate conflicts are as much about a contest of the pertinent parties' resolve as they are about a match of their relative capabilities. As stated earlier, the United States is still the world's predominant military power that no other country, including China, can come close to matching. But as we all know, stronger capabilities do not necessarily mean victory in war—as attested by the outcome of wars in Afghanistan, Vietnam, and Korea. How conflicts turn out also depends on the contestants' policy capacity to extract, mobilize, and deploy resources from its economy and society and on their respective willingness to endure hardship and suffer privation. In other words, interstate conflicts are also about the disputants' stakes in them, their dedication to their cause, and their stamina and perseverance.

When seen from this perspective, Moscow has undoubtedly more at stake in Ukraine and Beijing more at stake in Taiwan than Washington—just like the United States had a greater stake in the outcome of the 1962 Cuban Missile Crisis as this island in the Caribbean is much closer to the United States than the USSR. Similarly, Ukraine and Taiwan are practically on Russia's and China's doorstep, respectively. Geographic proximity is a good indicator of a state's stake in a fight and its resolve to stand its ground. This matters in protracted conflicts when the pertinent question is not who can apply more coercive pressure on whom to cause it to "say uncle" but more about who is likely to become impatient, distracted, and discouraged. Who is likely to outwait whom in these contests? The mistake made by the United States in the Vietnam War was that Washington thought Hanoi had a pain threshold and that, by inflicting heavy damages on North Vietnam by its air campaign, the United States could pressure it to give up its cause. The United States underestimated North Vietnam's tolerance for pain, and it overestimated its own staying power.

Nothing Washington can say or do will convince China that it cares more about Taiwan than Beijing does. Similarly, Moscow clearly has a larger stake in Ukraine's status than Washington does. It seems obvious that Moscow's game plan is to wait for the West to lose its interest in Ukraine. We are already seeing evidence that domestic politics is affecting US funding to support Kyiv. There already is much talk about disappointments over the results of Kyiv's much publicized counter-offensive in summer 2023 and about the eventuality of it having to negotiate with Moscow to end the current conflict without having recovered all its lost territory (e.g., Charap 2023; Haass and Kupchan 2023).

We have seen such cycles before, as shown by enthusiasm and support when the United States initially got involved in a foreign war (the rally around the flag syndrome), only to be followed in relatively short order by disappointment and impatience when the costs of war began to mount. When body bags start to come home, American people's support for war wanes. The longer a war lasts, the louder the voices demanding withdrawal. I mentioned earlier that Beijing and Moscow have drawn lessons from US attacks on Iraq, Serbia, and Libya. Another lesson is Somalia, as shown dramatically in the movie *Blackhawk Down*, and Washington's hasty withdrawal from Lebanon after the attack on US marine barracks by a suicide bomber in 1983, killing 231 of its soldiers.

I indicated earlier my guess that in the end the United States will eschew military intervention on Taiwan's behalf. Of course, Washington can be expected to provide material support for Taipei, but as the Biden administration had made clear before Russia invaded Ukraine, US boots on the ground would be a different matter. Washington has supposedly learned the lesson of never fighting another land war on the Asian mainland after Korea and Vietnam. But such historical memories can be forgotten quickly. In this context, my earlier discussion about the time-inconsistency problem is important to remember. It is difficult to limit one's support for an ally once a war has started. Wars often entail a decision of "all in" or "all out." It is also easier to start a war than to end it. Once in a war, the opposing party also acquires a vote in deciding how it will evolve and end. The same logic used to describe the increasingly interlinked nature of conflicts in different parts of the world also applies here. A war involving Taiwan may not be limited to a maritime conflict. Beijing has the choice of "jumping" and shifting the conflict arena to include, for example, the Korean peninsula. Again, such contests can involve a long game, a test of the respective parties' stamina and commitment to their cause. Beijing and Taipei do not need to be reminded of what happened in Afghanistan and Vietnam.

Graham Allison (2020, 34) quotes a *New York Times* report: "In 18 of the last 18 Pentagon war games involving China in the Taiwan Strait, the U.S. lost." One assumes that Beijing possesses similar knowledge. If such war games are predictive, one cannot help but wonder about the recent bellicose rhetoric emanating from Washington—except for hubris, which has led to self-injurious policies, as discussed earlier. Allison (2020, 38) quotes George Kennan saying, "there is more respect to be won . . . by a resolute and courageous liquidation of unsound positions than by the most stubborn pursuit of extravagant or uncompromising objectives." He goes on to remark, "If the balance of military power in a conventional war over Taiwan . . . has shifted decisively in China's . . . favor, current U.S. commitments are not sustainable. The gap between those commitments and the Unites States' actual military capabilities is a classic case of overstretch" (Allison 2020, 39).

It is also appropriate to ask what "winning" means in the case of Taiwan. The Falklands/Malvinas comes to mind as a possible parallel. These islands are located much closer to Argentina than Britain. The Kelpers (residents of these islands) depend on Buenos Aires for their many needs, just as Taiwan's economy is heavily dependent on the mainland, as indicated earlier. After Britain's military campaign retook these barren, wind-swept islands from Argentina, it was "stuck" with them, without any strategic or economic value to London. It is now saddled with sustaining and defending them—even though prior to the 1982 war it had tried various formulas to rid itself of this burdensome responsibility. How long will London be willing to continue its current policy? Time and location favor Buenos Aires.

When asked at a public forum whether he expected the United States to intervene militarily in defense of Taiwan, Singapore's former prime minister Lee Kuan Yew answered "no." His response was quick and short, and his reasoning was simple. The United States may prevail the first time. But what about the next time, the time after that, and then an even later one (https://www.youtube.com/watch?v=q_gr3dtBaic)? China is more dedicated to its cause, and it will be more able to play the long game, while the United States is more likely to become impatient, distracted, or disillusioned. This conflict is fundamentally lopsided in terms of each party's willingness to bear the necessary costs commensurate with their respective stakes. Lee's reasoning is obviously that if officials in Washington think in the long term and are not susceptible to short-term domestic political considerations, they would refrain from staking the US reputation on a dubious proposition and get their country into yet another foreign morass due to self-inflicted injury as in Vietnam, Iraq, and Afghanistan. Moreover, taking on China entails an entirely different magnitude of challenge compared to US adversaries in these other cases of military involvement.

Mitigating Steps to Avoid or Defuse Conflict

What can be done to lower the danger of a possible conflict and its potential for escalation? It would be easy to say that we should work to reduce or remove one or more of the ingredients for the dangerous brew mentioned above. The problem, however, is that these phenomena not only reflect and contribute to the current level of tension, but some are also the effects of deeper sources of antagonism and mistrust. Recent events have seriously undermined mutual trust between Washington and Beijing, and it will take a long time to restore this trust (Chan 2017a).

Trust can promote cooperation, but cooperation does not necessarily entail trust. As Robert Axelrod (1984, 174) has remarked, "there is no need to assume trust between the players: the use of reciprocity can be enough to make defection unproductive." There is currently a breakdown in mutual expectations of reciprocity—and not necessarily because of misperceptions. Rather, I tend to believe that leaders in Beijing and Washington understand each other quite well. As Iain Johnston (2011, 28) has stated, "there is evidence that the very top levels of both sides actually have a better understanding of each other's interests and red lines than is implied in public debates." That they know each other's bottom line well has paradoxically inclined them to often undertake brinksmanship, walking right up to the red line before pulling back. This is concerning because accidents can happen so that one of the "close encounters" can precipitate an unwanted crisis.

Recurrent confrontations, arms racing, and alliance ties do not happen suddenly out of the blue. They have a history and are embedded in a web of social, political, and historical contexts. This also means that they are not easily reversed in view of the influence of domestic political incentives, organizational inertia, bureaucratic interests, and politicians' own rhetoric and entrenched views. These various factors often tend to reinforce one another, and once they start to gain momentum, it becomes increasingly difficult to control or reverse them. Politicians are, in my view, more likely to become boxed in by their domestic politics rather than international relations.

The default is to continue the existing policies or practices. To change them requires political courage, conviction, and capital. Moreover, the leaders on both sides of a dispute can conclude that they have incompatible interests. It is not unreasonable for Chinese leaders to see the United States as being determined to thwart its rise and contain its influence. From Beijing's perspective, Washington's objective is to prevent China's dominance of its home region. Probably many in Washington would acknowledge this intention in a moment of candor. If so, the root cause of the ongoing tension pertains to whether China is entitled to a sphere of influence in its home region just as the United States has insisted in the Western Hemisphere.

Analysts such as John Mearsheimer (2006) have stated clearly that after establishing its own regional hegemony, a longstanding goal of Washington's grand strategy is to prevent the emergence of another regional hegemon, whether it be in Europe, the Middle East, or East Asia. This is a rather pessimistic view of the unfolding situation, suggesting that unless there is a fundamental change in the two sides' perceptions of their basic interests and relative power, they may well be on a collision course. Mitigation of the various elements contributing to the dangerous mixture elevating the danger of war can ameliorate the symptoms of their antagonism but not really address the basic cause.

Perhaps the easiest thing to do but the hardest to resist is tuning down the harsh rhetoric that is mostly intended for these countries' respective domestic publics. Such rhetoric demonizing the other side inflames public opinion, and it also tends to trap officials by their own words by making it difficult to retract their policy positions both politically and psychologically. This was one of the reasons why it was so difficult for Washington to extricate itself from the Vietnam morass because its officials and politicians had said loudly and repeatedly that US credibility and resolve were at stake in that conflict. Tuning down harsh rhetoric condemning or criticizing the other side cannot obviously resolve differences in the two countries' basic interests. But it does help to avoid the danger of creating an echo chamber, whereby the hostilities of each side's hardliners feed on each other, making these hardliners de facto partners in escalating and sustaining bilateral tension. Thus, prior to World War II domestic discourse in the United States with racist overtones reverberated across the Pacific, lending greater credibility and legitimacy to Japan's hardliners who saw Washington as determined to thwart their country's rise (Ward 2017). It is, of course, sometimes difficult to de-escalate one's rhetoric in the heat of domestic partisan battles when the political opposition tries to outbid the incumbent officials in demonizing foreign adversaries and to condemn these officials for being deficient in standing up to these adversaries.

Conclusion

Fuses are precipitants that can ignite a large conflagration, setting off a process of conflict contagion and escalation. These triggers can come in a variety of ways, and they can occur unexpectedly. They are therefore difficult to predict regarding their specific form, location, and timing. We can, however, point to the world's recurrent hot spots in the past such as the Arab–Israeli conflicts; wars between India and Pakistan, both of which are nuclear states; crises on the Korean peninsula; tension across the Taiwan Strait; sovereignty disputes in the South China Sea; the unsettled boundary between India and China; and instabilities involving Russia and its former constituent republics and erstwhile allies in eastern and central Europe. These areas represent the equivalent of fault lines for earthquakes. They have experienced repeated skirmishes and wars, and some are suffering from ongoing armed conflict such as the current war between Ukraine and Russia and that between Israel and Hamas in Gaza with the possibility of contagion to involve Hezbollah in Lebanon and its patron, Iran. The belligerents in these conflicts have their respective foreign supporters, and these outside parties are already indirectly involved and may further increase their involvement (such as US support for Israel and Ukraine, and Iran's support for Hamas and Hezbollah).

History shows that a disproportionately large number of militarized disputes and wars have originated from a small number of enduring rivals such as those involved on the list of "usual suspects" just mentioned. Although we obviously cannot rule out the possibility that interstate disputes can occur elsewhere to engage major states, the most likely places to start looking for fuses that might produce large, intense interstate conflagrations are naturally the chronic hot spots that the world has experienced in the recent past, especially those where major states—the United States, China, and Russia—are likely to become directly involved. This latter consideration in turn reduces further the number of likely cases of local conflicts that can serve as fuses to trigger a dangerous armed confrontation that threatens regional and even global peace and stability.

Because the Biden administration communicated even before the onset of the Russo–Ukrainian War that direct US military intervention is off the table, and because Biden himself has said publicly and repeatedly that the United States will intervene militarily should Taiwan come under attack, the evolving situation concerning that island's status comes to the top of the list of potential fuses endangering peace and stability. Short of a US attack on North Korea's nuclear and missile facilities, the situation on the Korean peninsula does not appear as dire. Washington had considered this option, but the window for taking action has probably closed, in part due to Pyongyang having already acquired the weapons technology necessary to undertake a forceful retaliation at least against South Korea and Japan. It also appears that North Korea is not facing an imminent danger of domestic disorder or collapse, which will have a much larger adverse impact on China and does not necessarily impinge US interests unless Seoul tries to exploit this opportunity by taking actions that endanger Beijing's stake in maintaining a buffer between its border and the presence of US military.

Relations between Beijing and Taipei have suffered a serious setback since the election of Tsai In-wen, representing the pro-independence Democratic Progressive Party. That relations between Beijing and Washington also deteriorated significantly during the Barack Obama administration, worsened further during the Donald Trump administration, and continued to decline during the Joe Biden administration points to the potential for these two countries becoming involved in a direct confrontation in a contingency involving Taiwan. In addition to this consideration of these countries' external relations, their respective domestic situations are also concerning.

Xi Jinping has consolidated unprecedented domestic power since the days of Mao Zedong and in a country where the absence of institutional safeguards to check mistakes by an omnipotent leader has led previously to national disasters such as the Great Leap Forward movement and the Cultural Revolution. There are also incipient signs indicating that the Chinese economy may be slowing, with youth unemployment rising to a politically unacceptable level and the real estate market facing severe financial challenges. Current and looming economic problems may incline the government to divert adverse public opinion by turning to a more nationalist and militant foreign policy posture, with Taiwan as the most obvious and likely target of this hostility. Beijing has already indicated that its patience is wearing thin. Having waited for 75 years and having also seen that its "soft" approach to entice Taiwan to rejoin the motherland has made little progress, it has said that the Taiwan issue cannot be deferred without a resolution to future generations forever.

In the meantime, public opinion in Taiwan has shifted increasingly in favor of supporting the island's eventual independence, although importantly, the majority prefers to continue the current situation because it worries about Beijing's military response should Taipei declare de jure independence. Both major political parties, the Kuomintang and the Democratic Progressive Party, appear to be stymied in the face of this public opinion. Neither can afford to appear compromising with Beijing to endanger their electoral prospects, nor can they afford to extricate the island from its heavy asymmetric economic dependency on China. In the face of growing Chinese military capabilities, US support is becoming even more indispensable to maintain the status quo across the Taiwan Strait.

As for the United States, there is abundant evidence pointing to its political dysfunctions. Yet despite all the partisan bickering, there is a strong consensus to confront the "China threat," a policy position that is also strongly supported by public opinion. Taiwan's status does not impinge on core US security interests as it does for China. As in the case of the Vietnam War, public rhetoric by leading politicians and officials has engaged US reputation and credibility in this dispute, thereby elevating Taiwan's status as a national interest because Washington has said so. What would otherwise be a sideshow has now become a central issue of contention between China and the United States, as Washington is perceived by Beijing to have broken its prior commitments and to be inching toward crossing China's red line. As in Taiwan, current public opinion and official rhetoric have increasingly boxed in the United States, constraining its policy space. The American public's general sense of malaise and disaffection incline politicians and officials to malign and even vilify foreign competitors, and this demonization can create its own reality and trap decision makers in their own rhetoric.

Thus, Taiwan appears to be the single most dangerous fuse that can bring about a confrontation between the world's two most powerful countries. As emphasized earlier, however, fuses can only create an explosion if the conditions that cause a tinderbox are already present. Matches do not easily ignite a large blaze in the absence of preexisting conditions that are conducive to starting and spreading a fire. As discussed earlier, Sarajevo is like streetcars that can come around and around. If not this time and this place, there are other occasions for another opportunity (if this is the right word) for a crisis to happen and spiral out of control. Any number of things can serve the function of a trigger or fuse. What is more important to recognize and more subject to efforts to mitigate the consequences of a crisis is the underlying conditions that constitute a combustible environment making a large, intense conflagration more likely and less manageable.

The underlying conditions characterizing the current Sino–American relations are therefore important to consider as the general context making it more likely for the United States to intervene in the Taiwan Strait. Washington clearly knows how to push Beijing's buttons, and moreover, to complicate matters it does not act as a unitary actor, as shown by Nancy Pelosi's 2022 visit to Taipei in apparent defiance of the White House's plea for her to abandon her trip. At the same time, Washington has often also used the "good cop, bad cop" routine (referring to the executive and legislative branches, respectively) to extract maximum concession from Beijing and to create excuses for not fulfilling promises made to Beijing by the executive branch by pleading legislative resistance. Beijing is not so dense as to overlook these possibilities as well as partisan motivations to gain votes and publicity by bashing China. It often feels that it has been put on a treadmill, whereby there is constant motion but no movement—indeed, in some respects, retrogression—on the Taiwan issue. Various trade, investment, and other favorable treatments extended to Taiwan have garnered few positive results for Beijing's "soft" approach, nor have talks over the years with Taipei and Washington made any progress. Reflecting on the Falkland/Malvinas War, Ned Lebow describes Argentina's frustration in these words: "[Buenos Aires] came increasingly to believe, and not without reason that they were behaving like the proverbial donkey, tricked into pulling the cart by a carrot on a stick dangled before him" (Lebow 1985, 104). The parallel to the situation across the Taiwan Strait should be obvious. Another parallel may come to pass. Britain had won its war with Argentina but is now stuck with defending and supporting those distant, barren, wind-swept islands with a small population and no economic and strategic value—islands that London had tried to unload before Argentina's invasion in 1982. Another lesson from the Falklands/Malvinas episode is that London, by framing the issue as self-determination by the Kelpers (the 1,800 or so residents of these islenads), it in effect gave them a veto over any negotiated settlement, creating a situation of the tail wagging the dog.

In this context, the real issues pertain less to Taiwan's status than the evolving relationship between China and the United States. Tension involving this island is more a symptom than the cause of the worsening relationship between Beijing and Washington. The Taiwan issue could be set aside and stabilized if this relationship is friendly and cordial, as shown for decades after the two countries established diplomatic relations in 1979 until the recent past. In contrast to my previous discussion of the incentive that the weaker contestant in an asymmetric local conflict can have to entice and even trap a foreign ally to intervene on its behalf, if war happens between China and the United States, it would be more Washington trapping itself than Taipei trapping it. The United States had no trouble abandoning Taiwan and unilaterally abrogating its defense treaty with Taipei when it decided to switch its diplomatic recognition to Beijing in 1979. China's authoritarian political system, its communist ideology, its one-party rule, its abuse of human rights, and its state-controlled economy were not obstacles to these countries' rapprochement at that time (Chan 2023a; 2023b).

These considerations are therefore also not persuasive as reasons for their worsening relationship in recent years. If anything, China's society and economy have become more open since the Maoist years: the average Chinese enjoys today greatly improved living conditions and personal freedom, Chinese society and economy have become more open, China has become much more integrated and embedded in the global economy, and China's foreign policy has become much less bellicose. Beijing no longer espouses a revolutionary ideology that supports armed insurgency to overthrow bourgeois governments abroad, it has abandoned its diplomatic isolation (during the Cultural Revolution) to become an active participant in multilateral diplomacy, and it has ceased its opposition to international arms control agreements (such as the ban on nuclear tests) and its denouncement of international organizations (such as the United Nations). In fact, it has now professed its support for the Westphalian principles of state sovereignty and noninterference in other countries' domestic affairs, joined negotiations on limiting Iran's nuclear program, even sponsored talks on limiting North Korea's nuclear program and signed many international treaties and arms control accords (even ones that Washington has declined to join, such as the United Nations Convention on the Law of the Sea), and it is now the largest contributor of personnel to United Nations peacekeeping missions.

These changes should have made China's policies and practices more congenial to declared US interests and values. But they have not. China has not fought a war since 1979. Nor has it undertaken any military intervention in any country. In contrast, the United States has engaged in several wars and a considerable number of military interventions abroad—even though Washington has complained about Beijing's aggressive and bellicose foreign policy. The United States has also spent far more than China on its military, and it withdrew from quite a few international organizations and treaties during Trump's administration, even though the Biden administration has decided to return to some of them. In early days of Trump's second presidential term, he has shown again his proclivity to undertake unilateral and assertive US policies. He has announced 25% tariffs on Mexican and Canadian goods entering the United States and another 10% of tariffs on China on top of those already introduced by the Biden administration (which had imposed a 100% tariff on Chinese electric vehicles). He made outlandish statements to reassert U.S. sovereignty and control over the Panama Canal, to purchase Greenland, to incorporate Canada as the 51st state of the United States, and to "take over" the Gaza strip after evicting the Palestinian population there. He has withdrawn the United States for a second time from the World Health Organization, the Paris climate accord, and the Human Rights Council of the United Nations (Biden returned the US to these institutions or accord after Trump's first presidential term). One wonders how US officials and public would have reacted to similar statements and actions by Beijing.

The one major change that could be the most plausible reason for worsening Sino-American relations is that China has narrowed the capability gap separating it from the United States. China has in recent decades made relative power gain, and the United States has suffered relative power loss. This power shift has been rapid and significant, although a power transition between the two countries—meaning China overtaking the United States—is still far from a certainty despite much handwringing among US officials and the popularity of power-transition theory and discourse on Thucydides' Trap among US academics. The current reality is that the United States is still preponderant in its command of military capabilities, and it still enjoys enormous structural power beyond the military dimension, as shown by its dominant position in international finance, its control over the production and supply of manufactures by US-based multinational corporations around the globe, and its command of mass communication, scientific knowledge, technological innovation, and the world of fashion, fads, ideas, and information—or soft power, if you will.

Power shift is therefore the driver behind the changing Sino–American relations. Seen in this light, the Taiwan issue is not really about Taiwan. That island's importance is not intrinsic to the United States but is rather derivative of its relations to China. Taiwan is important to the United States because it is important to China. It is a bargaining lever for Washington, and it is therefore better left unresolved rather than settled from its perspective. This reason is a partial explanation of the protracted nature of this dispute, as with some other disputes. Washington has seen fit to dial down or up its support for Taiwan, in large part reflecting the state of its relations with Beijing rather than developments inside Taiwan. US support for Taiwan was strongest when it was a garrison state ruled by martial law under the authoritarian rule of a single party, the Kuomintang. Commitment to democratic values or human rights did not appear to have mattered then. Although Taiwan has made steady progress in institutionalizing its democracy and advancing its people's personal freedoms, US support has fluctuated over time in ways that do not necessarily correspond to these achievements.

The larger context providing the enabling conditions for Sarajevo to spark the onset of World War I, of course, consisted of the power shifts between a declining Britain and a rising Germany and the intensified competition between these two countries. Power-transition theorists (e.g., Organski and Kugler 1980) are right in pointing to these dynamics as contributors to that large, devastating conflict, even though they are wrong in attributing it to an impatient and cocky latecomer eager to pick a fight to displace an existing hegemon and claim the mantle of world leadership from it. Germany started a preventive war to forestall a rising colossus to its east (namely, Russia). It ended fighting Britain not because it had wanted to but rather because it was unable to persuade London to stay on the sideline. Moreover, Berlin's agenda was more concerned with Germany's security position in Europe rather than its ambition to rule the world.

Besides the shifting power balance, pre-1914 Europe also saw tightening alliance formation, intensifying armament races, and recurrent crises in the Balkans and elsewhere (such as Morocco, the race to colonize Africa, and the

Great Game between Britain and Russia in central Asia). These conditions contributed collectively to a more tense and mistrustful Europe. They made it more crisis-prone and, when a crisis such as Sarajevo happened, more difficult to manage and contain its deleterious consequences. As discussed earlier, we are seeing signs pointing to the end of the world of détente and US unipolarity marked by the USSR's demise in 1989. Signs are now pointing to renewed alliance solidarity, bifurcated interstate alignment patterns, incipient armament competition, and movements to reduce economic interdependence and openness. To be sure these developments are still unfolding and have yet to reach full-blown trends. We do not yet see in East Asia today the development and entrenchment of rigid, opposing armed camps or rampant arms races. Thus, it is not yet the world of Hobbes, but it is also in some danger of reversing its march toward the world of Locke.

It is relatively clear where the initiative for this reversal is coming from. The loudest voices for economic decoupling and most potent forces to reverse globalization are coming from the West, especially the United States; and Donald Trump's second presidential term is likely to exacerbate this push. In contrast, Chinese president Xi Jinping has said on several public occasions that China is committed to globalization. China has also disavowed any intention of joining military alliances. This observation, of course, does not deny that incipient organizations such as the SCO and BRICS could someday develop into a more formal anti-Western coalition. This said, the initiation and impetus for creating, strengthening, and expanding formal and informal military coordination among allies and quasi-allies have clearly come more from the West. NATO expansion, which is the proximate cause of Russia's invasion of Ukraine, is one example. The revival of the Quad is another example. The latter group clearly has China as its target for containment, and as an exclusionary political club it represents a reversal of the idea of open regionalism propagated by ASEAN (the Association of Southeast Asian Nations) with its agenda including the liberalization of international trade and the promotion of joint economic development and interdependence.

Lest it be mistaken, the discussion above on power shifts should not be seen just in the context of a rising China and a declining United States. The last two decades of the 20th century and the first decade and a half of the 21st century were marked by unprecedented unipolarity in the modern era (Brooks and Wohlforth 2008). US supremacy has been unrivaled, and Washington's dominance of international political economy was, of course, accompanied and facilitated by the collapse of the USSR. Even though the USSR and subsequently Russia had made a series of consequential and unilateral concessions—including the voluntary dissolution of the Warsaw Pact, the breakup of the Soviet Union, the acceptance of a reunified Germany as a member of NATO, and even the accommodation of a US military presence in central Asia to combat international terrorism—Western countries did not relent from their pressure on the Kremlin and persisted in their effort to expand the European Union and NATO right up to Russia's border. These countries also bypassed the United Nations in carrying out various military operations, including those against Libya and Serbia, as well their invasion of Iraq and Afghanistan; and they supported various color revolutions to advance their declared agenda of regime change.

These actions did not go unnoticed by either Russia or China, not only arousing their suspicions of Western countries' trustworthiness but also teaching them that weakness and accommodation do not encourage cooperation but rather invite further pressure and demand for more concessions from the West. It is not uncommon to nowadays hear in the United States that by opening its market and providing China with technology and capital, the world and especially the United States had made it possible for China to reach its current level of affluence and development. To Chinese ears, such statements are gratuitous and one-sided, implying that trade relations have the practical and intended effect of benefiting just one of the two parties involved.

In a moment of candor or bravado, Barack Obama was quoted as saying, "America should write the rules. America should call the shots. Other countries should play by the rules that America and our partners set, and not the other way around" (VOA News 2016, n.p.). He also reportedly said, "If over a billion Chinese citizens have the same living patterns as Australians and Americans do right now, then all of us are in for a very miserable time. The planet just can't sustain it" (Hudson 2010, n.p.). How should the Chinese people and their leaders interpret this remark? Does it suggest that Americans and Australians should reduce their consumption levels or, conversely, that the Chinese people should be prevented from improving their living conditions?

It has been said that the current Sino–American relationship is different from the one between the USSR and the United States during the Cold War. First, Moscow was engaged in an ideological competition with Washington to spread communism abroad. In contrast, Beijing is not engaged in such competition with the United States. It has not sought to export its model of governance or its ideology—in fact, a common complaint about Beijing is that it does not require its economic partners to adhere to political conditions. It is, moreover, the United States and the West more generally that have sought to export capitalism and democracy, promote regime change, and support various color revolutions. Second, the USSR was not nearly as embedded or involved in the international economy as China is today. It traded primarily with its Warsaw Pact partners and a few others like Cuba. It had hardly any trade or investment ties with the West. Today's China presents the opposite situation, being the top trade partner or investment destination (or nearly so) for many Western countries and US allies and quasi-allies in East Asia. Third, as already mentioned, China has not organized an anti-West coalition—at least not a military alliance—in contrast to the USSR-led Warsaw Pact.

These observations are valid, but changes are occurring. Washington is framing its opposition to Beijing in terms of a struggle between democracy and autocracy, thus infusing this competition with a heavy dose of ideology. It is moreover undertaking a series of steps to decouple economically from China, imposing tariffs on Chinese goods, embargoing Chinese technological companies, banning China from receiving certain technologies and investments, and relocating supply chains from China to other countries. China has, of course, retaliated against these US actions, but there is little doubt on the question of which country is trying to cut or reduce economic ties. There is also little doubt about which country is trying to consolidate, strengthen, and even expand its alliance or security relationships and is leading in the export of weapons and related technologies. One does not see any Chinese action in the Western Hemisphere comparable to those undertaken by the United States in Asia.

This last observation brings us to the role that alliances—or security relations more generally—have played in enlarging and escalating what started as local bilateral conflicts. These ties have served as mechanisms for such conflicts to spread. The metaphor of chains has accordingly been used to describe the process whereby allies or security partners become embroiled in disputes that did not involve them initially. Sarajevo created a chain reaction that caused Germany and Russia to become engulfed in a dispute involving their ally Austria-Hungary and Serbia, respectively. France subsequently became involved because it was an ally of Russia and Britain because it was a member of the Triple Entente.

China has just one formal ally, North Korea; and it had fought alongside this ally in the Korean War in 1950. China has close ties with Pakistan and Burma. But it is unlikely that Beijing would intervene militarily on their behalf. In large part, China still lacks the necessary capabilities to undertake such intervention. Its military reach does not extend very far from its borders. In fact, no other country in the world except the United States is capable of direct, large-scale, and protracted intervention abroad. But even if Beijing should acquire such capabilities in some indefinite future, it does not have the level of stake in any other country that would warrant its military intervention on behalf of its security partners. Despite Western criticisms, Beijing has done little to support Russia in its current war in Ukraine. In short, the danger of embroilment in a conflict involving a third country—except for North Korea—is quite limited for China in the foreseeable future.

Quite the opposite characterizes the US situation. Washington has an extensive alliance portfolio, and it has an extensive record of foreign military interventions. These interventions are not necessarily the result of entrapment by an ally or client, and they were usually undertaken because of Washington's own agenda and motivations. However, from the case histories of those conflicts discussed in Chapter 2, we can certainly say that the danger of entrapment is far greater for the United States than China. Moreover, whether it is due to Washington's own volition or a partner's attempt to get it involved in a local conflict—these possibilities are not mutually exclusive. This said, Washington had also acted quite prudently in past situations that might get it into a direct conflict with Moscow or Beijing.

The danger of a Sino–American confrontation is the greatest in a contingency involving Taiwan. Should such a confrontation occur, it would not be because Beijing is itchy for a fight with the United States or because it wants to claim global hegemony or even just regional hegemony. Fighting the United States would be its last resort rather than its first preference. War with the United States would suggest that China's diplomacy to persuade Washington to stay out of its civil war has failed. Although the outcome of a confrontation over Taiwan will clearly have ramifications across Asia and even the world, the reason for China's decision to fight will have more to do with domestic political repercussions and the priority Beijing attaches to national reunification and the geostrategic importance of Taiwan than any ambition to displace the United States as the established global hegemon.

Beijing knows fully well that even if it can prevail militarily to force Taiwan's reincorporation into China, it would be a pyrrhic victory because a war would destroy the island's economy, alienate many of its people, divert Beijing from its goals of national rejuvenation and improvement of its people's lives, and set back its relations with Washington for decades. Thus, should Beijing choose war to settle Taiwan's status, it must have decided that its importance exceeds all these and other considerations. Although this book argues that such a possibility exists and is even becoming more likely in view of current trends, this argument does not dismiss the idea that there are other important considerations inviting Beijing to exercise restraint and bide its time. This remark also applies to Washington, whose cautious actions in previous situations involving the danger of a direct confrontation with Moscow or Beijing suggest that the probability of its military intervention to assist Taiwan may be considerably lower than most people expect.

For Beijing to choose war it must believe that it has exhausted all other options and that waiting would reduce rather enhance its bargaining position. For these reasons, should it resort to force, this decision means that it must have already considered and yet discounted these relevant factors and that it is more resolved to prevail this time. As the relevant literature suggests, although considerations such as possible foreign intervention should lower the danger of war in situations of general extended deterrence, they have the reverse effect in situations of immediate extended deterrence. Thus, everything else being equal, Biden's public pledge to intervene on Taiwan's behalf should discourage Beijing from using force. This phenomenon describes a situation of general extended deterrence. However, should Beijing still be prepared to use force in full knowledge of this pledge—which turns the situation into a case of immediate extended deterrence—its decision implies that it must have reasons that in its view override Biden's deterrence threat and that it must be more determined and/or optimistic about having its way this time. Thus, threats by a defending country to intervene on behalf of its protégé are likely to fail in situations of immediate extended deterrence (Fearon 1994; 2002; Huth 1988; Huth and Russett 1988).

Should such a war occur, it is unlikely that Beijing could persuade any country to join it in this fight. Even if it tried, such persuasion will not be successful. It can only hope that other countries would remain neutral in this fight and that those allied with the United States would refuse or at least limit Washington from using its military forces and installations based in their country (such as South Korea, Japan, and the Philippines) to fight China. In contrast to China, it is much more likely and even expected that the United States will lobby its allies to join this fight. Therefore, the forces and dynamics for a bilateral conflict to become multilateral will likely come from Washington rather than Beijing. Should Washington be successful in pressuring other countries to join it in a war against China, it would present a case of reversed entrapment. That is, it represents a case whereby smaller states become embroiled in a conflict initiated by their larger ally—the opposite of concerns about a moral hazard causing the stronger ally to be dragged into a war against its best interests.

How successful will the United States be in getting other countries involved in a military contingency involving Taiwan, and their likely level and kind of involvement will depend in part on Beijing's current conduct. The more it acts brashly and assertively, the more likely its neighbors will become concerned with its intentions. This is the backlash effect discussed earlier, referring to a country's own self-weakening or self-defeating policies causing its isolation and the formation of a countervailing coalition to contain or defeat it.

Other East Asian countries, however, would rather not have to choose sides in a conflict between China and the United States. They are the ones who must live with China, whereas the United States always has the option of going home. Moreover, they are better having China around to be a counterpoise to the United States than having to be left alone to deal with Washington, whose exercise of power will be less restrained in the absence of countervailing influence from Beijing. Although US rhetoric frames its defense of Taiwan in the name of freedom, democracy, self-determination, and human rights, most countries (including those in East Asia) will not be persuaded. They remember that Washington had supported an authoritarian Taiwan ruled by the Kuomintang that certainly did not have a shining record on human rights. They also remember that in the 1950s and 1960s Washington had claimed that the government in Taiwan represented China—the entire China, including the mainland that Taipei did not control. There was therefore a flip-flop of 180 degrees in Washington's position. Self-determination for the people of Palestine, Kashmir, Crimea, or, for that matter, Southerners in the Confederacy wishing to secede from the Union did not carry much weight in Washington.

In conclusion, the stars are lining up to present a confluence of several adverse trends auguring an increased danger of a Sino–American confrontation over Taiwan. To be sure, there may be mitigating factors, the most important of which is that both China and the United States have nuclear weapons, which can have a sobering effect on crisis escalation. Moreover, as Lee Kuan Yew indicated, Washington may conclude that the game is not worth the candle when taking into consideration the long haul. For its part, Beijing should also take to heart lessons from Wilhelmine Germany's brash and assertive behavior that caused a backlash effect ending in its self-encirclement, even though there are obviously some crucial differences between the world then and now. To avoid conflict, it takes both China and the United States to stop pulling the opposite ends of a rope to tighten the knot, especially with respect to Taiwan.

References

Albertini, Luigi. 1980. *The Origins of the War of 1914*, trans. Isabella M. Massey. Westport, NY: Greenwood.

Allison, Graham T. 1971. *Essence of Decision: Explaining the Cuban Missile Crisis.* Boston: Little, Brown.

Allison, Graham T. 2015. "The Thucydides Trap: Are the U.S. and China Headed for War?" *The Atlantic,* September 24. www.theatlantic.com/international/archive/2015/09/united-states-china-war-thucydides-trap/406756/.

Allison, Graham T. 2017. *Destined for War: Can America and China Escape Thucydides's Trap?* Boston: Houghton Mifflin Harcourt.

Allison, Graham T. 2020. "The New Spheres of Influence: Sharing the Globe with Other Great Powers." *Foreign Affairs* 99 (2): 30–40.

Arreguin-Toft, Ivan. 2005. *How the Weak Win Wars: A Theory of Asymmetric Conflict.* Cambridge: Cambridge University Press.

Arrow, Kenneth J. 1963. "Uncertainty and the Welfare Economics of Medical Care." *American Economic Review* 53 (5): 941–73.

Axelrod, Robert. 1984. *The Evolution of Cooperation.* New York: Basic Books.

Bachrach, Stanley D. 1976. *The Committee of One Million: "China Lobby" Politics, 1953–1971.* New York: Columbia University Press.

Baldwin, David A. 1979. "Power Analysis and World Politics: New Trends Versus Old Tendencies." *World Politics* 31 (2): 161–94.

Balot, Ryan K., Sara Forsdyke, and Edith Foster, eds. 2017. *The Oxford Handbook of Thucydides.* Oxford: Oxford University Press.

Barnhart, Michael A. 1987. *Japan Prepares for Total War: The Search for Economic Security, 1919–1945.* Ithaca, NY: Cornell University Press.

Beckley, Michael. 2015. "The Myth of Entangling Alliances." *International Security* 39 (4): 7–48.

Beckley, Michael. 2018. "The Power of Nations: Measuring What Matters." *International Security* 43 (2): 7–44.

Beckley, Michael. 2022. "Enemies of My Enemy: How Fear of China Is Forging a New World Order." *Foreign Affairs* 101 (2): 68–85.

Bennett, D. Scott. 1997. "Measuring Rivalry Termination, 1816–1992." *Journal of Conflict Resolution* 41 (2): 227–54.

Bennett, D. Scott. 1998. "Integrating and Testing Models of Rivalry Duration." *American Journal of Political Science* 42 (4): 1200–32.

Bennett, D. Scott, and Timothy Nordstrom. 2000. "Foreign Policy Substitutability and Internal Economic Problems in Enduring Rivalries." *Journal of Conflict Resolution* 44 (1): 33–61.

Benson, Brett V. 2011. "Unpacking Alliances: Deterrent and Compellent Alliances and Their Relationship with Conflict, 1816–2000." *Journal of Politics* 73 (4): 1111–27.

Benson, Brett V. 2012. *Constructing International Security: Alliances, Deterrence, and Moral Hazard.* Cambridge: Cambridge University Press.

Benson, Brett V., Patrick R. Bentley, and James E. Ray. 2013. "Ally Provacateur: Why Allies Do Not Always Behave." *Journal of Peace Research* 50 (1): 47–58.

Benson, Brett V., Adam Meirowitz, and Kristopher W. Ramsay. 2014. "Inducing Deterrence through Moral Hazard in Alliance Contracts." *Journal of Conflict Resolution* 58 (2): 307–35.

Bercovitch, Jacob, and Paul F. Diehl. 1997. "Conflict Management of Enduring Rivalries: The Frequency, Timing, and Short-Term Impact of Mediation." *International Interactions* 22 (4): 299–320.

Berghahn, Volker R. 1973. *Germany and the Approach of War in 1914*. London: Macmillan.

Bergman, Ronen, and Mark Mazzetti. 2021. "The Secret History of the Push to Strike Iran." *New York Times*, May 23.

"Biden: China Should Expect 'Extreme Competition' from US." 2021. Associated Press. February 7. https://apnews.com/biden-china-should-expect-extreme-competition-from-us-8f5158c12eed14e002bb1c094f3a048a.

Blanchette, Jude, and Ryan Hass. 2023. "The Taiwan Long Game: Why the Best Solution Is No Solution." *Foreign Affairs* 102 (1): 102–14.

Bobrow, Davis B., ed. 2008. *Hegemony Constrained: Evasion, Modification, and Resistance to American Foreign Policy*. Pittsburgh: University of Pittsburgh Press.

Boettcher, William A., III. 2005. *Presidential Risk Behavior in Foreign Policy: Prudence or Peril?* New York: Palgrave.

Bourne, Kenneth. 1967. *Britain and the Balance of Power in North America, 1815–1908*. Berkeley: University of California Press.

Brands, Hal. 2015. "Rethinking America's Grand Strategy: Insights from the Cold War." *Parameters* 45 (4): 7–16.

Brands, Hal, and Peter Feaver. 2016. "Should America Retrench? The Battle over Offshore Balancing: The Risks of Retreat." *Foreign Affairs* 95 (6): 164–69.

Brecher, Michael, and Benjamin Geist. 1980. *Decisions in Crisis: Israel 1967 and 1973*. Berkeley: University of California Press.

Brooks, Stephen G., G. John Ikenberry, and William C. Wohlforth. 2012/2013. "Don't Come Home, America: The Case against Retrenchment." *International Security* 37 (3): 7–51.

Brooks, Stephen G., and William C. Wohlforth. 2005. "Hard Times for Soft Balancing." *International Security* 30 (1): 72–108.

Brooks, Stephen G., and William C. Wohlforth. 2008. *World out of Balance: International Relations and the Challenge of American Primacy*. Princeton, NJ: Princeton University Press.

Brzezinski, Zbigniew, and John Mearsheimer. 2005. "Clash of the Titans." *Foreign Policy* 146 (January/February): 46–50.

Bueno de Mesquita, Bruce. 1981. *The War Trap*. New Haven, CT: Yale University Press.

Bueno de Mesquita, Bruce, and Alastair Smith. 2012. *The Dictator's Handbook: Why Bad Behavior Is Almost Always Good Politics*. New York: PublicAffairs.

Bueno de Mesquita, Bruce, Alastair Smith, Randolph M. Siverson, and James D. Morrow. 2003. *The Logic of Political Survival*. Cambridge, MA: MIT Press.

Burr, William, and Jeffrey Richelson. 2000/2001. "Whether to 'Strangle the Baby in the Cradle': The United States and the Chinese Nuclear Program, 1960–64." *International Security* 25 (3): 54–99.

Buzan, Barry. 2004. *The United States and the Great Powers: World Politics in the Twenty-First Century*. Cambridge: Polity Press.

Callahan, Michael. 2023. "Biden Administration Approves Potential $440 Arms Sales to Taiwan." CNN, July 30. https://www.cnn.com/2023/06/30/politics/us-arms-sales-taiwan/index.html.

Carpenter, Ted G. 2005. *America's Coming War with China: A Collision Course over Taiwan*. New York: Palgrave MacMillan.

Cha, Victor D. 1999. *Alignment despite Antagonism: The United States–Korea–Japan Security Triangle*. Stanford, CA: Stanford University Press.

Cha, Victor D. 2007. "Currents of Power: U.S. Alliances with Japan and Taiwan during the Cold War." In *The Uses of Institutions: The U.S., Japan, and Governance in East Asia*, eds. G. John Ikenberry and Takashi Inoguchi, 103–29. New York: Palgrave Macmillan.

Cha, Victor D. 2009/2010. "Powerplay: Origins of U.S. Alliance System in Asia." *International Security* 34 (3): 158–96.

Cha, Victor D. 2016. *Powerplay: The Origins of the American Alliance System in Asia*. Princeton, NJ: Princeton University Press.

Chan, Steve. 2008. *China, the U.S., and the Power-Transition Theory: A Critique*. London: Routledge.

Chan, Steve. 2009. "Commerce between Rivals: Realism, Liberalism, and Credible Communication across the Taiwan Strait." *International Relations of the Asia-Pacific* 9 (3): 435–67.

Chan, Steve. 2010a. "Major-Power Intervention and War Initiation by the Weak." *International Politics* 47 (2): 163–85.

Chan, Steve. 2010b. "An Odd Thing Happened on the Way to Balancing: East Asian States' Reactions to China's Rise." *International Studies Review* 12 (3): 386–411.

Chan, Steve. 2011. "Preventive War by the Weak: Loss Aversion and Strategic Anticipation." *Tamkang Journal of International Affairs* 14 (3): 1–41.

Chan, Steve. 2012a. *Looking for Balance: China, the United States, and Power Balancing in East Asia*. Stanford, CA: Stanford University Press.

Chan, Steve. 2012b. "Loss Aversion and Strategic Opportunism: Third-Party Intervention's Role in War Instigation by the Weak." *Peace & Change* 37 (2): 171–94.

Chan, Steve. 2013. *Enduring Rivalries in the Asia Pacific*. Cambridge: Cambridge University Press.

Chan, Steve. 2014. "So What about Power Shift? Caveat Emptor." *Asian Perspective* 38 (3): 363–86.

Chan, Steve. 2015. "On States' Status-Quo and Revisionist Orientations: Discerning Power, Popularity and Satisfaction from Security Council Vetoes." *Issues & Studies* 51 (3): 1–28.

Chan, Steve. 2016. *China's Troubled Waters: Maritime Disputes in Theoretical Perspective*. Cambridge: Cambridge University Press.

Chan, Steve. 2017a. *Trust and Distrust in Sino-American Relations: Challenge and Opportunity*. Amherst, NY: Cambria Press.

Chan, Steve. 2017b. "The Power-Transition Discourse and China's Rise." In *Encyclopedia of Empirical International Relations Theory*, ed. William R. Thompson. New York: Oxford University Press. http://politics.oxfordre.com/page/recently-published/.

Chan, Steve. 2019. "More Than One Trap: Problematic Interpretations and Overlooked Lessons from Thucydides." *Journal of Chinese Political Science* 24 (1): 11–24.

Chan, Steve. 2020a. *Thucydides's Trap? Historical Interpretation, Logic of Inquiry, and the Future of Sino-American Relations*. Ann Arbor: University of Michigan Press.

Chan, Steve. 2020b. "China and Thucydides's Trap." In *China's Challenges and International Order Transition: Beyond the "Thucydides Trap,"* eds. Kai He and Huiyun Feng, 52–71. Ann Arbor: University of Michigan Press.

Chan, Steve. 2021a. "Why Thucydides' Trap Misinforms Sino-American Relations." *Vestnik RUDN, International Relations* 21 (2): 234–42.

Chan, Steve. 2021b. "Challenging the Liberal Order: The US Hegemon as a Revisionist Power." *International Affairs* 97 (5): 1335–52.

Chan, Steve. 2021c. "In the Eye of the Storm: Taiwan, China, and the U.S. in Challenging Times." In *Taiwan's Political Economy*, eds. Cal M. Clark, Karl Ho, and Alexander C. Tan, 61–78. New York: Nova Science Publishers.

Chan, Steve. 2022. "Precedent, Path Dependency, and Reasoning by Analogy: The Strategic Implications of the Ukraine War on Sino-American Relations and Relations across the Taiwan Strait." *Asian Survey* 62 (5–6): 945–68.

Chan, Steve. 2023a. *Rumbles of Thunder: Power Shifts and the Danger of Sino-American War*. New York: Columbia University Press.

Chan, Steve. 2023b. "Bewildered and Befuddled: The West's Convoluted Narrative on China's Rise." *Asian Survey* 63 (5): 691–715.

Chan, Steve. 2024a. *Culture, Economic Growth, and Interstate Power Shift: Implications for Competition between China and the United States*. Cambridge: Cambridge University Press.

Chan, Steve. 2024b. *Taiwan and the Danger of a Sino–American War*. Cambridge Elements on Indo-Pacific Security. Cambridge: Cambridge University Press.

Chan, Steve. 2024c. "Power Shift, Problem Shift, and Power Shift: Reacting to China's Rise." In *The Sources of Great Power Competition*, eds. Patrick Rhamey and Spencer D. Bakich, 289-299. New York: Routledge.

Chan, Steve, Huiyun Feng, Kai He, and Weixing Hu. 2021. *Contesting Revisionism: China, the United States, and the Transformation of International Order*. Oxford: Oxford University Press.

Chan, Steve, Richard W. X. Hu, and Kai He. 2019. "Discerning States' Revisionist and Status-Quo Orientations: Comparing China and the U.S." *European Journal of International Relations* 27 (2): 613–40.

Chan, Steve, and Weixing Hu. 2023. *Geography and International Conflict: Ukraine, Taiwan, Indo-Pacific, and Sino-American Relation*. New York: Routledge.

Charap, Samuel. 2023. "An Unwinnable War: Washington Needs an Endgame in Ukraine." *Foreign Affairs* 102 (4): 22–35.

Chen, Jian. 1994. *China's Road to the Korean War: The Making of the Sino–American Confrontation*. New York: Columbia University Press.

Cheng, Evelyn. 2022. "Taiwan's Trade with China Is Far Bigger than Its Trade with the U.S." CNN, August 4. https://www.cnbc.com/2022/08/05/taiwans-trade-with-china-is-far-bigger-than-its-trade-with-the-us.html.

Chiozza, Giacomo, and H. E. Goemans. 2003. "Peace through Insecurity: Tenure and International Conflict." *Journal of Conflict Resolution* 47 (4): 443–67.

Chong, Ja Ian, and Todd H. Hall. 2014. "The Lessons of 1914 for East Asia Today: Missing the Trees for the Forest." *International Security* 39 (1): 7–43.

Christensen, Thomas J. 1997. "Perceptions and Alliances in Europe, 1865–1940." *International Organization* 51 (1): 65–97.

Christensen, Thomas J. 2001. "Posing Problems without Catching Up: China's Rise and Challenges to U.S. Security Policy." *International Security* 25 (4): 5–40.

Christensen, Thomas J., and Jack Snyder. 1990. "Chain Gangs and Passed Bucks: Predicting Alliance Patterns in Multipolarity." *International Organization* 44 (2): 137–68.

Chubin, Shahram, and Charles Tripp. 1988. *Iran and Iraq at War*. Boulder, CO: Westview.

Ciorciari, John D. 2009. "The Balance of Great-Power Influence in Contemporary Southeast Asia." *International Relations of the Asia-Pacific* 9 (1): 157–96.

Ciorciari, John D. 2010. *The Limits of Alignment: Southeast Asia and the Great Powers since 1975*. Washington, DC: Georgetown University Press.

Cline, Ray S. 2002. *The Power of Nations in the 1990s: A Strategic Assessment*. Lanham, MD: University Press of America.

Colaresi, Michael. 2005. *Scare Politics: The Politics of International Rivalry*. Syracuse, NY: Syracuse University Press.

Colaresi, Michael P., Karen Rasler, and William R. Thompson. 2007. *Strategic Rivalries in World Politics: Position, Space, and Conflict Resolution*. Cambridge: Cambridge University Press.

Colaresi, Michael P., and William R. Thompson. 2002. "Hot Spots or Hot Hands? Serial Crisis Behavior, Escalating Risks, and Rivalry." *Journal of Politics* 64 (4): 1175–98.

Collinson, Stephen. 2023. "The Number One Takeaway from Biden's Address." CNN, October 20. https://www.cnn.com/2023/10/20/politics/takeaway-biden-address-israel-ukraine-aid/index.html.

Copeland, Dale C. 2000. *The Origins of Major War*. Ithaca, NY: Cornell University Press.

Crawford, Timothy W. 2003. *Pivotal Deterrence: Third-Party Statecraft and the Pursuit of Peace*. Ithaca, NY: Cornell University Press.

Danilovic, Vesna. 2001. "Conceptual and Selection Bias Issues in Deterrence." *Journal of Conflict Resolution* 45 (1): 97–125.

Davis, William W., George T. Duncan, and Randolph M. Siverson. 1978. "The Dynamics of Warfare, 1815–1965." *American Journal of Political Science* 22 (4): 772–92.

DeRouen, Karl, Jr. 2000. "Presidents and the Diversionary Use of Force: A Research Note." *International Studies Quarterly* 44 (2): 317–28.

Deutsch, Karl W., and J. David Singer. 1960. "Multipolar Power Systems and International Stability." *World Politics* 16 (3): 390–406.

Diehl, Paul F., ed. 1998. *The Dynamics of Enduring Rivalries*. Urbana: University of Illinois Press.

Diehl, Paul F., and Gary Goertz. 2000. *War and Peace in International Rivalry*. Ann Arbor: University of Michigan Press.

Doherty, Kathleen. 2021. *Cyprus, Seeking Solution, A Case Study of the 2015–2017 Negotiations*. Washington, DC: Institute for the Study of Diplomacy, Georgetown University.

Doran, Charles, F. 1991. *Systems in Crisis: New Imperatives of High Politics at Century's End*. Cambridge: Cambridge University Press.

Doran, Charles F., and Wes Parsons. 1980. "War and the Cycle of Relative Power." *American Political Science Review* 74 (4): 947–65.

Drozdiak, Natalia. 2023. "NATO Pledges to Spend at Least 2% of GDP on Defense." Bloomberg, July 7. https://www.bloomberg.com/news/articles/2023-07-07/nato-agrees-on-new-pledge-to-spend-at-least-2-of-gdp-on-defense#xj4y7vzkg.

Dsouza, Vinod. 2023. "BRICS Countries Dump $123 Billion in U.S. Treasuries in 2023." Watcher.Guru, September 25. https://watcher.guru/news/brics-countries-dump-123-billion-in-u-s-treasuries-in-2023.

East, Maurice A. 1972. "Status Discrepancy and Violence in the International System." In *The Analysis of International Politics*, eds. James N. Rosenau, Vincent Davis, and Maurice A. East, 299–319. New York: Free Press.

Elman, Colin. 2004. "Extending Offensive Realism: The Louisiana Purchase and America's Rise to Regional Hegemony." *American Political Science Review* 98 (4): 563–76.

"Emmanuel Macron Warns Europe: NATO Is Becoming Brain Dead." 2019. *The Economist*, November 7. https://www.economist.com/europe/2019/11/07/emmanuel-macron-warns-europe-nato-is-becoming-brain-dead.

Etzioni, Amitai. 2015. "Spheres of Influence: A Reconceptualization." *Fletcher Forum of World Affairs* 29 (2): 117–32.

Evans, Paul, and Cheng-Chwee Kuik. 2023. "Middle-Power Agency in an Indo-Pacific Era." *Global Asia* 18 (3): https://www.globalasia.org/v18no3/cover/middle-power-agency-in-an-indo-pacific-era_paul-evanscheng-chwee-kuik.

Fang, Songying, Jesse C. Johnson, and Brett A. Leeds. 2014. "To Concede or to Resist? The Restraining Effects of Military Alliances." *International Organization* 68 (4): 775–809.

Farer, Tom J. 1979. *War Clouds on the Horn of Africa; The Widening Storm*, 2nd edition. New York: Carnegie Endowment for International Peace.

Farnham, Barbara, ed. 1994. *Avoiding Losses/Taking Risks: Prospect Theory and International Conflict*. Ann Arbor: University of Michigan Press.

Fearon, James D. 1994. "Signal versus the Balance of Power and Interests: An Empirical Test of a Crisis Bargaining Model." *Journal of Conflict Resolution* 38 (2): 236–69.

Fearon, James D. 1995. "Rationalist Explanations for War." *International Organization* 49 (3): 379–414.

Fearon, James D. 1997. "Signaling Foreign Policy Interests: Tying Hands versus Sinking Costs." *Journal of Conflict Resolution* 41 (1): 68–90.

Fearon, James D. 2002. "Selection Effects and Deterrence." *International Interactions* 28 (1): 5–29.

Fischer, Fritz. 1967. *Germany's Aims in the First World War*. New York: Norton.

Fortna, Virginia P. 2004. *Peace Time: Cease-Fire Agreements and the Durability of Peace.* Princeton, NJ: Princeton University Press.
Fravel, M. Taylor. 2007a. "Power Shifts and Escalation: Explaining China's Use of Force in Territorial Disputes." *International Security* 32 (2): 44–83.
Fravel, M. Taylor. 2007b. "Securing Borders: China's Doctrine and Force Structure for Frontier Defense." *Journal of Strategic Studies* 30 (4–5): 705–37.
Fravel, M. Taylor. 2008. *Strong Border, Secure Nation: Cooperation and Order in China's Territorial Disputes.* Princeton, NJ: Princeton University Press.
Fravel, M. Taylor. 2012. "All Quiet in the South China Sea: Why China Is Playing Nice (for Now)." *Foreign Affairs*, March 22. https://www.foreignaffairs.com/articles/china/2012-03-22/all-quiet-south-china-sea.
Friedberg, Aaron L. 1988. *The Weary Titan: The Experience of Relative Decline, 1895–1905.* Princeton, NJ: Princeton University Press.
Friedberg, Aaron L. 1993/1994. "Ripe for Rivalry: Prospects for in a Multipolar Asia." *International Security* 18 (3): 5–33.
Friedman, Max P., and Tom Long. 2015. "Soft Balancing in the Americas: Latin American Opposition to U.S. Intervention, 1898–1936." *International Security* 40 (1): 120–56.
Fukuyama, Francis. 1989. "The End of History." *The National Interest* 16: 3–18.
Fukuyama, Francis. 1992. *The End of History and the Last Man.* New York: Free Press.
Gaddis, John L. 1986. "The Long Peace: Elements of Stability in the Postwar International System." *International Security* 10 (4): 99–142.
Gannon, J. Andre, and Daniel Kent. 2021. "Keeping Your Friends Close, but Acquaintances Closer: Why Weakly Allied States Make Committed Coalition Partners." *Journal of Conflict Resolution* 65 (5): 889–918.
Gartner, Scott S., and Randolph M. Siverson. 1996. "War Expansion and War Outcome." *Journal of Conflict Resolution* 40 (1): 4–15.
Gartzke, Erik, and Michael W. Simon. 1999. "Hot Hand: A Critical Analysis of Enduring Rivalries." *Journal of Politics* 61 (3): 777–98.
Gelpi, Christopher. 1999. "Alliances as Instruments of Intra-Allied Control." In *Imperfect Unions: Security Institutions over Time and Space*, eds. Helga Haftendorn, Robert O. Keohane, and Celeste Wallander, 107–39. New York: Oxford University Press.
Gholz, Eugene, Daryl G. Press, and Harvey M. Sapolsk. 1997. "Come Home, America: The Strategy of Restraint in the Face of Temptation." *International Security* 21 (4): 5–48.
Gilpin, Robert. 1981. *War and Change in World Politics.* Cambridge: Cambridge University Press.
Gilpin, Robert. 1987. *The Political Economy of International Relations.* Princeton, NJ: Princeton University Press.
Glaser, Bonnie S. 2020. "Dire Straits: Should American Support for Taiwan Be Ambiguous? A Guarantee Isn't Worth the Risk." *Foreign Affair*, September 24. https://www.foreignaffairs.com/articles/united-states/2020-09-24/dire-straits.
Glaser, John, Christopher A. Preble, and A. Trevor Thrall. 2019. "Towards a More Prudent American Grand Strategy." *Survival* 61 (5): 25–42.
Gochman, Charles S. 1980. "Status, Capabilities, and Major Power Conflict." In *The Correlates of War II: Testing Some Realpolitik Models*, ed. J. David Singer, 83–123. New York: Free Press.
Gochman, Charles S., and Zeev Maoz. 1984. "Militarized Interstate Disputes: 1816–1976: Procedures, Patterns, and Insights." *Journal of Conflict Resolution* 28 (4): 585–616.
Goddard, Stacie E. 2006. "Uncommon Ground: Indivisible Territory and the Politics of Legitimacy." *International Organization* 60 (1): 35–68.
Goertz, Gary, Bradford Jones, and Paul F. Diehl. 2005. "Maintenance Processes for International Rivalries." *Journal of Conflict Resolution* 49 (5): 742–69.
Goh, Evelyn. 2007/2008. "Great Powers and Hierarchical Order in Southeast Asia: Analyzing Regional Security Strategies." *International Security* 32 (3): 113–57.

Goh, Evelyn. 2013. *The Struggle for Order: Hegemony, Hierarchy, and Transition in the Cold-War East Asia.* Oxford: Oxford University Press.

Goh, Evelyn. 2019. "Contesting Hegemonic Order: China in East Asia." *Security Studies* 28 (3): 614–44.

Goh, Evelyn. 2023. "New Mindsets Needed for an Era of Uncertainty." *Global Asia* 18 (3): https://www.globalasia.org/v18no3/cover/new-mindsets-needed-for-an-era-of-uncertainty_evelyn-goh.

Gorman, Robert F. 1991. *Political Conflict on the Horn of Africa.* New York: Praeger.

Gould, Stephen J., and Niles Eldredge. 1977. "Punctuated Equilibria: The Tempo and Mode of Evolution Reconsidered." *Paleobiology* 3 (2): 115–51.

Green, Michael J. 2001. *Japan's Reluctant Realism: Foreign Policy Challenges in an Era of Uncertain Power.* New York: Palgrave.

Grieco, Joseph M. 2001. "Repeated Military Challenges and Recurrent International Conflicts: 1918–1994." *International Studies Quarterly* 45 (2): 295–316.

Haass, Richard, and Charles Kupchan. 2023. "The West Needs a New Strategy in Ukraine: A Plan for Getting from the Battlefield to the Negotiation Table." *Foreign Affairs*, April 13. https://www.foreignaffairs.com/ukraine/russia-richard-haass-west-battlefield-negotiations.

Hallin, Daniel C. 1986. *The "Uncensored" War.* Oxford: Oxford University Press.

Hamilton, Richard F., and Holger H. Herwig. 2004. *Decisions for War, 1914–1917.* Cambridge: Cambridge University Press.

Happymon, Jacob. 2021. *The Kashmir Back Channel: India–Pakistan Negotiations on Kashmir from 2004–2007.* Washington, DC: Institute for the Study of Diplomacy, Georgetown University.

Harding, Harry. 1976. "Linkages between Chinese Domestic and Foreign Policy." Paper presented at the Workshop on Chinese Foreign Policy. Ann Arbor, Michigan, August 12–14.

Hart, Jeffrey. 1976. "Three Approaches to the Measurement of Power in International Relations." *International Organization* 30 (2): 289–305.

Hast, Susanna. 2014. *Spheres of Influence in International Relations: History, Theory and Politics.* Burlington, VT: Ashgate.

Haynes, Kyle. 2017. "Diversionary Conflict: Demonizing Enemies or Demonstrating Competence?" *Conflict Management and Peace Science* 34 (4): 337–58.

He, Kai, and Huiyun Feng. 2008. "If Not Soft Balancing, Then What? Reconsidering Soft Balancing and U.S. Policy toward China." *Security Studies* 17 (2): 363–95.

He, Kai, and Huiyun Feng. 2012. *Prospect Theory and Foreign Policy Analysis in the Asia Pacific: Rational Leaders and Risky Behavior.* New York: Routledge.

He, Kai, Huiyung Feng, Steve Chan, and Weixing Hu. 2021. "Rethinking Revisionism in World Politics." *Chinese Journal of International Politics* 14 (2): 159–86.

Hemmer, Christopher, and Peter J. Katzenstein. 2002. "Why Is There No NATO in Asia? Collective Identity, Regionalism, and the Origins of Multilateralism." *International Organization* 56 (3): 575–607.

Hensel, Paul R. 1994. "One Thing Leads to Another: Recurrent Militarized Disputes in Latin America, 1816–1986." *Journal of Peace Research* 31 (3): 281–97.

Hensel, Paul R. 1999. "An Evolutionary Approach to the Study of Interstate Rivalry." *Crisis Management and Peace Science* 17 (2): 175–206.

Herrmann, David G. 1997. *Arming of Europe and the Making of the First World War.* Princeton, NJ: Princeton University Press.

Higgins, Trumbull. 1966. *Hitler and Russia: The Third Reich in a Two-Front War, 1937–1943.* New York: Macmillan.

Hilgruber, Andrea. 1981. *Germany and the Two World Wars.* Cambridge, MA: Harvard University Press.

Hiro, Dilip. 1991. *The Longest War: The Iran–Iraq Military Conflict.* New York: Routledge.

Hoopes, Townsend. 1969. *The Limits of Intervention: An Account of How the Johnson Policy of Escalation Was Reversed*. New York: McKay.

Hudson, Phillip. 2010. "President Barack Obama Says Prime Minister Kevin Rudd Is 'Smart, Humble.'" *The West Australian*, April 15. https://www.perthnow.com.au/news/nsw/president-barack-obama-says-prime-minister-kevin-rudd-is-smart-humble-ng-fe9b5c28fefd4406de67cef56dd015ed.

Hufbauer, Gary C., Jeffrey J. Schott, and Kimberly A. Elliott. 1990. *Economic Sanctions Reconsidered*. Washington, DC: Institute for International Economics.

Hui, Victoria Tin-bor. 2005. *War and State Formation in Ancient China and Early Modern Europe*. Cambridge: Cambridge University Press.

Huth, Paul F. 1988. *Extended Deterrence and the Prevention of War*. New Haven, CT: Yale University Press.

Huth, Paul, and Bruce M. Russett. 1988. "Deterrence Failure and Crisis Escalation." *International Studies Quarterly* 32 (1): 29–46.

Ike, Nobutake. 1967. *Japan's Decision for War: Records of the 1941 Policy Conferences*. Stanford, CA: Stanford University Press.

Ikenberry, G. John. 2008. "The Rise of China and the Future of the West: Can the Liberal System Survive?" *Foreign Affairs* 87 (1): 23–37.

"It Is Not Up to the U.S. Alone to Evaluate Its Democracy: Yang Jiechi." 2021. YouTube, May 19. https://www.youtube.com/watch?v=ETOfymWVShM.

Jaffe, Seth N. 2017. *Thucydides on the Outbreak of War: Character and Contest*. Oxford: Oxford University Press.

Jervis, Robert. 1978. "Cooperation under the Security Dilemma." *World Politics* 30 (2): 167–214.

Johnson, Jesse C., and Brett A. Leeds. 2011. "Defense Pacts: A Prescription for Peace?" *Foreign Policy Analysis* 7 (1): 45–65.

Johnston, Alastair I. 2011. "Stability and Instability in Sino–US Relations: A Response to Yan Xuetong's Superficial Friendship Theory." *Chinese Journal of International Politics* 4 (1): 5–29.

Joseph, Joseph S. 1997. *Cyprus: Ethnic Conflict and International Politics*. New York: St. Martin's.

Kagan, Donald. 1969. *The Outbreak of the Peloponnesian War*. Ithaca, NY: Cornell University Press.

Kahneman, Daniel, and Amos Tversky. 1979. "Prospect Theory: An Analysis of Decision under Risk." *Econometrica* 47 (2): 263–92.

Kahneman, Daniel, and Amos Tversky, eds. 2000. *Choices, Values, and Frames*. Cambridge: Cambridge University Press.

Kahneman, Daniel, Paul Slovic, and Amos Tversky, eds. 1982. *Judgment under Uncertainty: Heuristics and Biases*. Cambridge: Cambridge University Press.

Kang, David C. 2003. "Getting Asia Wrong: The Need for New Analytical Frameworks." *International Security* 27 (4): 57–85.

Kang, David C. 2007. *China Rising: Peace, Power, and Order in East Asia*. New York: Columbia University Press.

Kang, David C. 2010. "Hierarchy and Legitimacy in International Systems: The Tribute System in Early Modern East Asia." *Security Studies* 19 (4): 591–622.

Kang, David C. 2012. *East Asia before the West: Five Centuries of Trade and Tribute*. New York: Columbia University Press.

Kang, David C. 2020a. "Thought Games about China." *Journal of East Asian Studies* 20 (2): 135–50.

Kang, David C. 2020b. "International Order in Historical East Asia: Tribute and Hierarchy beyond Sinocentrism and Eurocentrism." *International Organization* 74 (1): 65–93.

Kang, David C. 2023. "There Is No East Asian Balancing against China." Unpublished manuscript.

Kastner, Scott L. 2022. *War and Peace in the Taiwan Strait.* New York: Columbia University Press.

Kaufman, Chaim. 2004. "Threat Inflation and the Failure of the Marketplace of Ideas: The Selling of the Iraq War." *International Security* 29 (1): 5–48.

Kawasaki, Tsuyoshi. 2007. "Learning Institutions: The Logic of Japan's Institutional Strategy for Regional Security." In *The Uses of Institutions: The U.S., Japan, and Governance in East Asia*, eds. G. John Ikenberry and Takashi Inoguchi, 77–102. New York: Palgrave Macmillan.

Kegley, Charles W., Jr., and Gregory Raymond. 1994. *A Multipolar Peace? Great-Power Politics in the Twenty-first Century.* New York: St. Martin's.

Kennedy, Paul. 1980. *The Rise of the Anglo-German Antagonism: 1860–1914.* London: Allen & Unwin.

Kennedy, Paul. 1987. *The Rise and Fall of the Great Powers: Economic Change and Military Conflict from 1500 to 2000.* New York: Random House.

Kenwick, Michael R., John A. Vasquez, and Matthew A. Powers. 2015. "Do Alliances Really Deter?" *Journal of Politics* 77 (4): 943–44.

Keohane, Robert O. 1971. "The Big Influence of Small States." *Foreign Policy* 2: 161–82.

Khong, Yuen Foong. 1992. *Analogies at War: Korea, Munich, Dien Bien Phu, and the Vietnam Decisions of 1965.* Princeton, NJ: Princeton University Press.

Khong, Yuen Foong. 2004. "Coping with Strategic Uncertainty: The Role of Institutions and Soft Balancing in Southeast Asia's Post–Cold War Strategy." In *Rethinking Security in East Asia: Identity, Power, and Efficiency*, eds. J. J. Suh, Peter J. Katzenstein, and Allen Carlson, 172–208. Stanford, CA: Stanford University Press.

Kim, Claudia J. 2019. "Military Alliances as a Stabilising Force: U.S. Relations with South Korea and Taiwan, 1950s–1960s." *Journal of Strategic* Studies 44 (7): 1041–62.

Kim, Tongfi. 2011. "Why Alliances Entangle but Seldom Entrap States." *Security Studies* 20 (3): 350–77.

Klein, James P., Gary Goertz, and Paul F. Diehl. 2006. "The New Rivalry Dataset: Procedures and Patterns." *Journal of Peace Research* 43 (3): 331–48.

Koen, Ross Y. 1960. *The China Lobby in American Politics.* New York: Macmillan.

Kofman, Michael. 2018. "The August War, Ten Years On: A Retrospective on the Russo-Georgian War." *War on the Rocks*, August 17. https://warontherocks.com/2018/08/the-august-war-ten-years-on-a-retrospective-on-the-russo-georgian-war/.

Krebs, Ronald R. 1999. "Perverse Institutionalism: NATO and the Greco–Turkish Conflict." *International Organization* 53 (2): 343–77.

Krickovic, Andrej. 2017. "The Symbiotic China–Russia Partnership: Cautious Riser and Desperate Challenger." *Chinese Journal of International Politics* 10 (3): 299–329.

Krickovic, Andrej, and Chang Zhang. 2020. "Fears of Falling Short versus Anxieties of Decline: Explaining Russia and China's Approach to Status-Seeking." *Chinese Journal of International Politics* 13 (2): 219–51.

Kugler, Jacek, and Marina Arbetman. 1989. "Choosing among Measures of Power: A Review of the Empirical Record." In *Power in World Politics*, eds. Richard J. Stoll and Michael D. Ward, 49–78. Boulder, CO: Rienner.

Kuperman, Alan. 2008. "The Moral Hazard of Humanitarian Intervention: Lessons from the Balkans." *International Studies Quarterly* 52 (1): 49–80.

Labs, Eric J. 1992. "Do Weak States Bandwagon?" *Security Studies* 1 (3): 383–416.

Larson, Deborah W., and Alexei Shevchenko. 2010. "Status Seekers: Chinese and Russian Responses to U.S. Primacy." *International Security* 34 (4): 63–95.

Larson, Deborah W., and Alexei Shevchenko. 2019. *Quest for Status: Chinese and Russian Foreign Policy.* New Haven, CT: Yale University Press.

Layne, Christopher. 1994. "Kant or Cant: The Myth of the Democratic Peace." *International Security* 19 (2): 5–49.

Layne, Christopher. 2006. *The Peace of Illusions: American Grand Strategy from 1940 to the Present.* Ithaca, NY: Cornell University Press.

Lebow, R. Ned. 1985. "Miscalculation in the South Atlantic: The Origins of the Falklands War." In *Psychology and Deterrence*, eds. Robert Jervis, R. Ned Lebow, and Janice G. Stein, 85–124. Baltimore: Johns Hopkins University Press.

Lebow, R. Ned. 2000/2001. "Contingency, Catalyst, and International System." *Political Science Quarterly* 115 (4): 591–616.

Lebow, R. Ned. 2003. "A Data Set Named Desire: A Reply to William R. Thompson." *International Studies Quarterly* 47 (3): 475–78.

Lebow, R. Ned. 2010. *Why Nations Fight: Past and Future Motivations for War*. Cambridge: Cambridge University Press.

Lebow, R. Ned, and Benjamin Valentino. 2009. "Lost in Transition: A Critical Analysis of Power Transition Theory." *International Relations* 23 (3): 389–410.

Lebow, R. Ned, and Daniel P. Tompkins. 2016. "The Thucydides Claptrap: Prevailing Theory Argues that U.S. Conflicts with Rising Powers Are Inevitable. It's Also Flat-out Wrong." *Washington Monthly*, June 28. https://washingtonmonthly.com/author/richard-ned-lebow-and-daniel-p-tompkins/.

Lee, James. 2019. "Did Thucydides Believe in Thucydides' Trap? The History of the Peloponnesian War and Its Relevance to US–China Relations." *Journal of Chinese Political Science* 24 (1): 67–86.

Leeds, Brett A. 2003. "Do Alliances Deter Aggression? The Influence of Military Alliances on the Initiation of Militarized Interstate Disputes." *American Journal of Political Science* 47 (3): 427–39.

Leeds, Brett A., Andrew G. Long, and Sarah M. Mitchell. 2000. "Reevaluating Alliance Reliability: Specific Threats, Specific Promises." *Journal of Conflict Resolution* 44 (5): 686–99.

Leeds, Brett A., and Jesse C. Johnson. 2016. "Theory, Data, and Deterrence: A Response to Kenwick, Vasquez, and Powers." *Journal of Politics* 79 (1): 335–40.

Lefebvre, Jeffrey A. 1991. *Arms for the Horn: U.S. Security Policy in Ethiopia and Somalia, 1953–1991*. Pittsburgh: University of Pittsburgh Press.

Lemke, Douglas. 2003. "Investigating the Preventive Motive for War." *International Interactions* 29 (4): 273–92.

Leng, Russel J. 1983. "When Will They Ever Learn: Coercive Bargaining in Recurrent Crises." *Journal of Conflict Resolution* 27 (3): 379–419.

Leng, Russel J. 2000. *Bargaining and Learning in Recurring Crises: The Soviet–American, Egyptian–Israeli, and Indo–Pakistani Rivalries*. Ann Arbor: University of Michigan Press.

Levy, Jack S. 1987. "Declining Power and the Preventive Motivation for War." *World Politics* 40 (1): 82–107.

Levy, Jack S. 1996. "Loss Aversion, Framing and Bargaining: The Implications of Prospect Theory for International Conflict." *International Political Science Review* 17 (2): 177–93.

Levy, Jack S. 1997. "Prospect Theory, Rational Choice, and International Relations." *International Studies Quarterly* 41 (1): 87–112.

Levy, Jack S. 2008. "Preventive War and Democratic Politics." *International Studies Quarterly* 52 (1): 1–24.

Levy, Jack S., and Joseph R. Gochal. 2001/2002. "Democracy and Preventive War: Israel and the 1956 Sinai Campaign." *Security Studies* 11 (2): 1-49.

Levy, Jack S., and William Mulligan. 2017. "Shifting Power, Preventive Logic, and the Response of the Target: Germany, Russia and the First World War." *Journal of Strategic Studies* 40 (5): 731–69.

Levy, Jack S., and William R. Thompson. 2006. "Hegemonic Threats and Great Power Balancing in Europe, 1495–1999." *Security Studies* 14 (1): 1–33.

Levy, Jack S., and William R. Thompson. 2010. "Balancing on Land and at Sea: Do States Ally against the Leading Global Power?" *International Security* 35 (1): 7–43.

Li, Richard P. Y., and William R. Thompson. 1975. "The 'Coup Contagion' Hypothesis." *International Studies Quarterly* 19 (1): 63–88.

Lieber, Kier A. 2007. "The New History of World War I and What It Means for International Relations Theory." *International Security* 32 (2): 155–91.
Lieber, Keir, and Gerard Alexander. 2005. "Waiting for Balancing: Why the World Is Not Pushing Back." *International Security* 30 (1): 109–39.
Liff, Adam P., and G. John Ikenberry. 2014. "Racing toward Tragedy? China's Rise, Military Competition in the Asia Pacific, and the Security Dilemma." *International Security* 39 (2): 52–91.
Lu, Marcus. 2023. "Ranked: The Top Economies in the World (1980–2075)." *Visual Capitalist*, July 21. https://www.visualcapitalist.com/top-economies-in-the-world-1980-2075/.
Luttwak, Edward N. 1999. "Give War a Chance." *Foreign Affairs* 78 (4): 36–44.
Ma, Xinru, and David C. Kang. 2024. *Beyond Power Transitions: The Lessons of East Asian History and the Future of U.S.–China Relations*. New York: Columbia University Press.
MacDonald, Paul K., and Joseph M. Parent. 2011. "Graceful Decline? The Surprising Success of Great Power Retrenchment." *International Security* 35 (4): 7–44.
MacDonald, Paul K., and Joseph M. Parent. 2018a. "The Road to Recovery: How Once Great Powers Became Great Again." *Washington Quarterly* 41 (3): 21–39.
MacDonald, Paul K., and Joseph M. Parent. 2018b. *Twilight of Titans: Great Power Decline and Retrenchment*. Ithaca, NY: Cornell University Press.
Mack, Andrew. 1975. "Why Big Nations Lose Small Wars: The Politics of Asymmetric Conflict." *World Politics* 27 (2): 175–200.
Mackinder, Halford J. 1904. "The Geographical Pivot of History." *Geographical Journal* 23 (4): 421–37.
Mackinder, Halford J. 1919. *Democratic Ideals and Reality: A Study in the Politics of Reconstruction*. London: Constable.
Mackinder, Halford J. 1943. "The Round World and the Winning of the Peace." *Foreign Affairs* 21 (4): 595–605.
MacMillan, Margaret. 2013. *The War That Ended Peace*. New York: Random House.
Mahan, Alfred T. [1890] 1980. *The Influence of Sea Power upon History 1660–1783*. New York: Prentice-Hall.
Mandelbaum, Michael. 1988. *The Fate of Nations: The Search for National Security in the Nineteenth and Twentieth Centuries*. Cambridge: Cambridge University Press.
Maoz, Zeev. 1984. "Peace by Empire? Conflict Outcomes and International Stability, 1816–1976." *Journal of Peace Research* 21 (3): 227–41.
Maoz, Zeev, and Ben D. Mor. 2002. *Bound by Struggle: The Strategic Evolution of Enduring International Rivalries*. Ann Arbor: University of Michigan Press.
Marcella, Gabriel, and Richard Downes, eds. 1999. *Security Cooperation in the Western Hemisphere: Resolving the Ecuador–Peru Conflict*. Miami: University of Miami North–South Center Press.
Mares, David R. 1996/1997. "Deterrence Bargaining in the Ecuador and Peru Enduring Rivalry: Designing Strategies around Military Weakness." *Security Studies* 6 (2): 91–123.
Mazarr, Michael J. 2020. "Dire Straits: Should American Support for Taiwan Be Ambiguous? A Guarantee Won't Solve the Problem." *Foreign Affairs*, September 24. https://www.foreignaffairs.com/articles/united-states/2020-09-24/dire-straits.
McDermott, Rose. 1998. *Risk-Taking in International Relations: Prospect Theory in American Foreign Policy*. Ann Arbor: University of Michigan Press.
Mearsheimer, John J. 2001. *The Tragedy of Great Power Politics*. New York: Norton.
Mearsheimer, John J. 2006. "China's Unpeaceful Rise." *Current History* 105 (690): 160–62.
Mearsheimer, John J. 2019. "Bound to Fail: The Rise and Fall of the Liberal International Order." *International Security* 43 (4): 7–50.
Mearsheimer, John J., and Stephen M. Walt. 2003. "An Unnecessary War." *Foreign Policy* 134 (January/February): 51–59.
Mearsheimer, John J., and Stephen M. Walt. 2007. *The Israel Lobby and U.S. Foreign Policy*. New York: Farrar, Straus, and Giroux.

Mearsheimer, John J., and Stephen M. Walt. 2016a. "The Case for Offshore Balancing: A Superior U.S. Grand Strategy." *Foreign Affairs* 95 (4): 70–83.

Mearsheimer, John J., and Stephen M. Walt. 2016b. "Reply." *Foreign Affairs* 95 (6): 169–71.

Meernik, James, and Peter Waterman. 1996. "The Myth of the Diversionary Use of Force by American Presidents." *Political Research Quarterly* 49 (3): 573–90.

Mercer, Jonathan. 1996. *Reputation and International Politics*. Ithaca, NY: Cornell University Press.

Mercer, Jonathan. 2007. "Reputation and Rational Deterrence Theory." *Security Studies* 7 (1): 100–13.

Merom, Gil. 2003. *How Democracies Lose Small Wars: State, Society, and the Failure of France in Algeria, Israel in Lebanon, and the United States in Vietnam*. Cambridge: Cambridge University Press.

Merritt, Richard L., and Dina A. Zinnes. 1988. "Validity of Power Indices," *International Interactions* 14 (2): 141–51.

Merritt, Richard L., and Dina A. Zinnes. 1989. "Alternative Indexes of National Power." In *Power in World Politics*, eds. Richard J. Stoll and Michael D. Ward, 11–28. Boulder, CO: Rienner.

Modelski, George. 1987a. *Long Cycles in World Politics*. Seattle: University of Washington Press.

Modelski, George, ed. 1987b. *Exploring Long Cycles*. Boulder, CO: Rienner.

Moise, Edwin E. 1996. *Tonkin Gulf and the Escalation of the Vietnam War*. Chapel Hill: University of North Carolina Press.

Moon, Chung-in. 2023. "Asia-Pacific vs Indo-Pacific: Paradigm Shift or False Choice?" *Global Asia* 18(3): https://www.globalasia.org/v18no3/cover/asia-pacific-vs-indo-pacific-paradigm-shift-or-false-choice_chung-in-moon.

Mor, Ben D. 1993. *Decision and Interaction in Crisis: A Model of International Crisis Behavior*. Westport, CT: Praeger.

Morgan, Clifton. 1999. "Domestic Support and Diversionary External Conflict in Great Britain, 1950–1992." *Journal of Politics* 61 (3): 799–814.

Morgenthau, Hans J. 1985. *Politics among Nations: The Struggle for Power and Peace*, 6th edition. New York: Knopf.

Morrow, James D. 1993. "Arms Versus Allies: Tradeoffs in the Search for Security," *International Organization* 47 (2): 207–33.

Morrow, James D. 1994. "Alliances, Credibility, and Peacetime Costs." *Journal of Conflict Resolution* 38 (2): 270–97.

Morrow, James D. 2003. "Assessing the Role of Trade as a Source of Costly Signals." In *Economic Interdependence and International Conflict*, eds. Edward D. Mansfield and Brian Pollins, 89–95. Ann Arbor: University of Michigan Press.

Most, Benjamin, and Harvey Starr. 1989. *Inquiry, Logic, and International Politics*. Columbia: University of South Carolina Press.

Moyer, Jonathan D., Collin J. Meisel, Austin S. Matthews, David K. Bohl, and Mathew J. Burrows. 2021. *China–US Competition: Measuring Global Influence*. Washington, DC: Scowcroft Center, Atlantic Council; Denver: Frederick S. Pardee Center for International Futures, University of Denver. https://www.atlanticcouncil.org/wp-content/uploads/2021/06/China-US-Competition-Report-2021.pdf.

Murata, Koji. 2007. "U.S.–Japan Alliance as Flexible Institution." In *The Uses of Institutions: The U.S., Japan, and Governance in East Asia*, eds. G. John Ikenberry and Takashi Inoguchi, 131–50. New York: Palgrave Macmillan.

Murphy, Matt. 2022. "Dutch Government Apologises to Srebrenica Veterans." BBC News, June 18. https://www.bbc.com/news/world-europe-61855110.

Murray, Michelle. 2010. "Identity, Insecurity, and Great Power Politics: The Tragedy of German Naval Ambition before the First World War." *Security Studies* 19 (4): 656–88.

Murray, Michelle. 2019. *The Struggle for Recognition in International Relations: Status, Revisionism, and Rising Powers.* New York: Oxford University Press.

Mynott, Jeremy, ed. 2013. *Thucydides: The War of the Peloponnesians and the Athenians.* Cambridge: Cambridge University Press.

Nincic, Miroslav. 2011. *The Logic of Positive Engagement.* Ithaca, NY: Cornell University Press.

Nish, Ian. 1986. *The Origins of the Russo-Japanese War.* London: Longman.

Nye, Joseph S., Jr. 1990. *Bound to Lead: The Changing Nature of American Power.* New York: Basic Books.

Nye, Joseph S., Jr. 2002. *The Paradox of American Power.* New York: Oxford University Press.

Nye, Joseph S., Jr. 2004. *Soft Power: The Means to Success in World Politics.* New York: Public Affairs.

Nye, Joseph S., Jr. 2015. "Only China Can Contain China." HuffPost, March 11. https://www.huffpost.com/entry/china-contain-china_b_6845588.

Nye, Joseph S., Jr. 2019. "The Rise and Fall of American Hegemony: From Wilson to Trump." *International Affairs* 95 (1): 63–80.

Olson, Mancur, Jr. 1965. *The Logic of Collective Action.* Cambridge, MA: Harvard University Press.

Olson, Mancur, Jr. 1982. *The Rise and Decline of Nations: Economic Growth, Stagflation, and Social Rigidities.* New Haven, CT: Yale University Press.

Organski, A. F. K., and Jacek Kugler. 1980. *The War Ledger.* Chicago: University of Chicago Press.

Pape, Robert A. 1997. "Economic Sanctions Do Not Work." *International Security* 22 (2): 90–136.

Pape, Robert A. 2005. "Soft Balancing against the United States." *International Security* 30 (1): 7–45.

Paul, T. V. 1994. *Asymmetric Conflicts: War Initiation by Weaker Powers.* Cambridge: Cambridge University Press.

Paul, T. V. 2005. "Soft Balancing in the Age of U.S. Primacy." *International Security* 30 (1): 46–71.

Paul, T. V. 2018. *Restraining Great Powers: Soft Balancing from Empires to the Global Era.* New Haven, CT: Yale University Press.

Pelletierre, Stephen C. 1992. *The Iran–Iraq War: Chaos in a Vacuum.* New York: Praeger.

Pempel, T. J. 2016. "Soft Balancing, Hedging, and Institutional Darwinism: The Economic–Security Nexus and East Asian Regionalism." *Journal of East Asian Studies* 10 (2): 209–38.

Platias, Athanassios, and Vasilis Trigkas. 2021. "Unravelling the Thucydides' Trap: Inadvertent Escalation or War of Choice?" *Chinese Journal of International Politics* 14 (2): 219–55.

Posen, Barry. 2013. "Pull Back: The Case for a Less Activist Foreign Policy." *Foreign Affairs* 92 (1): 112–28.

Posen, Barry R. 2014. *Restraint: A New Foundation for U.S. Grand Strategy.* Ithaca, NY: Cornell University Press.

Powell, Robert. 2006. "War as a Commitment Problem." *International Organization* 60 (1): 169–203.

Pressman, Jeremy. 2008. *Warring Friends: Alliance Restraint in International Politics.* Ithaca, NY: Cornell University Press.

Priebe, Miranda, Bryan Rooney, Caitlin McCulloch, and Zachary Burdette. 2021. *Do Alliances and Partnerships Entangle the United States in Conflict?* Santa Monica, CA: RAND.

Putnam, Robert D. 1988. "Diplomacy and Domestic Politics: The Logic of Two-Level Games." *International Organization* 42 (3): 427–60.

Raiffa, Howard. 1982. *The Art and Science of Negotiation.* Cambridge, MA: Harvard University Press.

Rasler, Karen A., and William R. Thompson. 1991. "Technological Innovation, Capability Positional Shift, and Systemic War." *Journal of Conflict Resolution* 35 (3): 412–42.

Rasler, Karen A., and William R. Thompson. 1994. *The Great Powers and Global Struggle.* Lexington: University Press of Kentucky.

Rauch, Carsten. 2017. "Challenging the Power Consensus: GDP, CINC, and Power Transition." *Security Studies* 26 (4): 642–64.

Ray, James L. 1974. "Status Inconsistency and War Involvement among European States, 1816–1970." *Peace Science Society Papers* 23: 69–80.

Record, Jeffrey. 2007. *Beating Goliath: Why Insurgencies Win.* Washington, DC: Potomac Books.

Reiter, Dan. 1995. "Exploding the Powder Keg Myth: Preemptive Wars Almost Never Happen." *International Security* 20 (2): 5–34.

Renshon, Jonathan. 2016. "Status Deficits and War." *International Organization* 70 (3): 513–50.

Renshon, Jonathan. 2017. *Fighting for Status: Hierarchy and Conflict in World Politics.* Princeton, NJ: Princeton University Press.

Richards, Diana, T. Clifton Morgan, Rick K. Wilson, Valerie Schwebach, and Garry D. Young. 1993. "Good Times, Bad Times, and the Diversionary Use of Force: A Tale of Some Not-so-Free Agents." *Journal of Conflict Resolution* 37 (3): 504–35.

Richardson, Lewis F. 1960. *Arms and Insecurity: A Mathematical Study of the Causes and Origins of War.* Chicago: Quadrangle Books.

Ripsman, Norrin M., and Jack S. Levy. 2007. "The Preventive War That Never Happened: Britain, France, and the Rise of Germany in the 1930s." *Security Studies* 16 (1): 32–67.

Rising Power Initiative. 2021. "RPI Policy Alert: Rising Powers React to Contentious U.S.–China Relations: A Roundup." George Washington University. March. https://www.risingpowersinitiative.org/publication/rising-powers-react-to-contentious-u-s-china-relations-a-roundup.

Rooney, Bryan, Grant Johnson, and Miranda Priebe. 2021. *How Does Defense Spending Affect Economic Growth?* Santa Monica, CA: RAND.

Ross, Robert S. 1988. *The Indo–China Triangle: China's Vietnam Policy 1975–1979.* New York: Columbia University Press.

Ross, Robert S. 1999. "The Geography of Peace: East Asia in the Twenty-First Century." *International Security* 23 (4): 81–118.

Ross, Robert S. 2004. "Bipolarity and Balancing in East Asia." In *Balance of Power: Theory and Practice in the 21st Century*, eds. T. V. Paul, James J. Wirtz, and Michel Fortmann, 267–304. Stanford, CA: Stanford University Press.

Ross, Robert S. 2006. "Balance of Power Politics and the Rise of China: Accommodation and Balancing in East Asia." *Security Studies* 15 (3): 355–95.

Russett, Bruce M. 1969. "Refining Deterrence Theory: The Japanese Attack on Pearl Harbor." In *Theory and Research on the Causes of War*, Dean G. Pruitt and Richard C. Snyder, 127–35. Englewood Cliffs, NJ: Prentice-Hall.

Russett, Bruce M. 1970. *What Price Vigilance? The Burden of National Defense.* New Haven, CT: Yale University Press.

Ryan, Cornelius. 1977. *A Bridge Too Far.* New York: Popular Library.

Sabrosky, Alan N. 1980. "Interstate Alliances: Their Reliability and the Expansion of War." In *The Correlates of War II: Testing Some Realpolitik Models*, ed. J. David Singe, 161–98. New York: Free Press.

Sachar, Howard M. 1981. *Egypt and Israel.* New York: Marek.

Sacks, David. 2023. "Taiwan Announced a Record Budget: But Is It Enough to Deter China?" Council on Foreign Relations, August 30. https://www.cfr.org/blog/taiwan-announced-record-defense-budget-it-enough-deter-china.

Saltzman, Ilai Z. 2012. "Soft Balancing as Foreign Policy: Assessing American Strategy toward Japan in the Interwar Period." *Foreign Policy Analysis* 8 (2): 131–50.

Sartori, Anne L. 2003. "The Might of the Pen: A Reputational Theory of Communication in International Disputes." *International Organization* 56 (1): 121–49.

Schelling, Thomas C. 1966. *Arms and Influence.* New Haven, CT: Yale University Press.

Schroeder, Paul W. 1976. "Alliances, 1815–1945: Weapons of Power and Tools of Management." In *Historical Dimensions of National Security Problems*, ed. Klaus Knorr, 227–62. Lawrence: University Press of Kansas.
Schroeder, Paul W. 1994a. *The Transformation of European Politics: 1763–1848*. Oxford: Clarendon Press.
Schroeder, Paul W. 1994b. "Historical Reality vs. Neo-realist Theory." *International Security* 19 (1): 108–38.
Schroeder, Paul W. 1995. "History and Neorealism: A Second Look." *International Security* 20 (1): 193–95.
Schroeder, Paul W. 2004. "Embedded Counterfactuals and World War I as an Unavoidable War." In *Systems, Stability, and Statecraft: Essays on the International Theory of Modern Europe*, ed. Paul W. Schroeder, 157–91. York: Palgrave.
Schweller, Randall L. 1994. "Bandwagoning for Profit: Bringing the Revisionist State Back In." *International Security* 19 (1): 72–107.
Schweller, Randall L. 1997. "New Realist Research on Alliances: Refining, Not Refuting, Waltz's Balancing Proposition." *American Political Science Review* 91 (4): 927–30.
Schweller, Randall L. 1998. *Deadly Imbalances: Tripolarity and Hitler's Strategy of World Conquest*. New York: Columbia University Press.
Schweller, Randall L. 2001. "The Problem of International Order Revisited: A Review Essay." *International Security* 26 (1): 161–86.
Schweller, Randall L. 2006. *Unanswered Threats: Political Constraints on the Balance of Power*. Princeton, NJ: Princeton University Press.
Senese, Paul D., and Stephen L. Quackenbush. 2003. "Sowing the Seeds of Conflict: The Effect of Dispute Settlement on Durations of Peace." *Journal of Politics* 65 (3): 696–717.
Shambaugh, David. 2004/2005. "China Engages Asia: Reshaping the Regional Order." *International Security* 29 (3): 64–99.
Senese, Paul D., and John A. Vasquez. 2008. *The Steps to War: An Empirical Study*. Princeton, NJ: Princeton University Press.
Shavell, Stephen. 1979. "On Moral Hazard and Insurance." *Quarterly Journal of Economics* 93 (4): 541–62.
Shi, Jiangtao. 2020. "Destined for Conflict? Xi Jinping, Donald Trump, and the Thucydides Trap." *South China Morning Post*, May 21. https://www.scmp.com/news/china/diplomacy/article/3085321/destined-conflict-xi-jinping-donald-trump-and-thucydides-trap.
Shirk, Susan L. 2023. *Overreach: How China Derailed Its Peaceful Rise*. Oxford: Oxford University Press.
Shlaim, Avi. 2000. *The Iron Wall: Israel and the Arab World*. New York: Norton.
Simmons, Beth A. 1999. *Territorial Disputes and Their Resolution: The Case of Ecuador and Peru*. Washington, DC: United States Institute of Peace.
Singer, J. David. 1987. "Reconstructing the Correlates of War Dataset on Material Capabilities of States, 1816–1985." *International Interactions* 14 (2): 115–32.
Singer, J. David, Stuart Bremer, and John Stuckey. 1972 "Capability Distribution, Uncertainty, and Major Power War, 1820–1965." In *Peace, War, and Numbers*, ed. Bruce M. Russet, 19–48. Beverly Hills, CA: SAGE.
Singer, J. David, and Melvin Small. 1972. *The Wages of War: 1816-1965, A Statistical Handbook*. New York: Wiley.
Siverson, Randolph M., and Joel King. 1980. "Attributes of National Alliance Membership and War Participation, 1815–1965." *American Journal of Political Science* 24 (1): 1–15.
Small, Melvin, and J. David Singer. 1982. *Resort to Arms: International and Civil Wars, 1816-1980*. Beverly Hills, CA: Sage.
Smith, Alastair. 1995. "Alliance Formation and War." *International Studies Quarterly* 39 (4): 405–25.

Smith, Alastair. 1996a. "Diversionary Foreign Policy in Democratic Systems." *International Studies Quarterly* 40 (1): 133–53.
Smith, Alastair. 1996b. "To Intervene or Not to Intervene: A Biased Decision." *Journal of Conflict Resolution* 40 (1): 16–40.
Snider, Lewis W. 1987. "Identifying the Elements of State Power: Where Do We Begin?" *Comparative Political Studies* 20 (3): 314–56.
Snyder, Glenn H. 1984. "The Security Dilemma in Alliance Politics." *World Politics* 36 (4): 461–95.
Snyder, Glenn H. 1997. *Alliance Politics*. Ithaca, NY: Cornell University Press.
Snyder, Glenn H., and Paul Diesing. 1977. *Conflict among Nations: Bargaining, Decision Making, and System Structure in International Crisis*. Princeton, NJ: Princeton University Press.
Snyder, Jack. 1991. *Myths of Empire: Domestic Politics and International Ambition*. Ithaca, NY: Cornell University Press.
Snyder, Jack, and Keir A. Lieber. 2008. "Correspondence: Defensive Realism and the 'New' History of World War I." *International Security* 33 (1): 174–94.
Snyder, Scott. 2007. "The China–Japan Rivalry: South Korea's Pivotal Position?" In *Cross Currents: Regionalism and Nationalism in Northeast Asia*, eds. Gi-Wook Shin and Daniel C. Sneider, 241–55. Stanford, CA: Walter H. Shorenstein Asia-Pacific Research Center, Stanford University.
Sobek, David. 2007. "Rallying around the Podesta: Testing Diversionary Theory across Time." *Journal of Peace Research* 44 (1): 29–45.
Solingen, Etel. 2014. "Domestic Coalitions, Internationalization, and War: Then and Now." *International Security* 39 (1): 44–70.
Spykman, Nicholas J. 1942. *America's Strategy in World Politics: The United States and the Balance of Power*. New York: Harcourt, Brace.
Spykman, Nicholas J. 1944. *The Geography of the Peace*. New York: Harcourt, Brace.
Stein, Janice G. 1996. "Deterrence and Learning in an Enduring Rivalry: Egypt and Israel, 1948–73." *Security Studies* 6 (1): 104–52.
Stein, Kenneth W. 1999. *Heroic Diplomacy: Sadat, Kissinger, Carter, Begin, and the Quest for Arab–Israeli Peace*. New York: Routledge.
Stinnett, Douglas M., and Paul F. Diehl. 2001. "The Path(s) to Rivalry: Behavioral and Structural Explanations of Rivalry Development." *Journal of Politics* 63 (3): 717–40.
Stockholm International Peace Research Institute (SIPRI) Military Expenditure Database. 2020. "40 Countries with the Highest Military Spending Worldwide in 2024." https://en.wikipedia.org/wiki/List_of_countries_by_military_expenditures#As_a_share_of_GDP.
Stolper, Thomas E. 1995. *China, Taiwan, and the Offshore Islands: Together with an Implication for Outer Mongolia and Sino-Soviet Relations*. Armonk, NY: Sharpe.
Strassler, Robert B., ed. 1998. *The Landmark Thucydides: A Comprehensive Guide to the Peloponnesian War*. New York: Touchstone.
Suzuki, Susumu, Volker Krause, and J. David Singer. 2002. "The Correlates of War Project: A Bibliographic History of the Scientific Study of War and Peace, 1964-2000." *Conflict Management and Peace Science* 19 (2): 69–107.
Swaine, Michael D., and Ashley L. Tellis. 2000. *Interpreting China's Grand Strategy: Past, Present, and Future*. Santa Monica, CA: RAND.
Taber, Charles S. 1989. "Power Capability Indexes in the Third World." In *Power in World Politics*, eds. Richard J. Stoll and Michael D. Ward, 29–48. Boulder, CO: Rienner.
Taliaferro, Jeffrey W. 2004. *Balancing Risks: Great Power Intervention in the Periphery*. Ithaca, NY: Cornell University Press.
Taylor, A. J. P. 1954. *The Struggle for Mastery of Europe, 1848–1918*. Oxford: Clarendon Press.
Tellis, Ashley J. 2015. "Overview: Assessing National Power." In *Foundations of National Power in the Asia-Pacific*, eds. Ashley J. Tellis, Alison Szalwinski, and Michael Willis, 2–21.

Seattle: National Bureau of Asian Research. https://www.nbr.org/wp-content/uploads/pdfs/publications/sa15_overview_telllis.pdf.
Thompson, Peter. 2007. "The Case of Missing Hegemon: British Nonintervention in the American Civil War." *Security Studies* 16 (1): 96–132.
Thompson, William R. 1983. "Uneven Economic Growth, Systemic Challenges, and Global Wars." *International Studies Quarterly* 27 (3): 341–55.
Thompson, William R. 1990. "Long Waves, Technological Innovation, and Relative Decline." *International Organization* 44 (2): 201–33.
Thompson, William R. 1995. "Principal Rivalries." *Journal of Conflict Resolution* 39 (2): 195–223.
Thompson, William R. 2001. "Identifying Rivals and Rivalries in World Politics." *International Studies Quarterly* 45 (4): 557–86.
Thompson, William R. 2003. "A Streetcar Named Sarajevo: Catalysts, Multiple Causation Chains, and Rivalry Structures." *International Studies Quarterly* 47 (3): 453–74.
Thompson, William R. 2020. *Power Concentration in World Politics: The Political Economy of Systemic Leadership, Growth, and Conflict*. Cham, Switzerland: Springer.
Thompson, William R. 2022. *American Global Pre-Eminence: The Development and Erosion of Systemic Leadership*. Oxford: Oxford University Press.
Thomson, James C. 1973. "How Could Vietnam Happen? An Autopsy." In *Readings in American Foreign Policy: A Bureaucratic Perspective*, eds. Morton H. Halperin and Arnold Kanter, 98–110. Boston: Little, Brown.
Thyne, Clayton C. 2006. "Cheap Signals with Costly Consequences: The Effects of International Relations on Civil War, 1948–1992." *Journal of Conflict Resolution* 50 (6): 937–61.
Tierney, Dominic. 2011. "Does Chain-Ganging Cause the Outbreak of War?" *International Studies Quarterly* 55 (2): 285–304.
Toal, Gerard. 2017. *Near Abroad: Putin, the West, and the Contest over Ukraine and the Caucasus*. Oxford: Oxford University Press.
Toft, Monica D. 2017. "Why Is America Addicted to Foreign Interventions?" *The National Interest*, December 10. https://nationalinterest.org/feature/why-america-addicted-foreign-interventions-23582?nopaging=1.
Treisman, David. 2004. "Rational Appeasement." *International Organization* 58 (2): 344–73.
Tuchman, Barbara W. 1962. *The Guns of August*. New York: Random House.
Tyler, Patrick. 1999. *A Great Wall, Six Presidents and China: An Investigative History*. New York: Perseus.
Van Evera, Stephen. 1984. "The Cult of Offensive and the Origins of the First World War." *International Security* 9 (1): 58–107.
Van Evera, Stephen. 1999. *Causes of War: Power and the Roots of Conflict*. Ithaca, NY: Cornell University Press.
Vasquez, John A. 1993. *The War Puzzle*. New York: Cambridge University Press.
Vasquez, John A. 1996. "When Are Power Transitions Dangerous? An Appraisal and Reformulation of Power Transition Theory." In *Parity and War: Evaluations and Extensions of the War Ledger*, eds. Jacek Kugler and Douglas Lemke, 35–56. Ann Arbor: University of Michigan Press.
Vasquez, John A. 2009a. "Whether and How Global Leadership Transitions Will Result in War: Some Long-Term Predictions from Steps-to-War Explanation." In *Systemic Transitions: Past, Present, and Future*, ed. William R. Thompson, 131–60. New York: Palgrave Macmillan.
Vasquez, John A. 2009b. *The War Puzzle Revisited*. Cambridge: Cambridge University Press.
Vasquez, John A., and Marie T. Henehan. 2011. *Territory, War, and Peace*. New York: Routledge.
Voice of America (VOA) News. 2016. "Obama: US, Not China, Should Set Pacific Trade Rules." May 3. https://www.voanews.com/usa/obama-us-not-china-should-set-pacific-trade-rules
Wachman, Alan M. 2007. *Why Taiwan: Geostrategic Rationales for China's Territorial Integrity*. Stanford, CA: Stanford University Press.

Wallace, Michael D. 1973. *War and Rank among States*. Lexington, KY: Heath.
Walt, Stephen M. 1985. "Alliance Formation and the Balance of World Power." *International Security* 9 (4): 3–43.
Walt, Stephen M. 1987. *The Origins of Alliances*. Ithaca, NY: Cornell University Press.
Walt, Stephen. 2021. "China Wants a 'Rules-Based International Order,' Too" *Foreign Policy*, March 31. https://foreignpolicy.com/2021/03/31/china-wants-a-rules-based-international-order-too/.
Walter, Barbara F. 2002. *Committing to Peace: The Successful Settlement of Civil Wars*. Princeton, NJ: Princeton University Press.
Walter, Barbara F. 2003. "Explaining the Intractability of Territorial Conflict." *International Studies Review* 5 (4): 137–53.
Walter, Barbara F. 2006. "Building Reputation: Why Governments Fight Some Separatists but Not Others." *American Journal of Political Science* 50 (2): 313–30.
Waltz, Kenneth N. 1979. *Theory of International Politics*. Reading, MA: Addison-Wesley.
Waltz, Kenneth N. 1997. "Evaluating Theories." *American Political Science Review* 91 (4): 913–17.
Ward, Steven. 2017. *Status and the Challenge of Rising Powers*. Cambridge: Cambridge University Press.
Weitsman, Patricia. 2004. *Dangerous Alliances: Proponents of Peace, Weapons of War*. Stanford, CA: Stanford University Press.
Welch, David. 2015. "Can the United States and China Avoid a Thucydides Trap?" E-International Relations, April 6. https://www.e-ir.info/2015/04/06/can-the-united-states-and-china-avoid-a-thucydides-trap/.
Welch, David. 2018. "China, the United States, and the 'Thucydides Trap.'" In *China's Challenges and International Order Transition: Beyond "Thucydides's Trap,"* eds. Huiyun Feng and Kai He, 47–70. Ann Arbor: University of Michigan Press.
Wells, Tom. 1994. *The War Within: America's Battle over Vietnam*. Berkeley: University of California Press.
Werner, Suzanne. 1999. "The Precarious Nature of Peace: Resolving the Issues, Enforcing the Settlement, and Renegotiating the Terms." *American Journal of Political Science* 43 (3): 912–34.
Werner, Suzanne, and Amy Yuen. 2005. "Making and Keeping Peace." *International Organization* 59 (2): 261–92.
White House. 2024. "Remarks by President Biden and Prime Minister Kishida Fumio of Japan in Joint Press Conference." April 10. https://www.whitehouse.gov/briefing-room/speeches-remarks/2024/04/10/remarks-by-president-biden-and-prime-minister-kishida-fumio-of-japan-in-joint-press-conference/.
Whiting, Allen S. 1962. *China Crosses the Yalu: The Decision to Enter the Korean War*. Stanford, CA: Stanford University Press.
Wohlforth, William C., ed. 2003. *Cold War Endgame: Oral History, Analysis, Debates*. University Park: Pennsylvania State University Press.
Wohlstetter, Roberta. 1962. *Pearl Harbor: Warning and Decision*. Stanford, CA: Stanford University Press.
Wolf, Reinhard. 2014. "Rising Powers, Status Ambitions, and the Need to Reassure: What China Could Learn from Imperial Germany's Failures." *Chinese Journal of International Politics* 7 (2): 185–219.
Wright, Jasmine. 2021. "Biden Commits to 'Free, Open, Secure' Indo-Pacific in Rare Op-ed with 'Quad' Members." CNN, March 14. https://www.cnn.com/2021/03/14/politics/biden-modi-morrison-suga-quad-op-ed/index.html.
Xi, Jinping. 2021. "China Welcomes Helpful Suggestions but Won't Accept Sanctimonious Preaching." Xinhua, July 1. http://www.xinhuanet.com/english/special/2021-07/01/c_1310037332.htm.
Yicai Global. 2017. "China 'Lacks the Gene' to Fall into Thucydides Trap, Says Xi Jinping." Medium, September 20. https://yicaichina.medium.com/china-lacks-the-gene-to-fall-into-the-thucydides-trap-says-xi-jinping-ccade48ac392.

Yuen, Amy. 2009. "Target Concessions in the Shadow of Intervention." *Journal of Conflict Resolution* 53 (3): 745–73.

Zakaria, Fareed. 2020. "The New China Scare: Why America Shouldn't Panic about Its Latest Challenger." *Foreign Affairs* 99 (1): 52–69.

Zakaria, Fareed. 2023. "Iran's President on Anti-hijab Protests." CNN, September 23. https://www.cnn.com/videos/world/2023/09/23/gps-0924-president-raisi-on-womens-rights.cnn.

Zakaria, Fareed. 2024. "How Trump and Biden Hiked Up Inflation." CNN, April 14. https://www.cnn.com/videos/politics/2024/04/14/fareeds-take-trump-biden-inflation-gps-vpx.cnn.

Zhao, Lijian. 2022. Foreign Ministry Spokesperson Zhao Lijian's Regular Press Conference on May 30, 2022, Ministry of Foreign Affairs, People's Republic of China, May 30. URL discontinued.

Index

For the benefit of digital users, indexed terms that span two pages (e.g., 52–53) may, on occasion, appear on only one of those pages.